DANCING WITH MYSELF

DANCING WITH MYSELF

BILLY IDOL

SIMON &
SCHUSTER

London · New York · Sydney · Toronto · New Delhi

A CBS COMPANY

First published in Great Britain by Simon & Schuster UK Ltd, 2014
A CBS COMPANY
Copyright © 2014 by Billy Idol

1 3 5 7 9 10 8 6 4 2

Note to readers: Some names and identifying details of
people portrayed in this book have been changed.

ISBN: 978-0-85720-558-2
Trade Paperback ISBN: 978-0-85720-559-9
Ebook ISBN: 978-0-85720-561-2

The author and publishers have made all reasonable efforts
to contact copyright-holders for permission, and apologise
for any omissions or errors in the form of credits given.
Corrections may be made to future printings.

Designed by Akasha Archer

Printed and bound by CPI Group (UK) Ltd, Croydon, CR0 4YY

For Joan and Bill Broad

CONTENTS

PART II: NEW YORK CITY

PART III: LOS ANGELES

THEY SAY IF YOU HEAR THE BANG, YOU'RE STILL ALIVE

BY THE MORNING OF FEBRUARY 6, 1990, I'd been living on a fine edge for more than a decade, always courting disaster to experience the biggest high. I'd been living the deranged life. I felt so nihilistic, yet why hadn't I just tuned in and dropped out? Instead, I followed Jim Morrison's credo, the credo of Coleridge and, at one point, Wordsworth, the credo of self-discovery through self-destruction I so willfully subscribed to until this moment:

Live every day as if it's your last, and one day you're sure to be right.

On this fateful morning, I'm standing wide-awake at dawn in the living room of my house in Hollywood Hills, overlooking the Los Angeles basin that falls and stretches away toward the high-rising pillars of downtown. I haven't slept, still buzzing from the night's booze and illicit substances lingering in my bloodstream, staring at the view of the city beginning its early morning grumblings. Daylight unfolds and casts shadows within the elevation, as if God is slowly revealing his colors for the day from his paint box, the hues of brown and green of earth and foliage offset by the bleached white of the protruding rocks that hold my home in place on the hillside.

Standing at my window, I hear sirens blaring in the distance. *Someone wasn't so lucky*, I think as I tune in to the rumble of cars ferrying tired and impatient commuters on the 101 freeway that winds through the Cahuenga Pass, the sound of a world slowly getting back in motion. The constant moan of the freeway echoes that of my tired and played-out soul.

Just the night before, after almost two years of work, we put the aptly titled album *Charmed Life* to bed. I'm feeling some pressure, home early from the de rigueur studio party. I say that as if we threw one party to celebrate the completion of the album, but the truth is that the party went on for two years. Two years of never-ending booze, broads, and bikes, plus a steady diet of pot, cocaine, ecstasy, smack, opium, quaaludes, and reds. I passed out in so many clubs and woke up in the hospital so many times; there were incidents of returning to consciousness to find I was lying on my back, looking at some uniformly drab, gray hospital ceiling, cursing myself and thinking that I was next in line to die outside an L.A. nightclub or on some cold stone floor, surrounded by strangers and paparazzi.

I've been taking GHB, a steroid, to help relieve symptoms of the fatigue that has been plaguing me and preventing me from working out and keeping my body in some semblance of good shape. If you take too much GHB, which I'm prone to do, it's like putting yourself in a temporary coma for three hours; to observers, it appears as if you are gone from this world.

When we began recording in 1988, we promised each other we'd be cool and focused, and not wholly indulge in drugs and debauchery. But as weeks stretched into months, Fridays often finished early with "drop-time"—the moment we all took ecstasy. And then Friday soon became Thursday and so on, until all rules were taboo. We somehow managed to make music through the constant haze. It seemed like every few days I was recovering from yet another wild binge, and it took three days to feel "normal" again. The album proved to be slow going and the only way to feel any kind of relief from the pressure was to get blotto, avoid all human feelings, and reach back into the darkness once again. Somewhere in that darkness, I told myself, there was a secret of the universe or some hidden creative message to be found.

We'd invite girls to come to the studio to listen to the music. Mixing business with pleasure seemed the best way to see if the new songs worked. We'd be snorting lines of cocaine, and then the girls would start dancing. Before long, they'd end up having sex with one or more of us on the studio floor. Once the party was in full swing, we walked around naked but for our biker boots and scarves. Boots and Scarves became the running theme.

The girls loved it and got in on the act. It helped that we recruited them at the local strip bars; they felt comfortable naked. We had full-on orgies in those studios we inhabited for months. It was like a glorified sex club. We were all about instant gratification, lords of the fix.

I'd like to think this was all in the name of song-searching: the sex and drugs amped up the music, the songs arriving in the midst of chaos, cigarettes stubbed out into plates of food, the bathroom floor covered with vomit, sweaty sex going on all over the studio as we tried out our guitar riffs and mixes. The sound of our mixes, turned up loud, drowned out the background noise of sucking and fucking. Songs must be written. The ideas must flow. The flow must go to one's most base desires. Without constraint.

Now that it's all said and done, I feel exhausted and shattered. The keyed-up feeling that prevents me from sleeping is the result of the care and concern I put into making a record that will decide the course of my future. That's the sort of pressure I put on myself every time. Then there's the fact that the production costs have been astronomical; the need to keep the bandwagon rolling has drained my spirit and sapped my will.

Months later, *Charmed Life* will go on to sell more than a million copies. The "Cradle of Love" single and video, directed by David Fincher, will both become massive hits. But I don't know this when I retreat to my home alone at 2 a.m., intending to get some rest after wrapping recording. The breakup of my relationship with my girlfriend, Perri, the mother of my son, Willem, has left me bereft, but finishing the album has been my only priority. "If the thing is pressed . . . Lee will surrender," Lincoln telegraphed Ulysses S. Grant at Appomattox in 1865. And then: "Let the thing be pressed." That's a rock 'n' roll attitude. The difficult has to be faced straight-on and the result forged out of sweat and tears. That's where I take my inspiration.

The wide-screen version of the last few years' tumultuous events plays in my subconscious and cannot be ignored. What can I do to keep away these blues that rack my thoughts and creep into my bones? It's a fine day, warming up, the sun burning off the morning smog. Still, I feel uneasy, dissatisfied in the pit of my stomach. With the album now finished, I'll have to take stock of life and contemplate the emptiness without Perri and Willem.

The bike will blow away these post-album blues, I think. As I open the garage door, the chrome of my 1984 Harley-Davidson Wide Glide gleams with expectation, beckoning me.

The L.A. traffic is thick and the warmth of the sun is fresh on my face, its glow spreading over my bare head. California has yet to pass legislation making the wearing of helmets compulsory, and I've always liked the feel of the wind in my hair. My bike clears its throat with a deep, purring growl. The gleaming black tank and chrome fixtures flash in the sharp, sacrosanct daylight. I've opted for all denim to match the blue-sky high.

The Harley's firm hold on the road this morning is comforting, and I begin to relax; its curves perfectly match the contours of the pavement below. I try to outrun the demons. The sweet, jasmine-honeyed air intoxicates my spinning mind. I rev the bike, which reacts easily to my commands as I sail breezily along the winding canyon road toward Sunset Boulevard. The lush greenery and trees lining the road refresh my thoughts, and my concentration wanders. My mind is filled with images of Peter O'Toole as Lawrence of Arabia speeding through the English countryside, testing his bike, pushing it to the limit, when—

WHAM!!!

An almighty explosion interrupts my silent reverie. I feel my body violently tumbling through the air, floating into a pure void. I black out before landing.

I SENSE BEINGS CROWDING AROUND ME. I hear voices, some very close and loud, others softer and farther away. The whirl of movement in this dark vortex tells me that other worlds exist; I can feel their magnetic pull. People have a gravity of presence, and I can feel their movement as I slowly regain my senses. I'm not sure if I'm alive or dead.

I'm transported to just above myself. There are no white tunnels or distant lights, rather a red dimension. Walking through the shadow world on the other side, I see the beings who grace the crimson night crowding around to greet me. They pour out their love. The strange dimension sends a beam of thought: *You're all right. We love you. Don't worry, here is love.* They press and push. The circle of people holds my soul in a warm embrace.

I can feel their minds, good thoughts passing through me. I am one with them, yet still an individual. The warm red permeates my mind; a florid sun must light this world. I am connected to others who no longer live, but who exist in this red dimension. Red is the color of life, the color of death, a red masque, a celebration. The male and female voices are soft and resonate in my soul. *We love you*, they say. There are no individuals, no identification.

Now I slip into a warp of darkness, pulled from this loving dimension. I hang in a slip of time between life and death; I slowly begin to regain consciousness. The screen behind my eyes has yet to come on. It's as if God has not yet spoken those immortal words "Let there be light."

I HEARD THE CRASH. BIKERS SAY that if you don't hear that crash, you're already dead. I open my eyes. Bright sunlight floods in. I'm staring at the curb, my forehead resting just an inch from the sidewalk's edge. I'm lying in a bloody heap in the street, my Harley not too far away.

I'm positioned awkwardly on my left side, on top of my left arm. I free my arm, only to see something is very wrong. My wrist is fucked up, leaving my fingers contorted, clawlike.

I lift up to look at the rest of my body and a terrific pain courses through my nerve endings. Any attempt at movement brings waves of agony that rack me to the core. Looking down, I see that my right boot is without a heel, smashed into the asphalt. I try to move my leg; nothing happens. I see a bloody, mangled stump sticking through my torn jeans. It looks as if my foot and my lower leg are separated from me, the denim lying flat on the pavement beneath my knee, a pool of blood quickly spreading from the soaked cloth. I lie there and wait for help.

The immortal biker slogan "There are those who have been down and there are those who are going down" reverberates through my brain as I watch a man walk across the street. Though he sees my condition, he asks, "Are you all right?" Ignoring the question, I blurt out, "I've got Blue Cross Blue Shield—take me to Cedars-Sinai," before passing out.

I'm zapped back to reality with a sharp jolt as the EMTs move me from the street to the ambulance on a stretcher. They start to cut my clothes off, and I actually think to myself, *Just as well I didn't wear my favorite leather riding jacket.* I had contemplated wearing it that morning but opted for the denim instead as it was such a beautiful day. Funny how shit like this runs through your mind no matter what the circumstances. I am super-aware, yet at the same time in almost unbearable discomfort.

The herky-jerky movements of the ambulance as it picks its way through traffic—slowing down then speeding up—combined with the blaring siren are strangely comforting. The actions of the two paramedics are cool, calm, and deliberate. I am in good hands. The speed with which they transfer me to the hospital gurney and take me to the emergency operating room reminds me of an experience I had in Thailand the year before, where I was escorted speedily out of the country by a platoon of the Thai Army, tranquilized and lashed to a military stretcher. By the time I reach the emergency room, the pain is so intense my thoughts are stopped cold as my injuries wreak havoc on my nervous system. I am probably screaming, but I am deaf to any sound.

THE FACT IS, I HAVE BEEN deaf to many things. The road I've taken may have been the one less traveled, but definitely not in a good way. It was littered with disregarded warning signs. Despite spiritual reassurance by those friendly beings regarding my mortality, back in the real world, it's payback time. It is not the first time nor the last that William Broad will be held to account and asked to pay a heavy price.

PART I

LONDON

I LET OUT MY FIRST REBEL YELL

Middlesex, London; and Long Island, NY

I WAS BORN WHEN GODS WALKED the earth—rock gods, that is. Two months after James Dean, the original rebel without a cause, died, I came to life on November 30, 1955, in North London at Edgware Hospital, Middlesex. Who knows what anybody ever thinks on taking that first breath, a breath that will turn into a cry, a cry that will become a voice. But your instincts are there at the start, all the accumulated experience of those who came before, all the personalities coming to bear.

WHEN I WAS A BOY / DADDY TOLD ME / GROW TALL / YES AND BILLY DON'T CRAWL /
TAUGHT ME HOW TO RIDE / SET ME OUT ON MY OWN / AND I NEVER CAME BACK.
—"PRODIGAL BLUES"

Everything in my past seems so far away and long ago, but this dream of life goes back to my first friends, my mum and dad, Joan and Bill Broad.

My dad, William Alfred Broad, was born July 6, 1924, in Coventry, near Birmingham, in England. His father, Albert Broad, was a news-agent who also ran a pub and hotel before dying from liver disease, undoubtedly from drinking. I never met him. My dad—along with two brothers, Bob and Jack, and a sister, Joan—was brought up by his mother, Naomi Heslop-Broad. At eleven, he received a scholarship to the prestigious Solihull School, which was a big deal. After finishing his education, he became a typewriter salesman, and later sold slotted angle shelving, called Handy Angle. He built up the company's sales force from one to more than forty and was promised by the owners they'd make him a director, which never happened. Instead, he packed up my mom and me and moved to America.

My mum, Johanna O'Sullivan, was born in Ireland, February 24, 1928. She had three brothers, Michael, John, and Donal, and two sisters, Mary and Vera. After being schooled at the hands of tough, disciplinarian nuns, Joan arrived in Sheffield, England, to become a nurse. She ended up a theater sister, handing the surgeon his tools and running the operating room, making sure all was right for a successful surgery. She met my dad in 1950 and converted from Catholic to Protestant to marry him in 1953, thus alienating her parents, who refused to speak to her until I was born. My mum always pointed out that her Protestant church was actually called the Catholic Church of England, so she never felt as if she did change religions. It was just that kind of brilliant Irish topsy-turvy logic that would stand me in good stead during my subsequent adventures. Contrary to my mother's view of the world, my dad has always been a confirmed atheist as far back as I can remember.

Before making the transatlantic voyage to the U.S., we stopped over in Cork, Eire, to see Granddad, who had a proclivity for the drums, and Granny O'Sullivan, who could play any number of instruments, including the piano, accordion, banjo, clarinet, and violin. My mum's brother Donal favored the sax, while she sang and played piano. The whole group would put on shows at the hotel pub my mum's family owned, with Granny writing out the musical parts for the songs she composed in the attic of their house.

I arrived in Eisenhower's America in 1958, not quite four-years-old, with a banjo on my knee, given to me by my maternal grandparents. When I first stepped off the *S.S. America* in the States, I wore that banjo proudly, a foreshadowing of my musical destiny. We rented an apartment in Rockville Centre, a suburban community on Long Island, where most of the residents were commuters who took the railroad to Manhattan for their jobs. That I wound up living in a town with "rock" in its name now seems yet one more harbinger of my future. Truth hidden in the soul?

We would often walk through our neighborhood and past the home of then heavyweight boxing champion Floyd Patterson. Mum remembers him saying hello to us, my very first brush with fame. My mum's approach to people was always open and friendly. If we were waiting in a line, she would get to know everyone we were standing with by the time we reached our destination. Sometimes it embarrassed me, but it would hurt her if I said anything about it. My mum was teaching me by example how to be outgoing; the lesson would prove an invaluable one.

Some of my earliest memories of visiting Manhattan involve the canyons of skyscrapers that towered above me, menacingly glowering, reaching into the sky and pulling me into the future. In the city, we visited my uncle John, my mum's brother, and his family, who were always in a good mood—even when Uncle John had to work nights. All my Irish relatives had a healthy glow about them, and there was always music in the air. Much of my mum's family now lived in the States, which I'm sure was one of the reasons we moved. When Dad got a job as sales manager for Blue Point Laundry, we moved to Conklin Avenue in Patchogue, all the way out in Suffolk County, not far from Fire Island, just before the island splits into two fins, terminating at the wild breakers of Montauk Point.

Winters there would prove to be disorienting, with freezing blizzards and six-foot snowdrifts whipped up by sometimes tornado-force winds. The snowplows would come through to create huge mounds on the sides of the streets. But I recall the summers being long and hot, the tarmac on the roads melting under our thick, rubber-tired push-bikes. Big, gaily colored cars with giant fins cruised the streets. Dad had a turquoise Dodge with just that kind of wings.

The burning sun proved a warm umbrella for my childhood activities. I was only four, but I felt a freedom that was right and natural.

I remember company picnics on Fire Island, people docking their boats, the size and polish denoting their status. Tartan coolers and Bermuda shorts were permanent features in our Kodachrome-colored, late-'50s home movies that picture a young English family enjoying and coming to grips with life in America. The deep reds and greens of the color palette saturated my young mind, leaving an indelible imprint.

In back of our house was a creek that led out to the ocean. It was quite narrow in spots, and someone had fastened a rope to a tree so we could swing over and into the water. I learned to swim from the Red Cross, taking to the water easily, despite the occasional sting from a stray jellyfish, which a trip to the lifeguard would cure. We would surf the big, powerful Atlantic waves with car-tire inner tubes.

My dad's hobbies included golf, hunting, fishing, diving for clams, and catching swordfish. He tried to teach me to fish, but I hated the thought of the hook in the fishes' gills. I would often watch as he wrestled with and finally ensnared one, frozen by watching pain coursing through its body. I didn't care much for the gutting part, either.

I made friends with David Frail, who lived next door. His father suffered from multiple sclerosis and was confined to a wheelchair. I was especially impressed that the family had a maid and not just one but two vacuums—one for upstairs, the other for downstairs.

Once, my dad's boss invited all his favorite employees to his big house for a Sunday afternoon barbecue. We kids ran in and out of the water sprinklers. Life was good. The highlight of my young life, though, was when the Good Humor ice cream truck would roll through the neighborhood, the man in a white suit and black bow tie behind the wheel.

Television, especially color TV, was another huge discovery for me, a wonder with eight different channels as well as early morning, pre-school programming. I was attracted to the slapstick comedy of *Captain Kangaroo* and the history lessons of Walt Disney movies such as *The Swamp Fox*, which depicted the American Revolutionary War, portraying the British as fops and the Yanks as devilishly clever.

The realization that I was one of those fops, and considered the enemy, was a shock to me. I quickly lost my Limey accent and adopted cowboy slang to out-American the Americans. When I started school in 1960 at age five, however, I felt that, as a Brit, I shouldn't have to pledge allegiance to the flag at morning assembly. For me, the past and present weren't so far apart, and still aren't. Deep inside, I felt a connection to what has happened on earth through the ages, with history and music keeping me grounded.

Still, like many other youngsters, I fantasized about being little Joe in *Shane*. I wore a Davy Crockett coonskin cap, both Union and Confederate caps, and a Steve Canyon Jet Helmet. I was impressed with the sheer scope and size of America, which I'd gotten a taste of when Mum learned to drive and took me on a trip to Niagara Falls. After marveling at that natural spectacle, we crossed the border into Canada, where we saw the source of the Great Lakes. Was there no end to the wonders of this land? There was magnificence to America, but also a violence that colored its beauty, given the nation's history of American Indian tribes fighting for existence, squeezed between the frontier settlers and imperialistic British forces.

Violence, or the threat of it, colored my life in another way: I experienced fear in the slow-screaming, wailing, mournful sound of the early warning nuclear air-raid sirens, which reverberated on empty streets as we would "duck and cover." I contemplated deep, caliginous, silent thoughts that hinted of a darker America, one a child could only guess at. Pioneers had founded this prosperous country but at great cost, and their suffering gave birth to the blues and, eventually, to rock 'n' roll.

MY EARLY MEMORIES OF MUSIC ARE intermingled with wild, out-of-body experiences of my first presidential election. Eisenhower's eight years were up, with John F. Kennedy and Richard Nixon battling it out to succeed him. My mum, a Catholic in spirit, adored JFK. He was the new hope, a sort of independent thinker. She loved his election speeches and collected gramophone records of them. I can still recognize his words today, as he spoke to "a new generation of Americans."

My mum took me to see him on a campaign stop nearby. It was just a dirt road in the middle of nowhere, but soon enough, young Kennedy roared by. Sitting in the back of an open limo, he was smiling and waving, then gone in a flash. He carried the promise of America in that voice: "Ask not what your country can do for you—ask what you can do for your country." I felt him speaking directly to me.

I can still see my mom's albums of those speeches, big black hard plastic records, with various logos decorating the center labels, and serial numbers scratched in the vinyl where the grooves ended. When JFK won the 1960 election, it was a glorious day for my mum. No one in our family was eligible to vote, but it sure felt like we had something to do with his victory. These emotional journeys I shared with my mum made me feel really close to her. I dreamed wild thoughts that a whole nation's future lay in the grasp of a charismatic individual with brains.

My mum's record collection also included jazz, by greats such as Count Basie, Duke Ellington, and particularly Louis Armstrong, who I thought was fantastic. What a wild sound to his voice, which proved yet another musical instrument. She also favored Broadway musicals including *My Fair Lady*, *Camelot*, *South Pacific*, and *The Music Man* ("Seventy-six trombones led the big parade"). I discovered Richard Burton as King Arthur in *Camelot* and enjoyed the way he spoke-sung the musical's songs, little realizing I would use the same approach years later. He was the first person I heard sing about being bored, his lackadaisical tone inflected by a combination of acting and alcohol.

I listened to other albums, too, like Frank Sinatra's *Songs for Swingin' Lovers!* and Ella Fitzgerald. But I preferred the simplicity of Tex Ritter's acoustic guitar, the symbol of the people's freedom from all forms of oppression, the plucked strings the united sound of our spirits singing out for justice, for our rights as individuals. The guitar was the people's weapon, a soulful "gun," and "bullets" were the songs it created. As a child, I could feel without knowing, hear and understand without total comprehension. Tragedy! Promise lost! Death! Disaster! Hubris!

Tex was not necessarily the greatest technical singer, but he had personality, and his believability factor was great. Truth was in his voice. I was five when I first heard him, but the many parts that sum a person run deep and wide. "Billy the Kid" was one of my favorites. "Out in New Mexico long time ago / When a man's only chance was his old .44 . . . Shot down by Pat Garrett who once was his friend / The young outlaw's life had now come to its end." Tex also sang the theme song to the movie *High Noon* and performed children's songs, like "Froggie Went A Courtin' " and "The Pony Express."

Tex's voice was weathered by time; he wasn't young and good-looking, but his sound was warm, thanks in part to the old tube recording microphones that were in use then, and flavored by real-life experiences. Murder, betrayal, and death were his subjects, and the songs came off real dreamy to me, evoking the old American frontier, people livin' on the edge and singing about it. I wish you could feel the wild rush of pleasure I get from songs that mean so much to me. It starts in the pit of the stomach and flows outward, flooding the body with warm, pleasure-giving endorphins. The brain sizzles with well-being. I sing the body acoustic!

It's interesting that I fell for the guitar-and-voice combination, for it was just that which would set the modern world on fire: Robert Johnson, Bukka White, Woody Guthrie, and Hank Williams paved the way for Elvis Presley—The Hillbilly Cat—and Johnny Cash. If Western music was a modern musical frontier, I wanted to see the elephant, but back in 1960, I didn't know about rock 'n' roll. I had the usual kiddie songs on colored vinyl: "Three Little Pigs," "Scruffy the Tugboat," and "Popeye the Sailor Man." But my love of music started young.

My sister, Jane, was born November 22, 1959. I was fascinated with her, as one can see from our home movies. She could hardly see over her huge cheeks. We went on a family holiday through the Shenandoah Valley along the Blue Ridge Mountains, stopping at the Battle of Gettysburg site. I remember pushing the button on an information kiosk and hearing an actor speak Lincoln's famous words, "Four score and seven years ago . . ." This land set aside to commemorate such a terrible event played its way into my mind.

Although we were enjoying our stay in America, Dad got a job offer that returned us to England in 1962. He was hired by a company that sold medical equipment, including a new blood pressure machine called the Baumanometer. When we flew back in a large prop plane, I asked my parents where God was. If he was up in the sky, how come we couldn't see him? It would be a question that would plague me for the rest of my life.

CHAPTER TWO

ENGLAND SWINGS LIKE A PENDULUM DO

Dorking to Goring-by-Sea, England

GOOD OLD BLIGHTY, BACK TO ENGLAND, a return to my dad's old London stomping grounds, the place where I was first spat out into the world, one perilously in danger of suffocating under the claims of then Conservative leader Harold Macmillan that we "never had it so good."

What the fuck did I know about England? I was really an American kid. I had a Yank accent and a crew cut. I wore sneakers, not plimsolls. I said *man* instead of *mate*; *elevator*, not *lift*; and *cops*, not *bobbies*.

I felt like a fish out of water. We lived in the side rooms of a pub at the foot of Box Hill, which people climbed on weekends, but was pretty much empty Monday through Friday. I had a heavy Long Island accent with a cowboy twang, the outcome of a life led in a multilingo world gone twisted. I was called "Yank" during soccer matches, where I was "good-naturedly" tackled because the local boys knew I had no idea how to play the game. I was a foreigner in my own country, a stranger in a strange land.

One of the first things to catch my young, impressionable ear was Bernard Cribbins's novelty song "Right Said Fred," about three bungling workmen attempting to move an unwieldy yet unidentified item, eventually leaving it standing on the landing after all but demolishing the client's house (and drinking many cups of tea). It was produced by

George Martin, the very same gentleman who would go on to work with the Beatles. Funny that it was his comedy stuff that got to me first, as it did with John and Paul.

Music always pulled me through, voices laying out a tale of their lives, musicians riding the wave. I didn't know that a cultural revolution fueled by rock 'n' roll was right around the corner, to purge this land with sound. England's postwar recovery would reveal a new kind of comedy; a kick was on its way, a new thrill to push away the traditional British blues. Could a six-year-old really recognize the Abbey Road production team put together by George Martin by their feel and expertise? How could I know what was happening? "You know what you like," my dad would always say.

My ten-year-old cousin David Hofton came to stay with us and took me up Box Hill. I had my Excalibur sword because the Robert Taylor movie *Knights of the Round Table* was popular at the time. We were having a mock fight when a group of a dozen teenage boys in leather jackets and jeans descended on us. At first they just tried to scare us, but then they began talking about incomprehensible things that teenagers on the run from the "Smoke," as London was called, might talk about. That feeling of not quite knowing what was going to happen frightened me. When I was three, some boys playing cowboys and Indians had tied me to a tree and repeatedly punched me in the stomach, landing me in the hospital for a hernia operation. But nothing serious happened on this occasion, and soon we were all joking with one another. I realize today that they were just some lads trying to escape the sprawl of the suburbs that spread deep into Surrey. They let us go and we ran down the hill, but when I told Mum about what had happened, she called the bobbies nevertheless. They took us up the hill in their police cars, bells clanging. We rode along to show them where it had happened, with me in the passenger seat. It was quite exciting as we identified the boys, who were still where we'd left them. I felt a little sorry for them as they were driven away, but fear and excitement do go hand in hand.

When I was around six, my parents noticed that when I entered our living room and looked at the TV, I would squint. I always used to sit right underneath the telly, practically in the set (I suspect a lot of cath-ode ray kids did back then). So they sent me to an optician, who said I was badly shortsighted and that, horrors upon all horrors, I would have to wear those horrible National Health Service–issued round specs with tortoiseshell on the edge that all the old grandpas wore. For some reason, it was a really shitty and embarrassing feeling, leading to being called such names as "four-eyes" or "you squinty git" at school. For three years, I managed to get away with not wearing my glasses at school, and I sat near the back of the class. When I was nine, my par-ents found out and my dad sent a letter to the school telling them I had to wear my glasses and sit at the front. Blast, foiled again!

So I put on my glasses, sat at the front, and heard the calls of "four-eyes" for about a day, but gradually everybody got over it and they seemed to forget the fact that I was wearing them. A year or so later, John Lennon started wearing his own glasses openly. I found out later he'd always been blind as a bat, but he never wore his glasses—he'd been hiding it from most people, especially the fans. Then he thought, *Fuck it*, he wore them, and it became really cool. It just goes to show you: be a trendsetter. Don't follow what others think is cool. It taught me a lesson in a quite personal way. You are going to be who you are. Might as well embrace it or forever be at the mercy of the human fears and trepidations of life that can devastate and drag us down.

Not long after that, we left Dorking and moved to Goring-by-Sea, a neighborhood of the southern British coastal town of Worthing, a few miles from Brighton, a spot favored by the royals, as it was just an hour outside London. Year round, the wind-blasted trees stripped of their foliage bent and twisted their naked array, forced to lean back north away from the English Channel's fierce chilling winds and rains. The dark gray sky gave an angry face to any human walking around. Another gust of wind and I was nearly taken off my feet. This was nothing as fierce as the winters in Long Island or the hurricane I had witnessed in person from the Conklin Avenue kitchen window, which overturned cars and tore out trees, but British weather was unrelent-ing, its terminal gray broken only by the occasional brilliant lovely summer day. Then, for a second, hope shone through, only to be swal-lowed up.

Maybe there was something poetic in my dad wanting to move back to England that I couldn't grasp then, but now I think I do. That gloom can piss you off, which leads you to find things to do to cheer yourself up. It was another move, another home, another group of friends to make, and new turf to which to acclimate.

I was a young, fresh-faced lad. My hair, sun-kissed blond in the U.S., began to darken into a mousy brown with a tinge of red—my Irish side coming out, I guess, although Mum had jet-black hair. We lived at the southern end of Falmer Avenue, about one block and a hundred yards from the seafront, which had a grass verge that rose up to the few trees that could take the weather; then the land fell away into a stony beach that led down to the dark green of the murky British Channel. We had the second-to-last house on the east side of the road, with one house after us, then a long, high wooden fence that led into the backyard of another house you could see into. So began my lifelong penchant for living by the sea. Knowing there's a vast expanse that reaches out as a conduit to the rest of the world is exciting, even if it also appears like a great forbidding territory.

We lived in a four-bedroom house in a middle-class neighborhood with a garden, each of us with our own room. On bad winter days, I would indulge in the endless fantasy of childhood war games played out with my tiny toy soldiers. There were Civil War soldiers and whole divisions of World War I and World War II troops of British, American, French Foreign Legion, and Nazis. I would put the Confederate forces with the Nazis, even then understanding something of the similarity of their racial policies. For a kid, I knew a great deal about the history of all these wars, and had a firm grasp of the technical truths of each one, including battle histories and weaponry.

I would read a comic called *The Victor*, which had cover stories about soldiers winning different medals, such as the Victoria Cross, and where you could see the differences in the drawings of World War I and II armaments. My parents had no understanding that my childish imaginings were based in fact.

I was also fascinated with Winston Churchill, as we shared the same birthday. A few years later, the movie *Young Winston* showed him as a child, playing with his soldiers in a perfectly serious way, and

I knew how he felt. I read all about his early exploits in the Boer War at the turn of the century in some children's book, and I came to understand his importance to the British effort in both world wars.

Attending a Church of England school, to my mother's delight, I joined the Goring Cub Scouts and was chosen to represent the troop at an annual Baden-Powell meeting, a national meeting at which Churchill himself was to officiate. When we got to Albert Hall, to my dismay, he was ill and unable to attend, leaving his wife, Clemmie, to stand in for him. When he died a few years later at age ninety, I was saddened. Later, upon learning how vindictive he was towards the people of Southern Ireland and towards British workers, I realized people have many sides to their personalities and beliefs. Yet he was still a childhood hero to me.

I excelled at reading. I quickly devoured all the books on the library shelves. I pored through Enid Blyton fictions of the Famous Five and Secret Seven and all the history books about the Romans, the Stone Age and Bronze Age Britons, ancient Egyptians, old and new kingdoms, tales of the Norse and Greek gods, Odysseus's long voyage home after the siege of Troy. In particular, I enjoyed books about English seafarers like Sir Francis Drake and Captain Cook. History read like fantasy to me, but even better than fiction, because it all really happened and was constantly being revised as new information from archaeological digs was continually being unearthed after WWII ended. I once wanted to be an archaeologist, but I was never any good at languages.

At the same time, American comics began to be serialized in England. I loved the Marvel stories about the Fantastic Four, Thor, Hulk, and the X-Men. Sometimes I would find reissues of the 1940s *Captain America*, with Bucky vs. Hitler and the Nazi/communist Red Skull. I enjoyed Superman, but he seemed dated to us. Batman rocked on into kitsch with a kids' TV show starring Adam West. I watched *Dr. Who* every week. There was one episode that I watched alone, where a Dalek crawled out of its mechanical shell to reveal itself. As the camera's gaze lingered on the immobile dead cyborg, the Dalek's top flew open, and the fear of whatever horrible thing that might be inside drove me into hiding behind our couch, where I occasionally peeked over to try to catch a glimpse of whatever it was without it seeing me. That scared me; somehow, the fear of the unknown conjured by our imaginations can really put the fright in us. I don't believe it had any long-term effect or anything, but the deep terror I conjured up over that dead Dalek was palpable for a few days.

IN SCHOOL, TAKING MUSIC LESSONS, THE class would all sing folk and sea shanties like "A-Rovin' " or "What Shall We Do with the Drunken Sailor" and soldiers' marching songs like "Lillibullero." Throughout my life, one ear has been listening to what's being said while the other listens for music playing in the background, or for the melody and rhythm of a voice. Thank god for beautiful music, as it represents our human spiritual side expressing itself.

I never wanted to be in the school choir. In fact, I pretended to sing dreadfully when they held auditions for the choir in both school and church. Still, I enjoyed sing-alongs, and even today, I find some of those English folk songs have a resonance throughout the world. For instance, in *Dances with Wolves*, just before the scene where Kevin Costner first sees Kicking Bird trying to steal his corralled horse while he cleans his clothes in the watering hole, he is singing a version of "Soldier, Oh Soldier, Won't You Marry Me?" Many of those traditional songs have journeyed far and wide from their original source in the British Isles.

Movies were also an inspiration to me as a kid. One of the first great films my dad took me to see was David Lean's desert epic *Lawrence of Arabia*. Its gigantic, wide-screen Technicolor enraptured me, as did its story. England was in a bad economic way in 1962, our postwar recovery largely unaided by America, which was still busy helping the Germans get back on their feet a mere seventeen years after the fighting had ended. The U.S. needed a bulwark against communist expansion into Western Europe; we needed heroes, and Lean's film reminded us that we had selfless leaders. Lawrence was an archaeologist who helped free the Arabs from the Turkish yoke but was torn between his love of the desert, Arabian freedom, and loyalty to England. Although he became a political pawn in his home country, his encouragement of guerilla tactics would inspire the Irish freedom fighters to separate from

England in 1916. The movie uses the device of a motorbike to symbolize Lawrence's naiveté, his love of freedom, and his demise. The film begins with him prepping his Triumph for the ride that would lead to his high-speed accidental death.

"Let me tell you the secret of the world," Sean Connery as James Bond whispers to Miss Moneypenny before being interrupted by M in *From Russia with Love*. Swinging London was still a little way off, but with Secret Service agent 007 all the rage on both sides of the Pond, the "cool" pendulum was starting to swing in this direction.

Rock 'n' roll music was still very popular in England, though by the early '60s it was in a precarious position. Buddy Holly and Eddie Cochran were dead; Elvis had emerged from the army seemingly cowed, becoming a movie star in gimmicky Hollywood films and abandoning the edge and quality of his music. Little Richard had become a preacher, and Chuck Berry was in jail for consorting with a minor.

Most of the British stars were Elvis clones, like Cliff Richard or Johnny Kidd and the Pirates, with "Shakin' All Over," but neither managed to cross over to the States. Instrumentals were on the charts, too, the Bond theme leading the way with Vic Flick's noir/twang guitar–driven sound (he says he was paid $15 for recording it). Then there was Cliff Richard's backup band, the Shadows. "Theme for Young Lovers," "Peace Pipe," "Apache," "Wonderful Land"— all instrumentals with a Western feel, that wild Burns/Stratocaster *twaaaang*! I thought Hank Marvin, the Shadows' guitarist, was great. Even today, I still feel something spiritual in their mysterious sound. I liked Joe Meek's production of "Telstar." The theme from the TV show *Dr. Who* might have been one of the first truly electronic hits, with its pulses and outer-space swells.

You had to glean the good stuff from where you could, as the only radio station was the BBC, which was run by the government and played only a smattering of rock 'n' roll. I started hearing some music I liked, but nothing life changing just yet. There were several shows on Saturday morning featuring the "Mersey beat" and the new sounds coming from Liverpool or farther north.

Maybe that's where I first heard a suddenly popular British group, the Beatles, who already had a number one hit and were singing their second, "From Me to You." I didn't have enough money to buy the single, so I saved up for the next one, "She Loves You," which arrived in the summer of '63. It had me from the opening drumroll. *"Ddddderlin! Ddddderlin!* She loves you, yeah, yeah, yeah / She loves you, yeah, yeah, yeah."

It spoke volumes to a displaced kid about how life has the potential to be full of fun and energy. It has a hopeful, naïve aspect to it, something I could relate to. It allowed me to reunite with a world that, for me, had changed quite rapidly, and to which I had to adjust, just as the characters in the song had to be reunited to work out their problems. The Beatles' music seemed half-English and half-American, something I have always felt about myself—along with the part of me that was half-Irish.

I loved the music, the sound, and the crazy element the Fab Four brought to the scene. And I loved the fashion and style. They cared about being songwriters and musicians; they were innovative, but also wild and crazy. They were the single most important band in my life, because they made me want to do what they were doing.

I bought "She Loves You" for six shillings, three pence, and half a penny. When I went to bed, I would listen to my little transistor radio under my pillow, tuning my "trannie" to Tony Prince on Radio Luxembourg, who would play all the latest American and English rock 'n' roll hits on his chart show. Coming from across the English Channel, the signal would slowly fade out and come back over the course of a song, but it was the only way I could hear what was going on in music. Under my blanket, I would listen and pretend I was onstage, the heat on a warm night making me sweat and look the way the Beatles did during their performances.

The Beatles were new and so was I. Suddenly, it was great to be British! The groundswell was just beginning. I also loved Them's bluesy "Baby Please Don't Go," as well as the Rolling Stones, the Animals, the Kinks, and the Who. I could particularly relate to Pete Townshend songs like "My Generation" and "I'm a Boy," an unusual rock number about the cruelties of childhood.

More and more rock 'n' roll bands began appearing on TV shows like *Thank Your Lucky Stars* and *Sunday Night at the London Palladium*, variety programs that had numerous other acts, but it was magic seeing the four "moptops" when they played the Royal Variety Performance at the London Palladium. "Twist and Shout" brought the house down, as did John's irreverent "rattle your jewelry" comment to the aristocratic audience. In 1964, a show called *Ready Steady Go!* appeared on Friday nights, featuring performances by the latest hitmakers, changing the name of the particular episode to "Ready Steady Stones" or "Ready Steady Who," depending on the featured headliner. (The show would inspire a Generation X anthem years later.)

The Beatles would release singles in England that were not included on their albums, heightening the demand. But soon, they had rivals for the throne. The Dave Clark Five's single "Glad All Over" was touted as the new London sound. When they knocked the Beatles from the top slot, I cried. I liked their beefy sax sound, and Mike Smith was a throaty blues-rock singer, but they didn't prove to have the same staying power, much to my childish relief. That was how much I believed in John and Paul.

For my eighth birthday in 1963, my parents gave me the new Beatles single, "I Want to Hold Your Hand." The flip side, "This Boy," showcased their great harmonies, and how powerful John Lennon's voice could be. The wild musical middle took thrilling vocal leaps, which John later explained was his way of matching the youthful Elvis's savage vocal middle eights. Paul could do that type of thing more easily, but John's struggle to do so had you on the edge of your seat. And it came out so very sexy. The lads' passion for rock was quite evident with every release. The Beatles just got better and better, revealing the depth of their talent. I could sing along, although one step down in vocal range. The range of emotion is key.

On my sister's fourth birthday, November 22, 1963, I was watching TV when news of President Kennedy's assassination was reported. I went to tell Mum, "The president's been shot," and it took her a while to understand I wasn't talking about a TV show, but real life. I will always associate that tragedy with Jane's birthday, as it coincides with the death of our generation's innocence, including mine.

Less than three months later, on February 9, 1964, the Beatles officially conquered America when they appeared on *The Ed Sullivan Show*. In England, we only heard about their performance, but the media made sure we knew it was a triumph, and Beatlemania was in full swing in my old homeland. English people felt proud, and I knew from that moment on, as far as Americans were concerned, we were no longer "fops" but cool and happening. I even dropped my Yank accent and went back to speaking the Queen's English. In an echo of my childhood encounter with Floyd Patterson, the Beatles got to meet rhyming heavyweight contender Cassius Clay, who predicted with a couplet in which round he would knock out his opponent: "If he wants to go to heaven, I'll beat him in seven." The '60s were in full swing.

Another artist who captured my attention around that time was Roy Orbison, who had toured with the Beatles in '63. Songs like "Only the Lonely" and "Pretty Woman," with the Big O's soaring operatic vocals, spoke to the loneliness inside my heart. I found out Roy touched women deeply. His otherworldly image, vocal drama, sad subject matter, and real-life tales of the loss of his first wife in a motorcycle accident, along with his ever-present shades and black-and-white dress, all perpetuated this sense of loss and the cold, brutal truth that life can be harsh and success does not make up for it. But loss does give you something to write about.

I was captivated when the Beatles starred in their first film, *A Hard Day's Night*, which featured visuals to their music and the new sound of George Harrison's electric twelve-string guitar. The Beatles' irreverent humor spoke to a generation of youth sick of being ground up and used for workplace fodder by the rich and powerful. It motivated us to believe that our destiny was in our hands, if we so chose. If you ask me, these were the roots that would later evolve into the punk mentality. The Beatles' do-it-yourself approach and songwriting gifts endowed them with a freedom we all wanted, that would change the prevailing winds in postwar Britain and wow a fat America. The battle lines were being formed, but we had moral force on our side, one of the winning factors in any war, martial or cultural. We wanted the future and we wanted it now. The aristocracy had had its day: now it was our turn.

AROUND THIS SAME TIME, WHEN I was nine, I kissed my first girl
in the school playground, and later, on a trip with my grandparents,
I kissed the Blarney Stone. The girl was a neighbor, and her kiss was
warm and wet, and introduced stirrings of a sexual appetite; the Blarney Stone was cold to the touch but instilled in me the gift of gab. My
Irish granddad gave me a Ringo Starr snare drum, my second instrument after the banjo my grandmother had given me when we passed
through on our way to America. The gift was a momentous one, as the
drum initiated me into a world where being different was not only ac-
ceptable but required. My granddad and grandma seemed to recognize
that I shared their love for music.

When I was ten I complemented my snare drum with a marching-
band bass drum and a kick pedal. Playing the guitar, writing songs,
and singing them were my dreams. I was quite ambitious, even back
then. But I didn't really know anyone my age who was in a rock 'n'
roll group. When some eleven-year-olds put on a gig at the school
playground, performing the Mindbenders' "A Groovy Kind of Love,"
I noticed how the girls responded. The group wore winklepickers,
shoes that were very long and pointed, even more so than the Beatles'
Chelsea boots. In British rock, fashion was almost as important as the
music itself.

Most ten-year-olds were playing games and not instruments. But
here, right in front of me, were kids barely older than me, realizing
their own dreams by putting on a show. You could be in the audience
one minute and up on a stage the next. This was how it would be later,
in 1976, when punk invaded Britain.

In Goring, the Church of England school headmaster would play a
wide variety of classical music. He was serious about his love of music,
and that commitment resonates with me to this day. My family went to
church, and my sister and I attended Sunday school, where I found the
singing and stories about Jesus very entertaining. Mum had taken me
to a Catholic mass in Eire, where I found the Latin service and incense
slinging to be a bit too somber and weird.

It was around this time that I gave my first actual performance in front of an audience. Since I was a good reader, and my mum was connected to the Protestant Church, I was chosen to read a passage from the Bible at the lectern during the Christmas mass service. "While shepherds watched their flocks by night / All seated on the ground / The angel of the Lord came down / And glory shone around." Of course, all the kids would change that to "While shepherds washed their socks by night," which made it hard to keep a straight face. The reality of just how nervous I was kicked in, as the church would be filled with adults, children, and the vicar, all watching me. It was quite a large congregation, so I would need to speak very clearly and loudly, and sound like I really understood what I was reading. I would have to enunciate with as much authority as a ten-year-old could muster. To practice, I would stand at the top of the stairs in our house and read aloud to my mum, at the bottom, who gave me pointers on how loud I should be.

When the day arrived, needless to say, I was scared to death. Apart from having one line in a school pantomime (playing the part of a king), I had never really had to stand on my own, with everybody's gaze focused on me 100 percent. Of course, it all went all right, though it felt horrible while I read. Even afterward, with people saying I'd done well, it was hard to shake off the stage fright, which lingered well after mass ended. It certainly wouldn't be the last time I'd experience that uncomfortable feeling of stage fright, but I'd soon learn to ignore those fears.

"Expose yourself to your deepest fear; after that, fear has no power and the fear of freedom shrinks and vanishes. You are free."
—JIM MORRISON

CHAPTER THREE

ROCK 'N' ROLL HIGH SCHOOL: LONG HAIR, FLARES, AND HASH TOBACCO CIGARETTES

WORTHING HIGH SCHOOL SEEMED A BIT boring at first. There was an old school headmaster who was very strict and wouldn't allow any deviations from the school uniform, blazer, cap, and all. He retired after my first year, and the deputy, who was a pushover where the rules were concerned, took over. Fashion exploded, and we all started wearing flares and knee-high boots that zipped on the side to school. The coolest were those who had the boots that zipped up to the knee, covered by one's trousers until they were hiked up and the full glory revealed. We all started growing our hair way beyond what was allowed by the school's regulations. The whole school started sporting their own fashion choices, while the few skinheads enrolled boasted their No. 1 crops and cherry-red Dr. Martens kicking boots.

After the first year, I was put in the C-stream, which mainly comprised kids who were clever but didn't want to try too hard. If you were in A or B, you were too dull to hang with us, and if you were in D, too slow. In truth, I was pretty useless at school. History was the only subject that held my interest, and I was naturally proficient at religious instruction for some inexplicable reason that probably only God knows. I didn't like science or math much, and I couldn't really draw, so art was out after the second year. No one wanted to get stuck in music class with some old fuddy-duddy teacher who was serious about the pathetic music he liked. After all, more of us were getting into the rock 'n' roll sounds that were being developed at a very fast rate during this period.

On a scout summer camping trip in Devon, while we were setting up camp I can remember still that a radio played "Whiter Shade of Pale." Wherever I was, my ears were always attuned to the radio. We would slag off school and go to a record shop to listen to the new records, squeezing into a listening booth until we were thrown out.

Nineteen sixty-seven was a wild year in terms of music, with the release of the Beatles' *Sgt. Pepper's Lonely Hearts Club Band* and Jimi Hendrix's "Purple Haze" and *Are You Experienced*. After reading J. R. R. Tolkien's *The Lord of the Rings*, I began writing some fantasy stories, in which I could blend my love of history and fable to create an epic world of battles, kings, and armies defeating evil. I also made up titles for imaginary record albums, such as *Blurry Vision*, a high-concept record where all the songs related to what you might see with your third eye, a takeoff on my own shitty eyesight.

One day, my notebook full of stories and album ideas disappeared, only to end up in the deputy head's room, where I had to see him to retrieve it. I was a bit worried about getting it back, mainly out of childish embarrassment, as I had never shown these private thoughts or fantasies about music to anyone, other than mentioning some of those ideas to my mum. But the deputy headmaster was actually quite complimentary to me and, rather than laughing at me, discussed with me some of the ideas found in my notebook.

My parents still didn't see how committed to the new music I was and made me take violin lessons! At this point, I was already teaching myself to play a cheap £5.00 guitar. *Why can't I have guitar lessons?* I wondered. But it was not to be. I had to go to violin lessons twice a week, one on Wednesday, and, God forbid, the other on Saturday morning. I was mortified at the thought of anyone seeing me with the violin, as they'd think I wanted to play it by choice, so I cycled to my lessons by some completely roundabout route so that nobody would see me. Eventually, I was spotted and word got out, but at that point, I told my parents quite categorically that I didn't want to play the violin, but the guitar. I refused to practice, in order to prevent them from getting me to do what *they* wanted.

School became much more fun during the second term. I remember one kid, one of the hipper and more grown-up in the class, always taking something that seemed to pep him up. I asked what he was doing and he replied that he'd take the medicine-soaked cotton leaf out of a Benzedrex inhaler and eat it, which produced speed-like effects. He gave me one, and it did indeed pep me up.

I began making friends with some of the kids in the year above me, as many of them had long hair and flares and carried record albums with them. I began to hang out with one boy, Laurence Satchel—Lol to me—and his mates, smoking at the back of the open gym and talking music. They knew all about John Mayall's Bluesbreakers, Hendrix, Clapton, and Cream. Rock was starting to take off at this time: the years 1967 through 1970 were a giant leap-off point in modern music. I was still just a kid, but boy, what a great music/life education I was getting, so fuck school. I couldn't help feeling like that, as the new musical horizon coming into focus was so huge, varied, and wide in scope. Like a big bang, perhaps the rock music explosion, if it kept on happening, would see the world itself explode and erupt across the space-time continuum. What the older lads, schoolmates and fellow lovers of this new-world rock, seemed to offer was, somehow, a viable solution to the complete boredom and utter futility of the mundane, nine-to-five daily grind that existed for many people then and still does today.

I STARTED TO GO TO ROCK concerts with the older kids. On our way to a Juicy Lucy/Hawkwind gig, we saw John Lennon performing "Instant Karma!" on *Top of the Pops* through a shop window. Yoko Ono performed alongside him, knitting while blindfolded, occasionally holding up cue cards with one-word statements: SMILE, PEACE, HOPE, LOVE, BREATHE. Hawkwind were on the Hurry on Sundown tour for their first album at the time. One of my friends passed out from the effects of their white-noise machine, which created the rushing wind integral to their sound.

On Saturday and Sunday mornings, I used to caddie at my dad's golf club for pocket money, and every penny went to music. We started to go regularly to Worthing Town Hall to see all the up-and-coming bands on their way to Brighton or London. We saw Black Sabbath one month before their debut album came out, and I was right in front of Ozzy, his long-tassled jacket practically touching me. We knew many of the songs from John Peel playing them on his BBC radio show. They started with "Black Sabbath," playing the whole of the first album, and it seemed as if the very bowels of hell were opening up (in the most fun way, naturally). This truly represented a step forward in rock at the time, and to be alive and witnessing it firsthand, played by blokes who weren't that much older than me, was exciting and, to me, inspirational.

Lol and I saw Deep Purple with Ian Gillan, who had the biggest flares and showed them off by placing one foot on a monitor as he screamed the tortured ending to "Child in Time." Medicine Head, Uriah Heep, the Edgar Broughton Band, the Soft Machine, the Nice . . . the list went on and on.

In those hippie, heady days, everyone sat cross-legged on the floor for the concerts. Music appreciation was taken very seriously by that generation. What did the band have to say? What was their stance on life? Was it taking us forward into a freer age, or were we being trapped? Fans noted musicianship and skills, digging certain singers, guitarists, or drummers. Some guys and chicks were freaking out, silhouetted by the stage lights, twisting, wobbling, and contorting themselves in a strange dance that had a lot to do with Joe Cocker's stage movements during "With a Little Help from My Friends."

The crowd was mostly students or cool, groovy "heads," people who sold and took drugs. Hash rolled into tobacco cigarettes was smoked to enhance the music, with a piece of cardboard at the end to create a filter. To disguise it, kids claimed to be smoking herbal cigarettes, as most adults in England at the time didn't really know what burning pot smelled like. Of course, I wanted to try; hadn't the Beatles and Stones smoked pot and dropped acid? What was that really like? It was intriguing for a twelve- or thirteen-year-old kid sitting in the same room.

Those were the days, my friends. "I'd love to turn you on" was the mantra. Long hair, patchouli oil, burning joss sticks, and kaftans—stoners taking a ride into a positive future, or so it seemed. Coming up with a new way to live or a unique view of the world was our quest. Why waste time on normal life, a nine-to-five grind with a weary approach that seemed to bode nothing too exciting? Why give in to your parents' beliefs and fears about the future, which they'd inherited from World War II or the Depression? Why subscribe to a political system that looked down on you even as you became society's biggest consumers, providing them with the money to persecute you?

We would hang at different people's houses and listen to music ad infinitum, discussing it, partying to it, playing air guitar along to the break in Free's "All Right Now." I thought they were a really interesting band, as they were all very young and already at the top of the charts, with Paul Rodgers singing like he was an old soul bluesman and Paul Kossoff leaning back against the amp, his right leg bent at the knee held up near his guitar neck while he tortured his Les Paul into obeying his command to bend notes into screaming walls of blues pain. The bass player, Andy Fraser, played funk licks that were so innovative, I thought he was the best bassist since Paul McCartney. And Simon Kirke was an incredible drummer whose timekeeping was impeccable. He had a spare style of playing soulful and sexy, leaving plenty of space for the other musicians to work their particular brand of magic. He didn't play long, extended solos, which went against the grain of every other drummer who tried to outdo Led Zeppelin's John Bonham—which was pointless, since he owned that territory. Music was progressing fast.

Speaking of Led Zeppelin, of course I loved their first two records. What an incredible leap forward in musicianship and songwriting. With their powerful riffs, wailing singer, and possibly the heaviest drummer of all time, they outdid the Who at their own game. Jimmy Page had the guitar chops, production skills, and hair to get exactly what it was he was looking for. Led Zeppelin proved to everyone that musicians knew just as much as any producer or record label. The scope and sweep of their power blues went well beyond even what Sabbath was doing. Robert Plant had incredible vocal range, impossible for mortal men to match, plus he looked like the visual embodiment of the Norse/Tolkien beauty he sang about in his lyrics. Sex appeal certainly played into their magnetism.

Led Zeppelin hardly played in England; after debuting under the name the New Yardbirds at the Marquee on October 18, 1968, the UK music press complained they were too loud. The lads took their rock press slagging and immediately vanished to the States, assuming a new name, Led Zeppelin, only returning later to play huge gigs like Knebworth. For the moment, Zeppelin ruled, and power blues-rock was fresh and new. What could possibly disturb these new hopes and dreams? The answer loomed in some shitty economic decisions by the government, which brought on another depression; but for a moment, like a ship of fools, we basked in the days of peace, love, and rock 'n' roll.

Jimi Hendrix's career blossomed in public thanks to television and a blessing from the Beatles. I used to cycle to the house of a mate who had *Are You Experienced* and *Axis: Bold as Love*, which we listened to nonstop. I thought Hendrix's singing was great, though he apparently didn't think much of it himself. He sang with so much personality, who cared if he was actually speaking the words? Anyway, his guitar did the singing.

I CAN STILL RECALL HUMMING ALONG to the Who's "The Seeker" on my transistor radio one afternoon after school as I rode on my bicycle, with its cow-horn handlebars, to a girls' school, where Lol knew some of the students. They were all a year older than me, with budding breasts and bodies, their sexual drives way ahead of ours, as girls tend to mature so much faster than guys. I actually remember my first wet dream when I was nine. I woke up one morning to find my pajama pants stuck to me around my genitals, which was a bit disconcerting, but it didn't bother me too much. Soon after, I started wanking regularly.

I went out with a girl named Linda, who was part of the group we all hung with, and had my first grope of female anatomy. Back then in England, chicks didn't give blow jobs, but they didn't mind wanking you off. I had a skinhead friend in my class, Gaz Kingston, who knew all these skinhead girls who would wank you off at the drop of a hat, just for kicks. It was usually a group wank-off, as the skin chicks would jerk each of us off at the same time in some alleyway, where we would go to smoke and hide from adults, family, and teachers alike.

Gaz was actually a fantastic bloke who didn't seem to care too much that my friends and I had long hair and were ostensibly hippies in training, while he and his mates had their short hair in a No. 1 crop taken nearly down to the scalp, along with their de rigueur style accoutrements, including Ben Sherman shirts with skintight Levi's rolled up to display the tops of their high, laced-up, cherry-red Doc Martens. Gaz would cadge cigarettes off me sometimes at school, and as I offered them to him, he would say, "Good matesmanship, Bill," a phrase I use to this day when someone does me a favor.

Lol, a bunch of our mates, and I used to go to a bowling alley in Worthing just off the main street on weekends or school holidays. We would walk a few streets away to a subterranean coffee bar, which was tunnellike, small, and smoky, where the heads hung out. Jimi Hendrix's "Long Hot Summer Night" was on the jukebox along with Cream's "White Room," with Clapton's wah-wah, and "Badge," with its wobbly, Beatles-esque, vari-speed guitar as its centerpiece, all playing constantly.

The skinheads were everywhere in those days, seeing us, with our long hair and flares, as the enemy, forced to kick our heads in. They listened to Jamaican ska and reggae, both huge in England, while we listened primarily to rock. The skinheads also hated Jamaican immigrants and black people, which raised the question, how can you enjoy the music but despise the people who play it? One Saturday, as the strains of "Whole Lotta Love" blasted out from every shop doorway, we were strolling along the high street on our way to the coffee bar when, horror upon horrors, we ran right into a group of about thirty big tough skins, who immediately walked up to us intent on doing us harm. Showering us with verbal abuse, they were just about to get physical—and give us some "aggro" (slang for a good kicking), when from out of their midst, lo and behold, Gaz Kingston appeared and vouched for me as his mate. Thank God I let him cadge those ciggies off me. Guess good matesmanship pays off after all, as my mates and I got away without being fucked up horribly and ending in a hospital instead of hanging at the coffee bar that afternoon.

Girls, rock 'n' roll, revolution, clash of youth cultures: emerging teenagedom was in full flight for me, and I was loving it. It made school seem more and more irrelevant, except for the few subjects I enjoyed. In terms of the onward flow of my life, I was having a great time.

Lol was going out with the hottest girl in our clique, but she was a randy soul and was working her way through all of us. She seemed more mature than the rest of us and was throwing her nubile body at everyone. After Lol, it was my turn; in truth, we started out kissing behind his back. Soon he found out, and we had a falling-out. I put my finger on her tits and in her pussy, a hot first for someone my age. But not before she and I kissed in full view of the adults at a weekend summer Scout fair. It was an official function, but I was so turned on by her and not mentally giving a shit anymore about the Scouts, I necked with her without thinking of the consequences. The very next day, I was officially expelled from the Scouts. I didn't care, but Mum cried. And while it troubled me to see her cry, music and this new world I was on the brink of meant more to me at the time than her emotions. I'd done my time in the Scouts and had gotten all I was going to get out of it. *Time to move on, Mum*, I thought. *I'm not a little kid anymore.* But I knew I'd hurt her, and that felt just awful. Of course, the chick soon dumped me for someone else, and Lol and I laughed about both of us being duped. Good mates somehow survive birds!

Summer approached, and there was a small local faux Woodstock held one weekend on the outskirts of Worthing, called "Phun City." It had all the hallmarks of the hippie festival: good vibes, children cavorting at the side of the stage, people learning yoga, a guy blowing bubbles, tents with tie-dyed clothing or drug paraphernalia—all the stuff of hippie dreams on sale.

We camped out on the site, and now my scouting skills came into play, as I was the only one who really knew how to put up a cánvas tent with ropes and stakes. This minifest was magical. The Hells Angels were there, turning up on their choppers and walking around swinging baseball bats. The audience consisted of full-on longhairs sitting on the grass or blankets to "groove." Some danced or freaked out to the music. Peter Green had just left Fleetwood Mac and played along with a number of second-string bands, but then, suddenly, like a bolt out of the blue, came the MC5. Fuck, they were great! They seemed to be playing with a verve and commitment I hadn't quite seen in any of the other bands that day. The guitarists, in spangled clothes standing at either side of the singer, at certain points in the show would suddenly jump in the air and spin around while the vocalist, with an Afro, exhorted the crowd to wake itself up and "kick out the jams, motherfucker!" They were great, an alternative to the incense-burning, meditation-practicing, patchouli-oiled, kaftan-wearing, peace-and-love hippies. I didn't realize it then, but at fourteen years old, I had just witnessed the future of rock.

An amusing aside to this was when the compere/MC/DJ tried to provide info about first aid over the PA, in the event someone had a bum acid trip. Midway through the first afternoon of Phun City, he said, "Someone's been naughty and stolen the red-and-white-striped first-aid tent. Could you give it back, please?" A little while later, he announced that someone had been really naughty and stolen a Hells Angels chopper bike! As he spoke, around from back of the stage came a group of Angels, led by a very angry redheaded bloke who proceeded to wade right through the middle of the seated hippie audience, swinging his wooden baseball bat at the heads of all and sundry, creating a mass panic, and since the peace-and-love crowd were so densely packed, there really was nowhere to go. A few broken heads were added to the acid freak-outs in the St. John's Ambulance first-aid section. Luckily, my friends and I were not seated in the middle of that. Actually, by the second day, the festival was declared free through pressure from the Hells Angels and the hippies who couldn't get in. It was like a small-scale Isle of Wight, as that festival ended up being declared free the very next year. It was a sign of the times that people really believed in the freedom of the music and the lifestyle, the freedom to take drugs and, in some ways, to create chaos. Even though everything was declared to be "for the people," mayhem was too often the result.

By the summer of '70, we had tried hash, which I found very strong at first. It made me feel a bit super-aware and self-conscious, even paranoid at times, but I persevered, of course. Hadn't the Beatles smoked it all the way through the making of *Rubber Soul*? So, I hung in with it and gradually overcame that initial trepidation to discover a world of calm and bliss.

That summer, I also took my first acid trip, the first of many. I suppose, thinking back, I did have a few nerves about taking LSD, as there had been some strange stories about people having bum trips, going psychotic, and hurling themselves from windows of very high buildings in a crazed state. But that wasn't the impression one got from listening to the tales of musicians who had taken it, as they talked about acid giving them a whole new perspective about the world and their music. These lessons from my musical gods overrode any minor qualms or fears I had. The drug came on quite slowly at first, kicking in after about forty minutes, as I experienced a mild feeling of calm and a sensation of the world slowing down a touch. This gave me time to begin noticing details in objects or my features, which became tantalizing as I stared longer at the vista, which pulsated slightly to a hidden rhythm. As the effects grew stronger and the pulsing, multicolored, distorted vision took hold, I could begin to understand what some of the Romantic poets had described. I didn't see "Lucy in the Sky with Diamonds" images, but a more visceral, gossamer landscape that was still very real, not a fantasy at all. In fact, that was what could easily overcome you: the feeling of the corporeal world pulsing, breathing in and out at one with you. It was a strange, disconcerting sensation, one that could be either good or bad, as I would discover firsthand over the course of time. That first time, the trees all looked like their branches were covered in snow, giving the impression it was Christmas, though it was midsummer. At one point later, lying in bed alone, I heard my heart slow down as if coming to a gradual halt. I thought it had stopped for a moment as a thick bead of sweat fell with a dull echo from my forehead; but as I listened, it slowly whirred back into action.

One doesn't think logically. My first tab was called Yellow Sunshine, like Hendrix got Purple Haze from the name of another breed of acid.

I was getting to love this new world now opening up to me. *Come along, William*, this life beckoned, as the wilderness had once called out to Daniel Boone. But one morning my dad lowered the boom, and my little universe was shaken to its core. My father had lost his job when an American firm took over and sacked everyone, replacing them with their people. It meant another move was on for us, with Dad starting his own business, which meant leaving Worthing for Kent, near London.

He had decided to form a small power-tool hire/buy concern, U-Hire, which would service large and small construction companies. He would live in a small room above the office his business occupied in Charlton, South East London. His plan was for us to join him once things got up and running.

Bollocks, I thought, *just when I'm starting to hang around with some great mates!* But there was nothing I could do about it. He was firm about his plans; we needed to go where the money was. The only consolation was that I would be living a lot closer to the beating heart of southern England, swinging London.

Nevertheless, it was difficult saying goodbye to Lol and my other mates, though Bromley was only sixty miles away. I knew from my other moves just what the stark reality would hold for me in the forthcoming months: a new school, and new classmates. I would have to adjust, again. I'd just started finding my niche in Worthing High School, and now I would have no close friends nearby, and who knew if I would meet the same sort of pals as I'd just left? These thoughts were paramount in my mind. I've always had difficulty facing the unknown—who doesn't?—but the unknown was there to be faced. Once again, it was time to find a new path.

CHAPTER FOUR

SUCKING IN THE '70S

BROMLEY WAS A SMALL TOWN ON the outskirts of SE London, on the edge of the urban sprawl area, where it reaches into the Kent countryside to the south. It is a twenty-minute train ride from the main central London station, from where you can get to anywhere in England, and the world.

The old country lanes became modern roads that twist and turn illogically, lined by leafy oaks whose branches form a natural arch. We lived on top of a rise on Shawfield Park, which, from my mum and dad's bedroom, offered a twelve-mile view into the green countryside to the southeast and beyond. My walk to school took me down Tylney Road to my new school, Ravensbourne School for Boys. Although still a grammar school, it was slowly converting to the new comprehensive school system that would divide students by streams, not separate them into two distinct groups at age eleven.

I slowly began to realize that most of the teachers were allied with the old system; they seemed to have lost interest, and were just marking time until retirement. Right from the start, I knew something was wrong, as I was put in the highest level for math, where I'm hopeless, and the remedial class for history, when that was my best fucking subject. Some of the kids in my history class didn't even know how to read.

Fuck it. The one subject I'm really good at and love and they put me in with the slow learners. This made me begin to hate school. Thank God I didn't have to take biology, as I hate to cut things up, but took an alternative choice, Religious Knowledge, which entailed "a look into the historical background to the events of the New Testament," which meant I was seriously studying the history of the Holy Land at the time of Jesus along with the sociopolitical implications of his actions. Most people in the class were just malingering, but I, naturally, found it fascinating and still do.

I found out much later that the Beatles' producer, George Martin, had once been a student at Ravensbourne, but I had no idea back then. It was populated by what we called "suedeheads," onetime skinheads who'd grown out their hair but still followed the skins' creed. I had long hair and was into rock 'n' roll. There were only two or three other boys like me, which was the direct opposite of Worthing High. We really were the odd ones out, but fuck it. Feeling disenchanted, I started cutting school to play music with one of the two blokes I got to know well, my friend Bill Jenkins, in his basement, strumming a twelve-bar backup while he picked out blues leads.

Bill had long, dark hair with a tight wave toward his ears that just reached his shoulders and he always walked with his back up and his hands in pocket, leaning forward. My eyesight is so bad, I always remember people by how they walk, recognizing their gait before their features. Bill was shorter than me, a really good bloke, as we would say in England, and he loved music.

We didn't start hanging out at first, but over the course of a few weeks, I realized he played the guitar and was quite serious about it. He was into jazz and blues as well as rock, and we began to play together. The guitars were amplified by attaching a microphone to a reel-to-reel tape recorder stuck onto the voice box of the acoustic guitar with tape and then sticking a piece of cardboard in just the right spot so the mic would become live, putting the amplified sound out into the air instead of just recording it. We used a laughably few watts of power, but it gave our cheap acoustic guitars a semblance of an electric, though very crude, sound.

I would play rhythm as he played blues solos and wailed on a harmonica he had taped to a coat hanger that, when bent into shape, did the job of giving a solid platform for him to play both guitar and harp at the same time. Bill had a basement in the bottom of his house on Widmore Road, and we would take off from school in the early afternoon to go play music there. The first time I ever heard Velvet Underground's *White Light/White Heat* was in that basement. We listened to everything. We eventually found a bloke who played drums, and he set his kit up in Bill's basement, which gave us a place to hang out that most kids have would have killed for. Most houses in England didn't have basements, unlike those in America. I don't remember his parents bothering us much. They were out when we skived off school.

We shared plenty of shit together. One afternoon while jamming, we discovered that if we slid the tape recorder microphone up and down a female mannequin leg Bill had, the recording would take on a crude form of phasing.

I had first started to teach myself to play drums when I was seven, but as soon as I realized the drummer was always at the back and usually didn't write the songs, I graduated from my makeshift drum kit to a five-quid guitar I bought for myself with my caddie funds, as my parents refused to buy me musical instruments I actually wanted to play, rather than the violin they tried to force me to learn. Because of my long hair and bad attitude in school, my dad didn't talk to me for two years, from the time I was fourteen until I was sixteen. It was rough, his not speaking to me, but I knew he couldn't understand how I was so different from him, in terms of my learning abilities. He was a mathematician, and I was hopeless. He thought I just wasn't trying, that I lacked willpower, but today I'm sure I would've been diagnosed with ADD/ADHD. We waged a silent war—he hated my long hair hanging in my breakfast each morning.

I had picked up Bert Weedon's beginning guitar book from the music shop back in Worthing, and then other items I needed from the music shop in Bromley. I taught myself some chords—E, then A, and D, as you could play a song with those; then B, as E, A, and B are blues chords; and then D. Next I learned G, C, F, and so on, over the years eventually progressing to bar chords. It was all so I could accompany myself singing or to try to write a song one day. I bought myself a pitch pipe to help me tune an instrument. It was like a six-note harmonica, giving the basic tuning of E-A-D-G-B-E. I struggled through the fingerings on my own in my room, but in England in those days, there wasn't much to do, so you didn't mind sitting there for hours on end buggering around, coming to grips with trying to be a musician of some sort. I'm a shitty guitar player, but I had at an early age realized that I was learning to play the instrument for a purpose—not to be the lead guitar player, but so I could write, sing, and play in a rock band. Not that I was such a great singer, really, but I began making some vocal noise, singing along to songs one step down, which is lazy, but it gave me part of the sound people recognize today. It was a start, a hobby, really, a fascination, and something I truly cared about, and I was doing it for myself, not because anybody told me to.

While in Bromley, at sixteen, I saved up my morning double paper round money and bought an Epiphone Riviera electric guitar some bloke was selling. That guitar would be with me for many years to come (you can hear it on the Generation X version of Lennon's "Gimme Some Truth," and see it in the "White Wedding" video). I owned a rudimentary amp for a while, but at eighteen, I bought myself an HH solid-state amp.

The do-it-yourself approach leads you down a path that says, *This is about you, no need to compromise*. All those people—parents, authority, friends—probably won't ever understand completely what you're trying to do or why, but communication is a beginning, and by just doing what I was doing, my actions spoke volumes.

I occasionally played with some mates other than Bill Jenkins, as I never passed up an opportunity to practice and improve. Another lad I got to know from school in Ravensbourne was Andy Steer, who had the dubious distinction of being the tallest teenager in England. Andy would suffer pain from his heart as he was growing so fast. He used to throw up at the sound of the Lee Dorsey song "Working in the Coal

Mine," so his brother bought the record just to annoy him and make him vomit. Andy was a great visual artist who hoped to be an animator for Disney one day. After finishing at Ravensbourne at sixteen, I didn't have enough qualifications to go to university, so I attended Orpington College of Further Education for two years to redo my A levels and try to raise my grades.

I enjoyed Orpington College a lot more than Ravensbourne, as we were allowed to wear our own clothes and the teachers spoke to us like adults and were genuinely interested in teaching. These were more like college courses, and I responded by trying harder, as I had no idea what I would do for a living, but I knew it was death to get a job you didn't really like. I took English language, literature, and British Constitution, which was interesting because a teacher who was a Trotskyite taught it. Thanks to his efforts, I learned that there is always more to take into consideration than the face value of society.

Still, I missed my pals from Worthing, but Lol Satchel would come up to visit and I would go down there. But Bromley became my everyday reality. With Andy up in the clouds, Bill J.'s shoulders up to his ears, and me channeling John Lennon—long hair, round glasses, and all—we must have made an amusing sight standing out amongst a bunch of suedeheads.

I soon began to find more friends who shared my passion for rock 'n' roll. From hanging around the Bromley South train station after school, I met up with some like-minded blokes who were attending the more enlightened Bromley Technical High School. Among them was Steve Bailey, later to metamorphose into Steve Severin, the bass guitarist with Siouxsie and the Banshees; and Simon "Boy" Barker, who became a noted photographer going by the name "Six." I identified with these new friends, as they shared my passion for rock music, especially David Bowie, whom we all admired a great deal. We were always looking out for the new and interesting in art, music, and life, recognizing in one another, by the way we dressed and what we liked, kindred, outcast spirits. Steve had long, light brown hair down to his waist and a caustic wit. He lived in Bromley, just a short walk from my house on Shawfield Park. Simon Barker had long, dark hair and an acid sense of humor. Even though we attended different schools, we became close friends and began going to concerts together.

One of the shows we saw was Captain Beefheart at the Finsbury Park Astoria, now the Rainbow Theatre. It was one of my all-time favorite shows, the Captain an outrageous character who defied all bounds of middle-class taste with his Delta-blues growl and made-up language. We also attended a double bill of Hawkwind and Frank Zappa at the Oval Cricket Ground. We had tickets for the second night of a Zappa gig up in London the year before, but a bloke, jealous because his girlfriend had just confessed to being infatuated with Frank, pulled him from the stage and broke his leg, and the next evening's gig was canceled. We also went regularly to the Croydon Greyhound to see bands like Stray, a London-based melodic hard-rock band, and Osibisa, whose music was a fusion of Afro-Caribbean rock-jazz and R&B.

We were all real big fans of the savagely satirical, hybrid jazz/doo-wop/blues-rock played by Zappa and the Mothers of Invention, the German electronic band Can's albums *Monster Movie* and *Tago Mago*, and John McLaughlin's Mahavishnu Orchestra record *The Inner Mounting Flame*. The more out there, the better we liked it. It was only later that we began to appreciate the simpler, song-oriented new glam sound of David Bowie, Roxy Music, and the New York Dolls.

Around this time, I met a girl named Rebecca, whose brother was into groups like the Velvet Underground and Iggy Pop. I couldn't believe how outrageous songs like "Heroin" and the entire *White Light/White Heat* album were. I became obsessed with this new music, and rode my bike ten miles to a secondhand record store in Penge, where I found the Stooges' self-titled first album. I told Steve about this music from New York and Detroit, and we both started to believe it was the wave of the future. We read that David Bowie was hanging out with these bands in New York, chumming with Lou Reed and Iggy at Max's Kansas City. We gravitated toward these personalities who seemed far from the mainstream, with their own unique views on poetry and musicianship, evincing a do-it-yourself attitude opposed to the glut of "muso" bands dominating the rock landscape.

When we could afford to, we smoked hash and downed acid,

Tuinals, Seconals, and Mandrax. Sometimes we took speed. One friend who had a particular fondness for speed began losing his back teeth from overuse. Steve, Simon, and I lived drugs and music, dreaming of one day having our own group, which became our daily focus, even though I was the only one who actually owned a guitar and could play it.

We started to take acid bought from a bloke who sold it near a pub on Chislehurst Green. After partying, I would hitchhike home, fucked up on Mandrax. Sometimes I was so tired, on the verge of falling asleep when I got home, I didn't realize I had left a trail of Ritz crackers and cheese on my way up the stairs to my bedroom. Mum confronted me one night and I told her I was drunk, but I had no smell of booze on my breath, so she became exceedingly suspicious. Another time, the acid I took on a Saturday afternoon didn't start kicking in until I sat at home with my parents that evening. The carpet looked like it was rippling from a snake underneath, and when Mum put her head around the door to ask me a question, she and Dad looked like they were wearing Indian war paint. I excused myself as being tired, went up to my room, and hallucinated in bed for hours. My glow-in-the-dark crucifix was moving, and it looked like Jesus was dribbling a soccer ball at his feet. I remember listening to King Crimson's *The Court of the Crimson King*, having to lie back on the floor while an electric feeling coursed through my body. If I closed my eyes, it felt as if I were rushing backwards, and the picture in my mind was of me surrounded by a blue/white light. I stayed in bed until the trip gradually came to an end the next morning.

We went to as many concerts as we could afford and saw Roxy Music, Lou Reed on his Rock 'n' roll Animal tour, and Sparks at the Rainbow. We caught Lou Reed once more, this time opening for Beck, Bogert, and Appice on his '72 Transformer tour, and then again two years later at Charlton Football Ground, on his Sally Can't Dance tour, playing with the Who and Bad Company.

I also remember attending a massive three-day, twenty-four-hour outdoor music festival at Weeley, in the countryside north of London. In the spirit of Woodstock and the Isle of Wight, the lineup included

Crosby, Stills, Nash & Young; the Faces; the Groundhogs; King Crimson; Mott the Hoople; Lindisfarne; and Marc Bolan. It rained a lot during the weekend but it was still fantastic, everyone sitting on plastic covers on the ground, with all sorts of music, from rock, folk, and blues to hard rock, fusion jazz, and on and on. I fell asleep to King Crimson and woke up at seven the next morning to Mott the Hoople doing "Thunderbuck Ram" to a mostly comatose audience of 250,000, except for those still freaking out on the acid they'd taken the night before.

The largely hippie audience had already decided they hated Bolan and T. Rex, booing en masse when he took the stage, but I liked his simple rock, having been turned on to him when I dated a girl named Deborah in the early '70s. He actually wrote great melodies and used the regular guitar chords that I knew, instead of the more complex and slightly more sophisticated shapes of the Beatles, which was interesting to me. He also favored the twelve-bar blues, so he was returning to pop, blues, and rockabilly, but in a modern way. When T. Rex went on Bolan walked to the front of the stage and confronted the hooting mass by saying, "Fuck off!" Amazingly, the crowd shut up and listened to the band's set, including a mad, twenty-minute jam on "Ride a White Swan," during which Bolan bashed his guitar with a pair of tambourines. When he finished, the audience stood up as one and gave him a standing ovation that went on for quite a few minutes. Amazing to think he cowed a quarter million people with the words "Fuck off." This wasn't far from a punk-rock attitude, especially coming in the middle of the hippie era. I still think that somehow what he did that day was a turning point, a new attitude creeping back into rock that wasn't so touchy-feely.

Around this time, I started to go out with a girl named Valerie. I remember after another memorable party at someone's house, she was so drunk and fucked up that she took a shit in the bathtub and wiped her ass on the shower curtain. One day, while we were walking along the street with my mates, they asked Valerie if I had a big dick. For a moment, I was mortified. What would she say? If it was unfavorable, it could lead to years of ribbing, but, thank God, after a pregnant pause, she replied, "It's like his last name—Broad!" Phew, that was a dodgy moment, but she came through.

By now rock 'n' roll had taken over our lives. I was working a double paper route so I could afford to buy albums, see shows, or drop a tab of acid for the weekend. That's how I funded my extracurricular rock 'n' roll activities. But then, at seventeen, I had a decision to make. Either I had to join the workforce or go to university.

I had no intention of getting a nine-to-five job. Under pressure from my parents, I began attending the University of Sussex, near Brighton on the south coast of England, in 1974. This meant I would only be an hour from London, so I could still see all the concerts I wanted while there, and wouldn't be far away from my friends. My hair was now cropped short in a Lou Reed cut, and I wore black or denim drainpipe jeans, having completely transitioned from the flares and long hair of four years ago, still favored by most of the other students. Thanks to my short, dyed jet-black hair, some of my classmates thought I was on an army scholarship.

I didn't yet know just how intent I was on following my heart, but I knew I didn't want to be in anyone's power—not my dad's or that of the job marketplace. Never be in thrall to anyone but your own wants and desires, because only you can make yourself happy. Fly your own flag, and be true to it. Your soul is the true captain.

During my one year at Sussex University, my one true accomplishment was getting to play in a rock band. It didn't have a name, but we didn't care about that. We only played once a week on Fridays in the cafeteria, but at least we were playing. Talking about our set list and finding a place to rehearse took up the rest of our time. As far as I was concerned, we were tripping the light fantabulous. My dream of singing and playing guitar had started to come true. I had yet to learn that, in order to achieve your dreams, you must sometimes struggle to ultimately survive, and that to write meaningful songs, you must live, so that your experiences inform your words. These experiences must color the world you live in so that you can touch the ears and hearts of others. In 1975, I had yet to live enough life to know this.

My bandmates and I were looked down on and shunned by the other college groups, like the jazz fans. My attitude was, fuck 'em and their tired allegiance. I dreamed of storming barricades; they could keep their small-minded approach. I loved rock. I was being faithful to myself. Their dismissive nature hurt, but as I blared Iggy Pop and the Stooges' *Raw Power* in my dorm room, I had the future firmly in my grasp. All they had was past dreams, a fad disappearing into the backwaters of the music world. With rock, one could conquer the known and the unknown. With rock 'n' roll, one ruled the heart.

It was around this time my sister, Jane, recalls me asking her to attend one of my gigs at a pretty run-down church hall in Burnt Ash, just north of Bromley, where a group of greasers came in, shouted, and started throwing raw eggs and tomatoes at us as I kept playing, unfazed.

I was still a big fan of old rockabilly, '50s doo-wop, and rock, especially the stuff the infamous Morris Levy was reissuing on his Roulette label in the early and mid-'70s. It was pretty fantastic hearing Little Richard's Specialty sides or Jerry Lee Lewis's Sun recordings, plus Roy Orbison, Johnny Cash, Frankie Lymon and the Teenagers, Gene Chandler's "Duke of Earl," and the Cadillacs' "Speedo." It was a great relief to hear this rhythm-based music, short and to the point, the antithesis of the bloated prog rock of the '70s.

At the same time, I was listening to a lot of folk, as I appreciated the fingerpicking styles of playing guitar. I bought a twelve-string acoustic and listened to the Incredible String Band, Steeleye Span, Dylan's *Freewheeling* album, Linda and Richard Thompson's accordion-dominated Morris dance albums. I was musically educating myself.

Siouxsie Sioux was Susan Janet Ballion, a self-described loner who was a fan of the same bands I followed. She left school at seventeen, and her unique fashion style—fetish/bondage outfits that often featured her exposed breasts—turned heads when she began to follow the Sex Pistols after seeing them with Steve Bailey in February 1976.

Steve first met her in late '73 or early '74, when she lived in Chislehurst, near Bromley. They were really boyfriend and girlfriend, and I was always knocked out for Steve that he had met someone as cool as himself. I was never jealous of them, but in love with them as a couple and as friends, and this feeling grew the more I admired Susan as the type of girl one would wish to find for oneself. She had a larger-than-life personality and was brimming with ideas that flowed throughout her conversation. Susan didn't feel she had to suck up to males or their ideas or feel dominated by them. If anything, she gave any man she met a run for his money and could put him in his place with a sharp, witty saying that left him nonplussed or mouth agape. She is a liberated woman who is not bound by any other female's idea of what freedom is. She rules her universe like the deity she truly is. Don't get in her way, as the forces of the universe will be arrayed against you.

CHAPTER FIVE

AND THEN THERE WAS PUNK

100 Club, Oxford Street, London

"GET BACK TO LONDON!" THE FATEFUL postcard from Steve Bailey read. I took the train as soon as I could, and on March 30, 1976, at the 100 Club on London's Oxford Street, I saw the Sex Pistols play for the first time. On that night, the Pistols onstage were unlike anything we'd ever seen before. Johnny Rotten, with orange, razor-cropped hair, was hunched over, holding a beer and staring bug-eyed out at the crowd through tiny, tinted square glasses. He was wearing a ripped-up sweater, striped baggy pants, and big flat rounded shoes with thick rubber soles dubbed "brothel creepers." He was constantly bantering back and forth with the band's manager, Malcolm McLaren, who stood in the wings of the stage. While hardly moving, John radiated a defiant intensity that demanded your attention. I remember him noticing a few people in the audience with long hair and flares, then haranguing them for being out-of-date hippies, demanding they go back to their Melanie records. It all made a strong impression on me. The Pistols began a residency there every Tuesday night, and we would be there for the duration—Steve, Simon, Siouxsie Sioux, and the rest of the crew journalist Caroline Coon would later dub "the Bromley Contingent."

One particular night, Pistols guitarist Steve Jones showed up wearing a T-shirt from Malcolm's Sex shop with zippered slits revealing his nipples. Glen Matlock, looking like an urchin from a Dickens novel, played really good bass. At first glance, he could have been mistaken for a member of Small Faces. On another occasion, Glen turned up in a white outfit with paint splattered all over à la Jackson Pollock. That was the start of a fad that would be copied by the Clash. And then there was Paul Cook, whom Jonesy later dubbed "Cookie." He was a solid drummer, underrated, never wasting a move, everything counted—it was all in the beat!

Even at this early stage, the Pistols had their signature sound—tight and aggressive, with lots of blistering guitar riffs from Jones—but they were still playing covers, including the Monkees/Paul Revere and the Raiders' "(I'm Not Your) Steppin' Stone," the Who's "Substitute," and the Stooges' "No Fun." They had just begun writing some of their own material and, at a later date, I was on hand when they introduced "Anarchy in the UK." With the initial rolling bass riff and pounding drums, as Johnny snarled, "I am an Antichrist / I am an anarchist / Don't know what I want / But I know how to get it / I wanna destroy the passerby!" It was a long overdue call to arms.

John would take a song that said "I love you" and instead sing "I hate you," as he did covering the Small Faces song "Whatcha Gonna Do About It," where he'd opt for, "I want you to know that I *hate* you, baby, want you to know I don't care." To me, it revolutionized the kind of attitude a singer could take with a song. Johnny's whole demeanor was that the rest of the world was boring and complacent, and it was his duty to shake us up by administering a sucker punch in the gut.

In mid-'70s England, you couldn't get a shit job, let alone have a career. It didn't matter if you were a garbage collector or a college graduate. We didn't have any money to spend at expensive fashion boutiques. In those early days, Vivienne Westwood was the only designer doing stuff we could relate to—not that we could afford her clothes, either. To create your own image, you had to invent your own fashion, something original to put on your back. We needed something new to evoke the way we felt, and as fashion necessity turned fashion statement, we came up with our originals by cutting up old T-shirts or spray painting our own designs on them—anything we felt would set us apart.

When John's clothes fell apart, he safety-pinned them back together, or he took a Pink Floyd T-shirt and scrawled I HATE across the front. His look was more than mere fashion—it was a declaration of war against the self-indulgence and indifference that had come to permeate not only British bourgeois life but even what passed for the counterculture in the '70s. The Pistols' don't-give-a-shit attitude and their own extreme sense of style gave voice to what I was feeling and what I wanted out of life. They spoke to me. Steve Bailey was right. We had found what we were looking for.

What's more, the Sex Pistols seemed to be doing things on their own terms. It was a reaction to everyone who was telling people our age what we should do to succeed. After the Pistols' 100 Club residency came to an end, my Bromley friends and I would see the band at other venues several times that summer of '76, and we would come to believe that there was hope for our generation. Now it was up to us to start our own bands, following Johnny Rotten's example of how to make the ordinary extraordinary. The dull gray English skies suddenly opened up to a rainbow of possibilities. The fans embraced safety pins and spiky, razor-cut hair. Although the latter had been around since at least the mods and then David Bowie, Johnny started the home cut, the bad haircut that looked really good. This has remained the hair fashion statement among hip white kids to this day.

But punk was not all about hair color and clothes. John had brains and charisma, too. He spoke as if he knew something we could never know. He was wise beyond his years and dangerous to the establishment, a kid with his own ideas and way of thinking. He challenged England to get off its collective arse and demand something better than, as Rotten put it, a "holiday in the sun, a cheap holiday in other people's misery," a line that hit home for me, trying, as I was, to avoid the middle-class aspirations of my parents. The songs screamed with social consciousness. John warned us about the powers-that-be, that they promised "no future, no future for you!" Disgust poured from every rolled syllable, every upraised brow, every sneer, and every pop-eyed stare. No one was safe from his vitriol.

John was both old and young at the same time. I always thought he was older than me, but it turned out I was actually two months older than him. Seeing the Pistols plug their new songs into the set, gradually finding an audience, their fashions spreading, was thrilling. Soon we'd have a scene of our own to rival the '60s Merseybeat and trippy Carnaby Street pop explosions.

This was protest music retooled by youthful frustration and ambivalence, aggression with no outlet. The seething rage and spurned disgust we felt inside would inform the lyrics. Where the reigning arena-rock bands of the '70s stressed size, power, and superiority while keeping a healthy distance from their audience, punk embraced attitude, street smarts, and intimacy—much like our hero Bruce Lee, fighting with our bare hands. They had long hair and flares; we cropped our hair, dyed it, and wore pegged trousers. Forget My Generation. This was *Our* Generation. If you couldn't play your guitar like John McLaughlin or Frank Zappa, why not write a great song with three chords? Heck, Howlin' Wolf did it. And then the Rolling Stones copied him.

Still, a world that offered "no future" also required new artists and new rock stars. I finished out the year at Sussex University, returned home, and promptly informed my parents I would not be returning. Needless to say, they were horrified.When I told my folks I was quitting school and instead would be joining a punk-rock group, they experienced an onslaught of emotions. They were astonished, worried, confused, and hurt. They were from another generation, one that survived Hitler and the Blitz, and then the postwar reconstruction. They believed you couldn't dream of a successful future if you didn't have the right qualifications, the right education, and social connections. When I told them I wanted to be a rock star, it was their worst nightmare.

That summer, I worked at my dad's tool and hire company, responding to ads in *Melody Maker* placed by others who wanted to play this new brand of music, including a small ad from Tony James. He had been in the group London SS with Mick Jones, who would eventually form the Clash with Joe Strummer and Paul Simonon. I came from South East London and Tony from Fulham, but for both of us,

everything revolved around Kings Road and Wardour Street. We met
at the Ship, a pub on Wardour Street in Soho, London's West End. We
hit it off immediately and began to discuss putting a band together.
Tony was a clever, knowledgeable guitarist and bass player who liked
to write lyrics and riffs.

At that same time, I had answered a *Melody Maker* advert to audition for a band being put together by Acme Attractions, a Kings Road
clothing store and competitor to Malcolm McLaren's Sex. I went to the
tryout wearing my pointed Sex winklepickers, with watch buckles on
the side, skintight black drainies, a secondhand striped shirt with the
collar up, my hair short, flat, and dyed black. I strapped on my Epiphone semi-acoustic and played, not very well, but good enough to beat
out two long-haired musicians who complained I couldn't even tune
the guitar. Acme owner John Krevine, who organized the tryout, said,
"Yeah, but he's got the right attitude."

I could play and sing a bit, but I must admit to having been somewhat surprised to be offered the gig. It confirmed what I truly believed:
Follow your own course, be the captain of your soul. Also, I had an intimate knowledge of the burgeoning scene they wanted to plug into.
They already had a singer and drummer, so I brought Tony in to them,
claiming we wrote songs together, even though we hadn't actually
penned a single note at the time. I insisted I wouldn't be in the group
if they didn't hire Tony, too, which they agreed to. The singer was an
older guy named Gene October. Krevine came up with the name Chelsea, as everything that was cool emanated from Kings Road. Things
were starting to take off.

The Bromley Contingent continued to make the scene with a series
of wild parties, including one memorable bash at Bertie Berlin's house,
with Siouxsie, Steve Severin, Simon Barker, a bunch of workers from
Malcolm's Sex shop, and Johnny Rotten. Those were the fun times. We
were fine young cannibals, ready to conquer the universe, poised to become stars in our own right.

CHAPTER SIX

IN A REVOLUTION, ONE YEAR EQUALS FIVE

Louise's, a lesbian club in a basement just off Oxford Street, London

"YOU'LL NEVER FIND, AS LONG AS you live, someone who loves you, tender like I do," the bass voice intoned. Slickly, the DJ moved the ladies around the downstairs dance floor at Louise's, a basement club off Oxford Street frequented mostly by lesbians.

One had to enter through a narrow side street, which opened into a small reception room with a few scattered tables and chairs. Toward the back was a stairway that led downstairs to the bar and dance floor. The clientele was mostly butch women and fashionable lipstick lesbians.

For the Sex Pistols and our small Bromley Contingent of early punks, it was a much-needed haven. Back then, the way we dressed would have started a riot if we had set foot in any normal club or pub. The DJ often played Lou Rawls's "You'll Never Find Another Love Like Mine," and it would always pack the dance floor. It was an anthem for those ladies, and I would casually watch their slow dances and hot, intimate touches from my spot on the edge of the dance floor.

The people who ran Louise's accepted us, due to the fact that we were part of the group of people from Malcolm and Vivienne's store, Sex. We were also friends with a dominatrix named Linda, who went to Louise's regularly with her coterie of girls. Benjamin Franklin once offered advice to his fellow revolutionaries: "We must all hang together, or assuredly we shall all hang separately." We were a small group of people bored with the repeated clichés of modern life and its stagnant, putrid waters. That is what brought us—and ultimately bonded us—together.

I delivered tools for my dad in the daytime and went to rehearsals and gigs and hung out at Louise's every night. I would get home at 4 a.m., wake up at eight, and start all over again. This accelerated lifestyle would eventually take its toll, but I had a purpose that drove me to succeed. Referring to overthrowing the czar in Russia, Lenin said, "There are decades where nothing happens; and there are weeks where decades happen." Revolution was on our minds, too.

We nursed ourselves on the lesbians' rebellious milk, growing strong and attracting like-minded souls. We all congregated there, drinking and socializing, plotting our rebellion. It was our midnight meeting place, our sanctuary. We all walked the same path at that time. Many of the classic-rock bands talked about musicianship but had little to offer us, the disenfranchised and disenchanted. We were youth thrown on the scrap heap.

There was at least one veteran band that spoke to us. The Who insisted, "We're all wasted," while the likes of Lou Reed, David Bowie, and Iggy Pop seemed in touch, but what about our own scene?

Those nights at Louise's gave us hope and made me feel that something special was indeed afoot. I first heard Steve Jones utter the now-iconic phrase "Never mind the bollocks!" there as he sat with Rotten, Paul Cook, and Malcolm. The lost generation was back from the dead! As the gay ladies danced and loved one another, we devised our plans and consolidated a movement. By being like-minded, we ruled the night. We would rock London to its core. The lesbian bar was our spiritual "upper room," and we, the new aristocracy of the poor, knighted with fire, sallied forth and followed Johnny Rotten into the unknown!

For now, the "unknown" turned out to be Paris, where the Sex Pistols were to play their first-ever gig outside England, at the opening of the Club de Châlet du Lac, Paris, September 3, 1976. I drove my dad's Ford delivery van and we boarded the ferry at Dover that would take us across the Channel to Calais. Crowded into the van were Steve Bailey, Siouxsie, Si Barker, and Michael, one of a set of twins who hung out with us and who first used the expression "Never mind the bollocks" before Jones, with his don't-give-a-shit attitude, brought it to life for a whole generation.

We met up with the Pistols at Sartre's old hangout, Les Deux Magots, on the Place Saint-Germain-des-Prés, and occupied an outdoor table on the busy sidewalk. John was wearing a black beret and a red kids' jumper slit up the side. Parisians have always had a sense of pride when it comes to fashion, so it was great fun seeing the befuddled looks of surprise on their faces when confronted with a group of oddly dressed punks. This wasn't just a challenge to their sense of style and taste that could be chalked up to the generation gap; it was an assault on their ideas and attitudes.

That attack continued into the night at the gig, when Siouxsie wore her "Night Porter" outfit, complete with a swastika armband and SS cap. She'd taken the look from Liliana Cavani's controversial 1974 film of the same name, in which Charlotte Rampling played a concentration camp survivor who falls in love with her Nazi guard/torturer, played by Dirk Bogarde. Siouxsie's hair was cropped short, as Rampling's was in the film, and her makeup was extreme. She would become both famous and infamous for the getup. We were all used to strange looks, but the crowd's response to Siouxsie's outfit at the Club de Châlet du Lac that night was particularly unpleasant.

The French audience had no way of knowing in those early days that clothing as a performance art statement was part of the punk culture and couture. We all co-opted images and logos that, when mixed together, would force an observer to react and feel the rejection of all things human that we felt. We tried to challenge preconceived notions. Some of Vivienne Westwood's designs mixed communist and fascist imagery to assault the onlooker. Just as we felt marginalized, we wanted to lash back and hurt so that we could, as the Doors' Jim Morrison put it, "break on through to the other side."

All we wanted to do was shock, because that was all we felt was left to us. During those early days, within our little universe, an understanding of other people's interpretations of our actions was beyond us. On this night, though, the taunting crowd was becoming downright hostile.

The Pistols came onstage, with Rotten sporting a Westwood-designed black parachute bondage outfit with straps from elbow to elbow, leg to leg. We felt repressed in every way, so the prism of sexual bondage spoke to our belief that most people simply embrace and accept the chains and whips of society.

"The problem is you—whatcha gonna do?" John taunted the crowd in "Problems." The French audience watched the show impassively while scowling at us. "We hate long hair and we don't wear flares." Rotten twisted, turned, and grimaced as he leaned on the microphone stand. The black outfit of restraint seemed to electrify his look and galvanize his attitude. A true star, John dominated the room with his presence and wild stare, punctuating his lyrics by burning a hole in the audience with his eyes. He might ignore them one moment, then launch into a tirade the next, practically frothing at the mouth, following it up with a look of disgust at the lack of response from the overwhelmed crowd.

Meanwhile, the Sex Pistols were coming together as a band. Steve Jones was getting noticeably better, and Cookie was adding beat, becoming tighter timewise. Glen Matlock held his end down well, adding tasteful runs that Sid Vicious, his eventual replacement, could and would never accomplish.

"We're vacant and we don't *caaaaaare*," caterwauled John. We had been led into a nowhere world where black was white and white was black, where no one fit if you challenged the norm. Proof of that was this Paris audience, getting increasingly incensed at us. Obviously, *The Night Porter* wasn't very big in France.

As the band thundered to the end of the set, things started to get even uglier. We tried to ignore the rowdy crowd, but Siouxsie was glaring and giving back as good as she got. Soon, a whole section of fans started throwing stuff at us. When it looked like they were about to attack us, we managed to run across the stage and find refuge with the band in their tiny dressing room. We later found out it was the anniversary of the day France declared war on Germany in 1939. Siouxsie sure had balls; she refused to remove the offending armband, and continued to wear it the rest of the evening at the after-party.

The City of Lights held a wild promise. To walk through the "rue Morgue" and drink in the Gallic nightlife was stimulating, but the gig I had just seen stayed with me, lodged in my brain. I don't remember too much after it except waking up in the driver's seat of my van looking onto the River Seine, a peaceful Saturday morning, the calm before the proverbial storm.

CHAPTER SEVEN

GENERATION X MARKS THE SPOT:
WILLIAM BROAD BECOMES BILLY IDOL

Portobello Road, London

THE SUMMER MONTHS OF DRIVING FOR my dad during the day and rehearsing at night reinforced the desire in my heart and mind for an artistic life. I couldn't stand the idea of working for someone else's dreams. Even the fairly benign slavery of working for my father was not my idea of a life. I had come to the realization that I had no interest in selling a product unless the product was *me*. I had the blues about society and wanted to express myself, even if I didn't quite yet know completely how to accomplish it all.

Rehearsing with Chelsea was a beginning. My company of like-minded souls from Bromley fortified these ideals, as all we wanted was to control our destinies, and rock 'n' roll was one helluva way to do it. The Pistols served as our flagship, showing us the future, that the world could be ours if we so chose.

We couldn't just blame our parents. It was on us. We knew we wanted to put society on trial whether or not anyone would listen. We congregated and started making music to express this self-inflicted mission, to stand next to the greats, display our hand, and take on the world.

Growing up, I developed a lack of self-esteem that tortures me with doubts about my ability. At times, it cripples me, but alternatively it sets me free. My focus is much different from my parents'. It sees possibilities where they see doom and disaster. It hates with passion, where they simply dislike or ignore. It struggles over decisions that they would easily make. My ideas of right and wrong are skewed, where they see things clearly. But I'm ultimately set free by a dream for a life that overcomes my limitations and can make me glory in any success I might have that proves me right.

Where did all these feelings of alienation start? Lou Reed said, "I know I'm not dumb because I know I'm not smart." My fear was of mediocrity, of being just another cog in the relentless system that would eventually grind our spirits down to dust. I refused to be a prisoner in a gilded cage from which there was no escape, like Patrick McGoohan's Number Six in *The Prisoner*. I was determined to overcome my limitations, to stare my mediocrity in the face, to step up and dare to fail big, to go for the gold, live on the edge of uncertainty. At least I'd be alive to feel my own pain, as John Lennon had commanded. Dive rather than sink, and dare the current to take you!

AT THAT TIME ENGLAND WAS A soulless world of few possibilities, especially for its young. Gangs of police roamed London and the major cities, inflicting hell on the immigrant population, which had been reviled for taking jobs away from "those who needed them." They patrolled the streets, armed with the "sus" law: the suspicion of anything—drugs, weapons, any wrongdoing—provided sufficient grounds to stop people and harass or detain them. They harassed the young who were out of work and on the dole, while real criminals roamed free. The feelings of freedom, love, and peace engendered in the '60s had given way to a police-state mentality. A cold wind froze the hope and shriveled the testicles. We would need to grow bigger balls to deal with it.

One night, the police pulled us over, driving in my dad's van. They had their truncheons out, but burst out laughing as Siouxsie, Steve Severin, Si Barker, Bertie Berlin, and Little Debbie all tumbled out of the van, one after another, dressed in fashions too wild for them to understand. We set out to confuse the straights with our look and attitude. We were not going to take it anymore.

The left-wing liberalism of the previous decade had given way to a reinvigorated right wing that appeared to be gaining in strength and fanaticism in England's hour of need. The glam-rock and prog-rock movements were tolerated because they posed no threat to the establishment, with both offering escapes into either fantasy or musicianship. The politicized reggae of the Jamaican soul movement, thanks to mass immigration, was beginning to emerge in Britain. Dub-style dance-hall sounds reinforced the experimental nature of breaking down a recorded track into a wild, abandoned experiment into the possibilities of sound deconstruction, a new edge right on our own doorstep.

Amid this maelstrom, Chelsea rehearsed in a warehouse owned by John Krevine, our manager and the owner of Acme Attractions, located at the end of Portobello Road, near the Jamaican area in London. This was where dreadlocks lived in red, gold, and green, their Rastafarian looks representing a nonconformist style, the stores blasting "a wide selection without objection" of reggae. There was an uprising on the street that would inspire the Clash song "White Riot," where the dreadlocks were made to retreat in the face of police superiority in numbers "down the back end of Portobello." We watched from the top-floor window of our rehearsal space as rocks were thrown and scuffles broke out. The incident inspired our song "Youth Youth Youth," a punk-rock call-to-arms anthem, as the rude boys and rebels were referred to as "youth" in reggae culture. It was the second song Tony and I wrote, after "Ready Steady Go," a rallying cry for our band and for the young people out there in bedsit land.

Don Letts, a young dreadlocked London rude boy, worked behind the counter at Acme Attractions, playing his mixtape cassettes of all the latest and far-out reggae, then giving me copies. This new music was a far cry from the skank of the '60s. The deep, slow-moving rhythms passed from the mind deep into the soul, encouraging us to refresh rock 'n' roll and make it relevant again, as they had done with reggae.

A girlfriend offered to strip my hair of color and dye it black with blue highlights. But she forgot to bring the right stuff, so I left it peroxide blond. Gene October went nuts at the next rehearsal, insisting I change it back, which made me resolve to keep it that way, if it had that much of an effect on him. My small single-pickup guitar was black, so it looked good in contrast. My new look was the first inkling of my new identity.

Just as we had claimed, Tony and I had started writing songs together. We were all mightily influenced by the Ramones' eponymous first album. Only the Pistols didn't speed up their tempos; they kept to their original midpace speed. We rehearsed and played our first gig at the Chelsea Potter pub. I played guitar, tuning it up before the gig and hoping it didn't go out while I played. Of course, it was punk rock, so it hardly mattered. I remember we did a version of the Equals' "Baby Come Back" at superspeed, so I could play straight eights.

I still remember the wild excitement and adrenaline rush of nerves we all shared at that first gig. We only had a twenty-minute set at the time, which we could stretch to a half hour by playing songs twice. There weren't any originals in the set except for "Ready Steady Go."

Gene was the lead singer, and I joined in on backup vocals with Tony on bass and John Towe on drums. The semi-drunken audience leered at us, and we leered right back. Sometimes you have to plant your feet and deliver your ideas with as much personality as you can muster. Stare into the jaws of defeat and snatch victory. It was weird playing our first show on the floor along the side window of the Potter, but I was used to performing in the canteen coffee bar at Sussex, so it was no problem. And then it was all over in a flash.

I WAS VERY NEARLY IN AN early version of Siouxsie and the Banshees. I told Malcolm McLaren during the Screen on the Green Festival in Islington, August 29, which featured the Sex Pistols, the Clash, and the Buzzcocks, that he should book the band Siouxsie, Steve, and I were forming for the show he was promoting at the 100 Club on September 20. By the time of the 100 Club show, I was already committed to Chelsea and couldn't play with both, so the band performed with Marco Pirroni (later of Adam and the Ants) on guitar and Sid Vicious playing drums, which set the Banshees legend in motion.

John Krevine also managed the art-rock performance band Throbbing Gristle. Our next gig was supporting them during an art exhibit at the London Institute of Contemporary Arts on October 18, which consisted of, among other things, used bloody Tampax placed in frames along the walls. We called ourselves L.S.D. for that particular gig, though we went back to Chelsea afterward. The gig was reviewed by *New Musical Express*'s Tony Parsons, the first time I'd ever been mentioned in the music magazines that I had been reading, like gospel, since I was twelve.

Before the Internet, music publications like *Melody Maker* and *NME* carried the desperate hopes of a large number of adolescents in England, for whom music was a primary interest. Ever since Elvis Presley, youth culture started to have a true voice of its own. John Lennon was spot-on when he said, "Before Elvis, there was nothing." Teenagers with money had become a cultural force, using music and the arts to express their inner feelings. Rock 'n' roll gathered power with every changing of the guard, and now it was our turn.

The malignant power of rock 'n' roll turned me on. Being onstage was like a quick wet fuck—short and sweet, scary, but oh so neat. The magic of punk—or its blessing—was that nobody really knew what it was, exactly. Like a theory or an undiscovered land, it was there to be explored in rehearsal and onstage. That's where it happened, a deepening sense of the possible, a tidal wave of emotional politics set loose in Merry Olde England. It was all we were left as Britain descended into hell. We were forced to act. The loss of a future meant we had to carve one out with our own actions. Punk had been explored in rock in the early '60s, and its very simplicity rendered it the perfect vehicle for young adult bile and spleen.

Chelsea played a gig at the Electric Circus in Manchester that was our one and only gig outside of London. Our next gig was at the Nashville on November 21 supporting the Stranglers, the last one Tony and I would ever play as Chelsea. After writing "Youth Youth Youth" in rehearsal one day, Tony and I looked at each other and realized that Gene couldn't sing the song because he was already thirty. For a twenty-year-old, that was ancient. I didn't want to be an adult. I didn't want to be in control.

We realized we were writing songs for me to sing. Tony was writing a lot of the lyrics, and I worked on the chords and melody. Gene didn't like the fact that a young kid with peroxide-blond hair was upstaging him as we began to attract more fans of the new punk music. He wanted us to write a song with the title "Mad Dog," which we just couldn't do. It felt forced, and not in line with the idea Tony and I had for a group named Chelsea.

The inevitable break with Chelsea was a good thing for us. It brought Tony and me back to our original idea of a group with a social conscience, but brash and fun, with more of an up-to-the-moment image than Chelsea's '60s style. We wanted to play this new music for our twenty-something souls. We didn't want to be in any retro group. Though we gained some valuable experience out of the association, it was time to break off from Gene. We kept John Towe as drummer and Krevine as manager for the time being.

At this point, it seemed like everyone was reinventing themselves, cutting their hair, altering their look and their names. I thought changing my name would free me from the shackles of family and also protect them from possibly being embarrassed by my wicked ways. I intended to use the name Billy Idle, which had been bestowed on me by a disapproving chemistry teacher who had written on my report card: "WILLIAM IS IDLE!" in giant block letters, I-D-L-E. I had been using that name on the ID card required for entry into Louise's. But Monty Python's Eric Idle already had this name. When *Melody Maker* journalist Caroline Coon interviewed me for a story she was writing about the Bromley Contingent, she asked me to spell my name. I realized I couldn't be I-D-L-E. I had to decide right then and there. It occurred to me that I-D-O-L would work just as well. With his bleached blond hair and punk-rock pedigree, Billy Idol emerged.

Tony and I were at my house one day, working on song ideas, when I showed him a book called *Generation X* about '60s youth culture in Britain that my mum had found at a garage sale a couple of years earlier. We immediately thought it could be a great name for this new band, since we both felt part of a youth movement bereft of a future, that we were completely misunderstood by and detached from the present social and cultural spectrum. We also felt the name projected the many possibilities that came with presenting our generation's feelings and thoughts.

I asked most of my friends what they thought of the name, and since no one liked it, I decided it must be good. Tony began to write some lyrics for the song that became "Your Generation."

TRYIN' TO FORGET YOUR GENERATION / USING ANY WAY I CAN / THE END MUST
JUSTIFY THE MEANS / YOUR GENERATION DON'T MEAN A THING TO ME

Then I started writing the chords and melody. A B-bar chord with the fingers lifted—D-A-D-A-D-A-D-A—led to the familiar pattern of what would turn out to be our first single. It was a takeoff on "My Generation," but for the moment, we chose to deny our musical influences and embrace the now.

IT MIGHT MAKE OUR FRIENDS ENEMIES / BUT WE GOTTA TAKE THAT CHANCE.

Tony and I wanted a real hot-shit guitarist for Generation X, but the punk scene was still pretty small and there weren't that many good players around. Where would we find a fourth member? We decided to just hang out on the scene and hope to hell we'd discover one. Had I blown my chance by turning down the Banshees' gig at the 100 Club? I sure hoped not.

The punk scene began growing in leaps and bounds, with ten becoming twenty and then a hundred. You could reach out and touch it. To us, it was everywhere. The Pistols' "Anarchy in the UK" would soon hit record-store shelves, and the Damned's "New Rose" had just been released and was selling well, alongside a trickle of records by a number of lesser-known English punk bands. Every night was a non-stop party.

One evening, I ended up with some North London punks we knew at Fulham Youth Club, where a band called Paradox was playing. They were doing covers of Jimi Hendrix and Deep Purple, and they turned out to be pretty good. I took notice of the group's guitarist, a seventeen-year-old whiz kid named Bob "Derwood" Andrews, who had this serious, cool charisma. Afterward, I complimented his playing and asked if he'd like to try out for our new band.

The following day, Derwood joined me, Tony, and John at the Portobello rehearsal space, and we went through our repertoire, along with some covers. We thought he was great. Symbolically, I gave him the black single-pickup guitar I'd been using, proclaiming the group a whole.

Derwood was a true punk, six years younger than Tony. His nickname referenced the '60s TV show *Bewitched*: Derwood was what Agnes Moorehead, playing Elizabeth Montgomery's mom, would mistakenly refer to her son-in-law, Darrin, as played by Dick York. Funnily enough, I learned years later that "Derwood" wasn't his real nickname—it was "Dobbin," and that he only told us it was Derwood as a retort to Tony and me when we asked if he would change his name, as so many in punk were doing. He was taking the piss out of Tony and me with a fake nickname, and he's been stuck with Derwood ever since.

Bob was the real deal, the same age as the Sex Pistols sang about in "17." He had a motorbike he fixed himself, and a naturalistic look that was unself-consciously cool. He was technically a better musician than both of us. Bob made Generation X viable because of his personality as much as his ability, which was considerable. He was good-looking in a way that really, really appealed to the girls—and bird-pulling power should never be underestimated when putting a band together.

Now we started to feel we had the makings of a band that could really play, and that opened up the field of possibilities in terms of songs and the forms the music could take. Despite the idea that punk songs should be short, fast, and to the point, we felt that some subjects required a longer time length. We refused to limit ourselves to an outlook that precluded all possibilities. We hadn't done a thing yet, so why rule out anything?

The warm autumn days gave way to the frosts of November, but in our trade, "Have leather jacket, will travel" is the rock 'n' roll motto. I was hanging out more and more with Tony. We saw quite a few of the earliest Clash gigs. Tony was best mates with the band's Mick Jones from their days together in the band London SS. The group was beginning to cause their own revolutionary stir on the scene with their political rock, featuring exciting, fast-paced songs like "Hate and War," "I'm So Bored with the USA," and "Garageland." I saw their second-ever public gig with my Bromley pals at Screen on the Green and was at their infamous show at the ICA on October 23 with Tony when Shane MacGowan (later of the Pogues) got his earlobe bitten off. I was standing right behind him as the girl he was with took a chunk out of it. There were probably no more than fifty people in the audience at the time. I could see the blood, and while there was no real violence, the journalist who wrote about it exaggerated it into yet another sensational punk-rock gore story, an urban legend that grew in retelling from just the lobe to the entire ear being chewed off.

A punk-rock circuit was beginning to form. A few more bands started cropping up, like Slaughter and the Dogs, coming down from the north of England. It was great to know more people who cared about punk music. The stuff Mick and Joe Strummer were writing for the Clash had a fervor that made me want to work even harder to write great punk-rock anthems that could change the world—or at least the one we inhabited.

The Pistols, the Clash, and the Damned embarked on a small tour of England as we prepared for Generation X's first gig at the Central School of Art and Design on Friday, December 10. Our set list consisted of originals like "Youth Youth Youth," "Your Generation," "Ready Steady Go," and a song called "New Order." The gig went well, although my nerves were off the charts at the beginning, falling away as my adrenaline rush took over. All those Friday-night gigs at the university cafeteria and the few we'd done with Chelsea had gotten me used to playing in front of people. This was my dream, and it was beginning to come true.

THE NOTORIETY AND POTENTIAL FOR VIOLENCE was beginning to concern the club owners. The final straw was when the Sex Pistols and Siouxsie appeared on British TV, on Bill Grundy's *Today* on December 1, 1976. Grundy was a square talk-show host looking to boost his ratings with some outrageousness, but he got more than he bargained for. He was clearly egging on Johnny Rotten when the frustrated singer muttered, "Shit," under his breath. Provoked by the host to say it again, John obliged. When Grundy tried to incite Siouxsie by talking suggestively to her, Jonesy called him a "dirty fucker"!

Britain predictably reacted with outrage—the headline THE FILTH AND THE FURY blared across the Fleet Street tabloid the *Daily Mirror* and would later become the title of a 2000 documentary about the band, directed by Julien Temple. The story made the front page of every national paper. Follow-up stories the next day included one about a lorry driver who, in a moment of disgust at what had become of England's youth, threw a brick through his TV screen. Grundy was soon fired, and the Sex Pistols turned into a national sensation—or nightmare—overnight. Suddenly, what had been a tiny scene exploded into the consciousness of every young British kid. Club owners, fearful of staging punk shows with the added concerns of protests and security, reacted with an unofficial ban that included London's Marquee and the 100 Club. Suddenly, there was no place to play.

CHAPTER EIGHT

A NIGHT AT THE ROXY

Neal Street, Covent Garden, London

CULTURE'S ROOTS REGGAE LANDMARK *Two Sevens Clash*, a political statement record, was on my turntable, as the Rasta reggae rebels anticipated the significance of the two sevens in the coming year. Our new band, Generation X, was just starting to get going, but, like all the other punk bands, we needed somewhere to play, someplace to call our own. The punk scene was growing fast, because what else was there? The Bay City Rollers? Yet there was no authentic, purely punk club run and staffed by punks and featuring punk rock, a place where you could wear your safety-pin bondage pants, DESTROY T-shirts, and crazy-colored hair with pride barefaced to the world.

Looking back today, I can see that punk caught on when it did because it would be the last time there would be a generation gap between parents and their kids, where social and political disagreements ran according to age, before today's uneasy détente. We didn't want to listen to the music of our parents. It was the last time the wants, needs, and belief systems of a generation would be so opposed to those of the one that preceded it. We had seen at Louise's what it meant for those lesbian girls to have a place to indulge themselves without judgment. After violence erupted during two Pistols gigs at the Nashville and the Marquee, the unspoken ban on punk by the London club owners had become doctrine. Starting our own venue was the only option.

Tony and I had always agreed that a band should have a place to hang out and rehearse. If we wanted to play and capture the feeling of English youth at the time, we'd need a home base. We wanted to start afresh, exploring this new music that was taking the country by storm. This new location would give us a headquarters, somewhere we could congregate, a place to play and work.

Gene October and I knew of a club that had closed down in London's Covent Garden area called Chaguaramas, a seedy gay club and soul-boy hangout that had long since fallen into disrepair. I told Malcolm McLaren's accountant, and our soon-to-be manager, Andy Czezowski, about it. He and Tony's friend Barry Jones, who would be running the place, checked it out and then agreed to rent it from the owner. We all believed that, with the number of punks and bands looking for a place to gather and play, it would generate enough income to guarantee the place would turn a profit. With the two of them handling the business, Tony and I were left free to write songs and focus on the band.

In the coming months, the sweat would mingle with blood, spit, and sexual juices in this tiny room, which was redubbed the Roxy. The club had a small entrance off Neal Street, where patrons would walk past a pair of small offices, a coat-check room, and a small couch, which served as a reception area, before descending down into the bowels of the basement club.

Around this time, I embarked on a torrid romance with Jeannette Lee, whom I first met at the Kings Road shop where she worked with her boyfriend, the aforementioned DJ Don Letts. We spent a great deal of time together in the squat I shared with Steve Strange, another early figure on the punk scene. It was dingy, but we didn't care. We were together. The world could have stopped revolving and we wouldn't have noticed. At that time, Jeannette was the coolest chick I had ever been with.

Yes, she was somebody else's girl, but we forgot about that momentarily as I stared into her depth of being. She embraced a way of thinking that was far more mature than any I had experienced. Her tight minidress; small, shapely, beautiful figure; and stunning smile—my mind could not take it all in without rushing to a sensual overload. We would meet in this sordid love nest while we pretended the outside world didn't exist, and time was suspended in that forgotten downstairs room on a filthy mattress with sheets stained with love.

But the Roxy and the future soon called, which distracted me. They broke me from faraway love, tore me from her embrace, dashed my hopes on the rocks of desire as the sea poured into our kingdom, washing her from me. The cold, stone-green sea greeted with envy my belief that hopes can come true, even for the briefest of dreamy moments in which we murmured our deepest thoughts and spoke unsaid visions of a love that was forbidden. Jeannette and I had to move on.

In my mind, I still see her small frame disappearing around a corner of the West Hampstead tube station. Just a glimpse of a smile and she was gone. A possible future for me disappeared with her, but my deep desire to make music overrode my emotions, as always. I had learned this skill—overriding my emotions—when I was young, as my family continually moved around. I'd had to learn to adjust to each new home. We were uprooted every few years, through no fault of my parents, but the moves always hurt a little. I was accustomed to living with loss by disposing of it into the ether.

TONY AND I WENT TO MEET Barry Jones and Andy Czezowski at our new hangout. We discussed building a stage at one end of the dance floor in the lower basement. The idea that in the Roxy we were creating our own Max's Kansas City or Cavern Club spurred us on. It was a place for the new scene to take root. Don Letts supplied his mixtapes of far-out roots reggae and a selection of punk old and new from New York and London, and any previous bands that seemed relevant. Of course, the legal capacity was barely 250, but that would be stretched to the limit on many a night.

We took control of the keys for the place soon after and began to redecorate it into a hellacious punk hangout. I helped Barry with the stage, erecting a black backdrop that somehow said *anarchy*, and we beefed up the sound system. In the end, though, it would be the punks themselves who would decorate the Roxy—with spray paint, spit, semen, and blood from a junkie's needle.

AND MY SPRAY CAN IS THE GUN THAT SHOOTS THE MAN.
—"WILD YOUTH"

We began to plan an opening of sorts. We'd been using the club as a rehearsal space for Generation X and really wanted to play a show that reflected the do-it-yourself nature of punk long before *indie* was a word in today's rock vernacular. We set up our gear on the basement floor. We usually gathered in a circle to best communicate musically with one another, eye contact and body language being very important to help catch those spur-of-the-moment happy accidents that can come and go in the blink of an eye if you're not paying close attention. We rehearsed "Youth Youth Youth," "Your Generation," "Ready Steady Go," "Listen," "Prove It," "Save My Life," and others.

Tony and I were writing constantly in order to have enough songs for a forty-minute set, which would often shrink to less than half an hour when we played fast enough. Tony would come up with a lyrical idea, and I would follow with the chords and tune, although trade-offs often occurred where, in search of the best idea, we both threw in suggestions from all over the musical spectrum. True collaboration ruled: it was all for the music and achieving the maximum effect live.

We planned a preemptive, low-key opening in December to get word of mouth started. I talked to Siouxsie Sioux and Steve Severin, who said the Banshees would open the club with us. We were hoping the bill would be a good draw, since punk was something a majority of punters had heard about but hadn't actually seen, due to the lack of available venues. Manchester's Slaughter and the Dogs opened for us the following night. We made some homemade posters advertising the club and went around in the dead of night posting them in Notting Hill Gate, Portobello, Deptford, and Kings Cross, as well as any other areas of London where punks might hang out. Hardly anyone showed the first evening, but word spread. The combination of advertising and word of mouth traveled fast, and the various hip cliques, hungry for somewhere new, quickly decided that this was the place to see and be seen.

Don Letts was the DJ, and Jeannette was back with him, so I had
to control my emotions. She was his girl, but I couldn't help feeling we
had something personal and special, too. Still, this allowed me to play
the field, which was growing larger every day, as punk became an unstoppable wave.

For much of the '70s, a battle had played out between the government and the unions. An ongoing garbage workers strike buried
London in piles of rotting rubbish. Trafalgar Square was a mountain
of black garbage bags twitching with rats. Girls turned up at the Roxy
in black garbage bin liners, high heels, and ripped black hose with
the over-the-top goth eye makeup popularized by Siouxsie. The Roxy
became a hive of activity, spinning the fresh sounds of punk. New
acquaintances kept arriving from all over London and other parts of
England with the era's equivalent of viral messages. The place's energy
was fueled by former outcasts jazzed at finally finding a place where
they were welcome. The feeling was so palpable, it hung in the air, in-
fecting all with an excited lust for whatever was coming next.

Free to pursue my own romantic interests, I was taken into the
toilets by a girl named Zowie, who proceeded to give me a suck in full
view of everyone, performing the deed with relish. My eyes bulged like
those of a wolf in a Looney Tunes cartoon as orgasm overwhelmed me.
If this was rock 'n' roll freedom, give me more, more, more. I learned
Zowie felt lost, but in punk had found a purpose, a direction, a way to
think, a belief system, a philosophy. Many women of that era saw punk
as the next step in sexual liberation. Women were liberating themselves
and then doing the same for us. Zowie scowled at the world around
her but beamed upon hearing Patti Smith's *Horses*. I was a fan too, and
we would fuck our brains out to "Rock n Roll Nigger" from her *Easter*
album.

Zowie sank back into the bed in the same squalid squat where I had
lain with Jeannette. The door was open, as were our sexual adventures
in that dusky place, to the world outside. The booze helped ease our
shyness in the light of the afternoon sun as the day turned to dusk,
and shadows danced on our naked bodies as sweat dripped and songs
flipped, the winding bass hitting the spot. I couldn't touch her without

feeling the wild sensations that coursed through her body, which were overwhelming. Caught in an orgasmic warp, she experienced torrents of sexual ecstasy that took her to a special place I could only sit back and marvel at.

Zowie was sixteen, blond, and a bit of a scrubber, but the sort of girl you just can't stop fucking. Her sad blue eyes told a tale of misuse by men, but I enjoyed her undiminished love for them wholeheartedly. She'd hang around the Roxy while we rehearsed or go fuck off with her friends, only to return for the evening's performance, both musical and sexual.

The club swam with flotsam, jetsam, and various and sundry bodily fluids—every kind of activity went on in each corner of the place. People lived out the novel experience of being part of the London punk scene, many bringing their own personally created lifestyle and fashion choices to this violent playground in the heart of Covent Garden. Leather jackets and spiky hair for guys; girls in miniskirts or men's shirts as dresses, with a tie worn loosely at the neck, bondage leather wristbands, garish facial makeup, crazy-colored hair teased into formidable shapes when not hacked off, and towering fuck-me pumps to finish the overall effect.

Both sexes pounded back the booze and danced in spasmodic fashion with exaggerated moves, paying little attention to anyone else getting in their way. They'd ditch the dance floor for the back alley, vomit, then resume the ritual. Speed fueled the intensity, making their eyes bug out of their heads as they spun uncontrollably like tops to the sounds of the crash-dive music. The interior of the Roxy resembled a centrifugal nightmare, as if a painter had squeezed all the colors of his palette into a flow of spatter onto the canvas of the club walls. Graffiti became the artwork sprayed in defiance. The new art needed no frame to separate it from the outside world, because it was part of the ever-expanding punk cosmos. The look of punk, its mishmash of rock 'n' roll styles with sheer defiance, would become the style of the future. Someone smashed his head through a glass window, adding blood to the mélange, while the human detritus collided with the furniture, destroying it in their frenzy.

The pogo was the dance of choice as punks aped Sid Vicious jumping up and down at the 100 Club, banging into whoever was around him, including fellow members of the Bromley Contingent. Vicious thought we posed too much instead of simply letting go to the music, and this precursor to the American slam dance was his way of getting everybody to participate with wild and joyous abandon. It seemed we were beginning to find our voice as we came of age.

The Roxy scene continued to grow despite attempts by the local authorities to shut us down. The dim lights of the bar threw amorphous shapes onto the faces of punks who drank hard, trying to squelch the effects of the speed they had just swallowed. Future Pogues star Shane MacGowan, missing an earlobe, danced in a pool of booze before throwing up in the middle of the tiny dance floor. Johnny Rotten scowled disconcertingly at a scene that was taking its own shape, but he felt that way about most everything. The Pistols were the kings of the scene, but the underlings were busy doing their own thing and played on regardless. Hadn't Johnny said he wanted a scene full of all different types of punk bands? Here it was, taking shape before his very eyes, and he didn't look too pleased about it. Sure, at times it turned ugly, but it was the bastard child of the hopes and dreams of a disenfranchised British youth that was promised "no future," so how could it be otherwise?

A MORE ELABORATE CLUB OPENING WAS planned for New Year's Eve to ring in 1977. Tony got the Clash to agree to play with the notorious Heartbreakers from New York, featuring ex–New York Doll guitar-slinger Johnny Thunders. Generation X was the support group for both nights. Everybody who was anybody on the scene came to check out the official opening: Johnny Rotten and the Pistols, Malcolm McLaren and Bernie Rhodes (who managed the Clash), Siouxsie Sioux and Steve Severin, and the Damned and Keith Levene (who had just left the Clash). The blood from the hypodermic needles was splattered over the toilet cubicle walls, creating fresh Rorschach patterns to be discerned. Punk graffiti. This was all captured by Don Letts with his ever-present camera, which he used to document these passing times before they were gone for good. The young faces filled with passion flooded his lens and found their way into the future, where we can see them today. I was one of those captured in Super 8 and 16mm Kodachrome for posterity. The crush of the crowd downstairs was pretty bad, with what seemed like a thousand punks packed shoulder to shoulder. As we played, from my vantage point onstage, I could see the gathered glitterati of punk, their faces turned toward a twenty-one-year-old Bromley kid sweating on a stage he built with his own hands, trying to find his way, his own sound and expression. As a performer and a singer fronting a band, I was so new to this, I was learning as I went along.

After the New Year's Eve gig, Mick Jones, Tony, and I stood on the steps of the Roxy alone. The crowd was gone. We laughed and joked about the scene we felt so much a part of and all its vagaries. We surveyed the past wild year, which had seen our bands rise where nothing stood before. Was it all a dream? Would we awake tomorrow and find it was just a passing fancy? "Not bloody likely!" would have been our answer. If this was a dream, I just wouldn't wake up, because this dream was too good. We parted, and I turned in to the night to traverse the wet, winter London streets, a vampire lover of a nubile sixteen-year-old who loved to fuck. I was alive to stalk the dank evening.

With the Roxy as our base, we could easily meet and bounce up the motorway to any of the out-of-town gigs around London or that were starting to multiply in the midlands, such as Leeds, Birmingham, Manchester, Halifax, or Liverpool, where local colleges were anxious to book the new punk bands for one of their social nights. We might have had "no future," but the present was about to become ours.

CHAPTER NINE

PUNK COMES OF AGE WHEN THE TWO SEVENS CLASH

West Hampstead, London

PUNK WAS JUST STARTING TO BECOME the driving cultural force of the New Year, pulling in not only the British youth but adults as well, as the twister carried aloft the whole country. *Two Sevens Clash* called for action in this year of predicted unrest. Punk seemed to fit the bill as much as the soul rebel reggae, which connected us in the struggle. Punk was inclusive, but there were a large number of reactionary forces that would rear their collective hydra heads in England—fascists, in the form of the skinhead revival, and the teddy boys, who were lovers of old '50s-style rockabilly as well as the queen and the royal family, conservative in their politics—reactionary forces directly opposed to our beliefs about social and political liberation.

We were also faced with the "muso" bands of the '60s and '70s, who felt threatened by the new music and put up fierce resistance from inside the record industry, always putting down the new music and keeping us from the gatekeepers at radio and television except for the most sensationalistic stories. The opening of the Roxy had given us a central London address and a place to play regularly. We were the house band for months, and this gave us valuable preparation time. From our very first gig in December, we received offers from a variety of record labels, but Tony was really savvy about our business strategy. All the major companies wanted to cash in on punk, but we didn't want some short-term commitment. We preferred holding out for a longer deal. Tony had previous dealings with Bernard Rhodes, who managed the Clash, as I had with the Sex Pistols' shrewd mentor, Malcolm McLaren. Both men had a plan when it came to dealing with offers, and we learned plenty from them. In addition, we had each read practically every rock 'n' roll book, detailing other bands' successes and mistakes in business as well as in music. We studied the past lest we repeat it.

One of Tony's acquaintances was Neil Aspinall, who ran Apple for the Beatles. He started out as a roadie but became an accountant dealing with some of the band's business after the death of manager Brian Epstein. His advice also was to hold out for the best deal. If we had "it," it wouldn't disappear, and if we believed in ourselves, we could have a nice, long career. So we decided that was what we should do. Neil was nice enough to meet with us at his house, and it was great to meet someone on the inside of the Beatles' dealings.

At this point, I was still living at home with my parents in Bromley, although when I wanted to stay in London, I squatted in West Hampstead with Steve Strange, along with Jean-Jacques Burnel of the Stranglers and Wilko Johnson, who was playing with a pub-rock band called Dr. Feelgood. Steve had no money, either, and was hanging out on the punk club scene as well, with a bleached-blond look just like me. Staying there allowed me to rehearse and then go clubbing at night. Steve was a tireless networker who knew what was going on, eventually forming the New Romantic group Visage, riding a camel down Sixth Avenue in New York when the band was later signed. Punk was everywhere.

I really enjoyed seeing Wilko, a great guitarist with an exciting, unique stage presence. It was fun getting to know these people one-on-one as a colleague, a member of a band, not just an awestruck fan. Since there was only a single bed in Steve's room, we slept together, which gave the others in the flat the idea that somehow we were lovers. I was the last to realize this, but I didn't care, because for me, it was a means to an end. In fact, I quite liked the idea that people had thoughts about me that emboldened my image. It was the beginning of blurring the lines between William Broad and Billy Idol. I could see that sometimes you had to not give a fuck what others thought or you'd never do anything to advance yourself. I also got a small sense of how bisexual or gay people feel as society makes its judgment, and they have to live with it. In my case, I was mates with Steve and that was all that mattered to me. This was a brave new world, and it was fun to shake everybody up, however you did it.

Generation X played the London pub the Hope & Anchor on January 11, and then began to venture outside the city. We played the Middlesbrough Rock Garden on January 22, and Liverpool's Eric's on the 28th, then arrived back in London the next night to play at the Roxy, where we were supported by a new, female-fronted Newcastle band, Penetration. Everything was new and exciting, as the punk scene began to explode and we all discovered one another for the first time. By playing gigs, we were networking. It was all brand-new, the excitement, the camaraderie, rolling up the motorway in a rented Ford transit van packed with our gear, playing the gig, then returning to London at dawn. We drew lots to see who would get to lie on Tony's long bass cabinet or in the front seat on the trip back, because those were the most desirable places to sleep.

During these early, heady days of punk, the band and fans were bonded as one. Our youth, desires, and needs and the rush of energy engendered by the joining of like minds crested into a tidal wave of exploding passion. We did a brief interview with *New Musical Express*'s Tony Parsons, which came out the last week of January 1977. He wrote: "Generation X may well be the 'punk rock' group that many people have been waiting for; songs with lyrics about change and revolution, but with melodies cute enough for 'boy meets girl.' "

I don't really think we were singing about political revolution—more a personal one, though we certainly demanded real social change. In "New Order," we sang about rock 'n' roll giving us a purpose. By rocking out, we were saving lives, giving kids like us hope for something better. I felt we left the more overt political commentary to bands like the Pistols and the Clash, who were already doing it so well by making it part of their individual band manifestos from the start.

Generation X was a book about sociology. We felt we should make that study of British youth culture the basis for our song ideas. These were the things affecting us as young adults.

The English winter dragged on through the early part of the New Year, its freezing rain stinging the eyes and reddening the noses of the populace, but we didn't notice, rehearsing in the afternoon warmth of the Roxy's empty womb. Getting to know each other and putting our ideas into action dominated our time, filling our moments.

Adding to the rise of the punk scene was the voice of the fanzine. Mark Perry, a young lad from Deptford in London, put out a xeroxed, stapled publication called *Sniffin' Glue*, and other homemade zines sprang up, like *Ripped and Torn* out of Glasgow and Shane MacGowan's *Bondage*. All reported on everything that was happening, including information about the latest bands on the scene, the stuff that didn't make it into *Melody Maker* or the *NME*. They represented the beginning of word-of-mouth and viral marketing, and allowed us to spread the punk gospel.

Bands kept sprouting like grass after a rain shower. The Saints from Australia; the Vibrators; the B-52's from Georgia; Glasgow's Rezillos; the Police, another dyed-peroxide trio with Sting, Andy Summers, and Stewart Copeland; and Paul Weller's Who-style mod power trio the Jam. Wayne (now Jayne) County, the transgender star from New York's Max's Kansas City, played the Roxy along with Cherry Vanilla. A young preteen band called Eater put out an album. Tony and I went to see Iggy Pop play at the Aylesbury Friars with his post-Stooges band, including the Sales brothers and David Bowie on keyboards, doing stuff from Iggy's Berlin-inspired album, *The Idiot*, which anticipated the electronic dance music scene by about three decades. Jimmy Osterberg was the granddaddy of the punk scene, even though he had just turned thirty.

Tony and I drove our usual trasportation to the Iggy gig, the blue Ford van I used to deliver tools for my dad. On our way back through Bromley, a drunk driver barreled through a red light and smashed into the right-hand passenger side of the van, directly in the center of the brittle chassis frame, which probably saved Tony's life. Turned out the guy was going sixty miles an hour and was well over the legal limit for intoxication. It was yet another brush with death, at least for Tony, if not me. The vehicle was totaled. It was the same set of wheels I'd been driving since the summer, the very van we'd taken to Paris for the Sex Pistols, to Louise's, and to Chelsea rehearsals.

We continued playing in and out of London. One memorable gig was at the University of Leicester on Friday night, March 11. Punk was drawing detractors as well as hard-core fans. On this night, some heavy metal fans started to throw glasses at the stage. At the start of "Ready Steady Go," a wineglass hit Derwood in the head. He kept playing those fast eighth notes as he collapsed to the floor, with blood oozing from the cut on the top of his forehead. I thought it commendable that he didn't miss a beat, even as his eyes closed and he blacked out. I was standing right next to him as the beer cans and bottles rained down. He had to have medical attention. War between rival rock music fans was just beginning. People were starting to get polarized by the different scenes around them.

On March 28, I saw Sid Vicious play with the Pistols for the very first time at a gig in Leicester Square. Sid replacing the Dickensian Glen Matlock proved to be a real turning point for the band, with a darker tone creeping in. Sid was concentrating and played great that night. If only he had managed to sustain it. Having seen the Pistols from the very beginning, I felt they were ready to take it to the next level, maybe even conquer America. We went to a nearby pub with them afterward, and I could see that John already seemed bored of being fawned over by his admirers.

On Thursday, March 31, after a gig in Plymouth at the Leisure Centre, we played the Marquee for the first time, an industry showcase. To impress the label reps on hand, we brought in our own punters to cheer us along. Usually, you had to have a record out to play the prestigious venue: the fact that a punk showcase was booked at the Marquee was emblematic of punk's evolution from marginalized subculture to emerging commodity. The punks went absolutely nuts.

By this time, the Sex Pistols had already been thrown off EMI, their first label, and signed to A&M, but they were paid off to leave that company due to their outlandish behavior just before the release of "God Save the Queen." That single ended up coming out on Richard Branson's Virgin Records, going to number one on the BBC chart. But the powers that be refused to list it, leaving the space blank when the chart was shown on *Top of the Pops*. That year was the Queen's Jubilee, and the Pistols were now the band most feared by the authorities, the epitome of bad taste. The Clash put out their first single, "White Riot," in March, and their debut album the following month. Both bands put a lot of preparation and time into their music so that it wasn't released until it was just right, giving us further incentive not to throw out something half-assed. The proof was right in front of our faces: the credibility factor for both the Pistols and the Clash was gigantic. The excitement was running high. Because of his friendship with Tony from their London SS days, the Clash's Mick Jones always shared his thought process with us. He didn't pull any punches when giving us advice, but he was also incredibly kind and supportive.

He told us about recording the Clash's third single, "Complete Control," with the legendary reggae producer Lee "Scratch" Perry, who "smoked a lot of pot and waited for the vibes to be right." In fact, Jah himself had to come down before they could begin recording. To this day, when we're working on something in the studio and it's not quite right, I say, "We just have to wait for Jah to come down."

Tony and I were fascinated by this mix of cultures, wondering if the reggae dub echo and spin ideas could be used in rock 'n' roll. But we were, first and foremost, a punk club band, with raw energy and the message "Believe in yourself," direct and up front.

As in the Wild West, in punk rock, the uglier the scene was, the more romantic it became. I was gradually shedding my past. We played gigs through the sweat and stench of beer and vomit mixed with the sounds of fighting and people having sex in the middle of a dirty floor, a grime-encrusted dream. We took that world of piss and shit—like IRA prisoners scrawling their message on the walls of their cells—to mark our territory and spell out our resistance. The sounds of dry humping, the grunting, twisting, turning, and squeezing of flesh became a world of white heat, the kind Lou Reed sang about at

Warhol's Factory in New York back in his "sucking on my ding-dong" days. Speeding, drinking, and staying up all night. Surviving on a mixture of booze and babes, we were paid in liquor and sex. The nights blended into one another as the dream continued. We got by on our adrenaline, and then, helping us discover the way, powerful chemicals.

CHAPTER TEN

YOUTH YOUTH YOUTH: BREAK ON THROUGH TO THE OTHER SIDE

London

BRITISH YOUTH WERE DISAFFECTED. MOST WERE unemployed or on the dole. If they had a job, it amounted to some soulless work that deadened their minds, like being stuck on the London Underground Circle Line going round and round in circles with the same timetable day in and day out. In contrast, we believed we were fighting for our freedom on the stage across the country every night.

Punks would do anything to subvert the status quo, spawning the disgusting act of gobbing—or hocking a loogie of saliva at the performer. The first known instance took place during a show by the Damned at the Red Cow in Hammersmith, where Captain Sensible spat on the audience, who immediately returned the favor, launching what became a repulsive ritual. After that, all the bands played in a hail of spit. Christ, it was revolting, but then again, so was punk at times. Thank God it never caught on in the States, because it was a filthy habit. One night I had blood on my T-shirt from someone spitting his bloody meningitis at me. Derwood would have to chisel the dried flob from in between his frets so he could hold down the chord. The tops of the cymbals shone green in the light from the freshly deposited grolly. Oh, bollocks!

By June, we had become dissatisfied with drummer John Towe's playing, or maybe it was his curly hair, so we replaced him with Mark Laff, who had previously played in Subway Sect, a group connected with the Clash. Laff was a great bloke with a fun personality and a fantastic outlook; he wouldn't let life get him down too much if it threw him a curve. Derwood's musicianship required a more adept style of drumming, and we needed to continually step up or die in the fast-paced punk scene. There could be no passengers on this punk-rock locomotive. Grow stronger or be consumed. The fire needed constant fueling. Laff was our Keith Moon, as Tony used to say. With his short, mousy hair, Mark even looked like Moonie, who was his idol. The Who's drummer was one of the wildest, but also most innovative, musicians of his time.

Tony and I increasingly looked to the Who as a guide when attempting to suss out our development. I listened to their albums *My Generation* and *The Who Sell Out* a lot because I loved "I Can See for Miles," "Tattoo," and "Rael." The last began the story of Tommy, a serviceman who dies before he can reach his family. In this case, the protagonist is a ship captain; in *Tommy*, he's the son of a World War II bomber pilot. I also loved Pete Townshend's schoolboy vocal on "Odo-rono" and his singing on "Our Love Was." The conceptual story lines, the faux commercial vignettes, and the pirate radio station adverts in between cuts were great, with the memorable segue "More music, more music, more music . . ."

The Who celebrated the quasi-legality of the pirate radio stations because access to this new cultural force was like manna from heaven. The band was very into fashion, op art, pop art, and kinetic art in their clothes. They'd co-opt English military medals and turn their meanings inside out. I discovered a Pete Townshend Eel Pie songbook with notations for some incredible chords and progressions. I used this book as a guide, taking off from Townshend's ideas with some of my own, making it up as I went along. I wanted our songs to ring out as if they were a call to arms. We craved and needed that kind of energy.

We had gained enough notice to attract a real full-time management team. Jonh Ingham was a tall, well-spoken American who knew everything about what made great rock. An established music journal-

ist for *Sounds* magazine, Ingham, along with Caroline Coon, had been
at least partly responsible for breaking punk in the UK. Stuart Joseph
was his partner, brought in to handle the money. In hindsight, I'm
not sure that Joseph was the best choice for the job. But he had a great
deal of energy and was hungry to do something in the burgeoning
punk-rock world and was so broke at the time, he was living in his car.
Vivien Goldman, another *Sounds* writer, worked with the two of them
for about a month before deciding to split. She later told me she was
concerned at the time that they were strictly in it for the money. I knew
from the rock books I'd read that bands always got ripped off at the
start of their careers. My thinking at the time was that it was simply the
price you paid to get the necessary experience before eventually you got
a handle on it—if you lasted that long. At this point, midway through
1977, we were just glad and amazed we had any managers at all.

One of the first things we did under our new management team
was record a demo of four songs so that we had something to play for
interested record companies. We demoed "Ready Steady Go," "Day by
Day," "Your Generation," and "Youth Youth Youth." It was my first
time in a studio recording anything. We allowed the engineer to do
pretty much what he wanted. The demo was fairly rough, but it had
that punk spirit. In that same vein, we decided to bootleg it ourselves
but pretend we had nothing to do with it. It was as if we were so hot,
someone had pirated our demo, not too far from today's online file
sharing. We had Steve Strange take some white labels to a few different independent retailers like Rough Trade, making them available in
a limited number. They sold out in a second. We had proved we could
sell out London clubs; now we proved we could sell records. The label
offers started going through the roof.

Being in Generation X and getting caught up in the punk scene
was my education. I was growing up in public. The band was naked
to the world as we began to learn our trade, but what an exciting way
to apprentice. I had always dreamed of being in a band, but now I was
acquiring the skills to succeed, with all of England watching.

CHAPTER ELEVEN

WHITE LIGHT, WHITE HEAT, WHITE RIOTS

Charing Cross Station, London

THE SUMMER OF '77 WAS BLAZING hot in England. One day, the temperature reached 84 degrees, prompting the newspaper headline PHEW, WHAT A SCORCHER! After we crashed the van in March returning from Iggy's gig, I would walk everywhere or use public transport, and I didn't mind the heat.

To get to rehearsal at the Roxy from Bromley, I would walk to Bickley station and take a train to Charing Cross, a twenty-minute ride, then walk up Charing Cross Road, across Piccadilly up Wardour Street to Neal Street. But I soon learned that danger lurked for a lone punk wandering the streets of London. One morning, I ran straight into a parade of chanting Scottish football fans coming right at me. They took one look at my bleached hair, tight jeans, earrings, and pointed shoes and saw a lone London punk, easy prey. For a second, I thought about running. Then, quite spontaneously, they burst into the Ramones' "Sheena Is a Punk Rocker," and what seemed like 20,000 singing Scots marched past me. I was lucky it was before their match, because they lost to England that afternoon, and if they had seen me then, I surely would have had my head kicked in.

The Pistols' "God Save the Queen" had offended all the royalists, including the teddy boys, lovers of '50s rockabilly, who by now had declared all-out war on the punks. Since Kings Road was so identified with punk, the teds would march every Saturday from World's End down Kings Road in their finest Edwardian-style drape coats and bright, multicolored crepe-soled "brothel creepers," looking for any hapless punks to kick the shit out of.

John Krevine's new store Boy London, on Kings Road, had its front window smashed. The police tried in vain to keep order. The teds also took exception to our co-opting their look. One day, while I was standing on the platform at Charing Cross station looking to see the arrival time of my train, something suddenly struck me on the left jaw with great force, knocking me to the ground. Through my haze, I saw the telltale sign of a pair of rather cool-looking black patent leather brothel creepers walking away. I'd been punched by an angry ted! I got up more dazed than hurt, and saw he was now standing over by a magazine store with a couple of mates, but he had lost interest in me. Another time, I turned a corner only to run into a gang of more than twenty teds hanging out on the south side of Hammersmith Bridge. They surrounded me, and their leader sneered, "Well what have we here, a little punk rocker. What shall we do with him, boys?" I nearly shat myself, expecting a quick demise. But after a moment of silence, they all burst out laughing, probably at the sight of me shitting a brick.

YESTERDAY BY THE PAPER STAND / I FELT THE POWER OF ANOTHER
RELIGION / REBELS WITH A CAUSE CAME OUT OF THE SUN /
AND SPOKE THE ONLY LANGUAGE THEY'D BEEN GIVEN.
—"RUNNING WITH THE BOSS SOUND"

Sworn right-wing enemies of the punks, the skinheads, who were aligned with the fascist National Front political party, were demonstrating on my train route one Saturday as I traveled to Charing Cross. Between the teds, the skinheads, and the punks, it seemed as if all of London was fighting. I passed by the skins' demonstration with their signs of hate on my way to meet some friends from North London I'd known from punk gigs. As we met at the Underground station, some teds came through the turnstile in force and we blokes took off, relying on discretion as the better part of valor, since there were too many to fight. I cowered in fright in the Main Line train station toilet stalls, which they searched. I waited a while to see what happened to the others. One of our group, Wendy May, fought a ted girl and kicked the shit out of her, which showed how wild she was—a punk girl sporting style and a don't-fuck-with-me attitude. The violence in the air was palpable, and it wasn't just the punks who were pissed off. The whole country was taking up our fiery rhetoric.

Punks continued to take their share of abuse in the streets. Johnny Rotten was attacked and cut with a razor; royalists beat up Paul Cook in the Earls Court Underground station. Punk was polarizing London with people wanting to enforce their wills by violence if they couldn't achieve those goals any other way.

Those of us in punk bands believed in the power of song. Like the Who's Pete Townshend sang in "Pure and Easy": "I listened and I heard music in a word / And words when you played your guitar / The noise that I was hearing was a million people cheering / And a child flew past me riding on a star." Our job was to make our statements in music and song. Others were called to use their fists.

The punk scene continued to evolve. The Vortex, a new club in Soho at the top of Wardour Street, opened in response to the numbers drawn to the Roxy and the Marquee. The Vortex was a bit bigger and provided even more bands with a venue to play. More hard-core right-wing bands like Jimmy Pursey's Sham 69 and Skrewdriver began playing these clubs. Professing their working-class roots and with a minimum of pretension, they appealed to skinheads as much as to punks, and played to the lowest-common-denominator goons in the audience. Sham 69 went on to be one of the most successful bands during this period, with singles like "Hurry Up Harry" dumbing down the punk message. They brought a more violent, soccer-crowd mentality to their shows, which, while amusing at first, turned increasingly fascist in nature.

More people began jumping on the bandwagon, because punk appeared to be a road to quick success. There was a huge difference in mentality between the punk bands who came before 1977 and those who formed after. The first-wavers sincerely believed in the music and created an audience where none had existed before. But now bands of all types appeared, many of their members recently long-haired hippies, tailoring their images to the burgeoning punk scene. This proved disheartening to those of us who had been there since the start. Still, they would soon bring about their own demise, by appealing to the thug mentality.

CHAPTER TWELVE

NOT SELLING OUT, BUT BUYING IN

Notting Hill Gate, across from Kensington Gardens, London

THE RECORD COMPANY OFFERS FOR GENERATION X were getting too attractive and lucrative for us to ignore. The best one came from Chrysalis Records, an independent label owned and run by Terry Ellis and Chris Wright. Terry was the more outgoing and charismatic of the two, while Chris was more the businessman. The two began promoting shows at their university in the mid-'60s, branching out into managing, then starting their own record company in 1969. They had started their label with one of their management clients, Jethro Tull. They also signed the New York punk band Blondie, fronted by Deborah Harry, who would eventually hit with a single from their second album, *Plastic Letters*, "Denis," a gender-swapping cover of the American doo-wop group Randy & the Rainbows' 1963 hit "Denise."

Our first dealings were with Terry and A&R executives Roy Eldridge and Doug D'Arcy. Roy was a nice, mild-mannered chap who actually lived near my parents' home in Bromley. Doug, also on the quiet side, always seemed deep in thought, weighing the pros and cons of every situation. He was almost a little too serious at times, but then again, he had a lot on his plate, running the label's day-to-day operations. Chrysalis was one of only a handful of "major" indies doing business in the UK at the time, the others being Chris Blackwell's Island Records, Richard Branson's Virgin, and A&M Records, owned by Americans Herb Alpert and Jerry Moss. After witnessing the problems between the Sex Pistols and EMI, we wanted to be with an independent label. We admired the freedom that the Ramones had with Seymour Stein's Sire Records, a label we nearly joined at one point. We finally decided on Chrysalis because it offered us the best of both worlds—an indie, British-based record company with strong ties to the U.S.

We signed with Chrysalis Records on July 20, 1977. We hired a lawyer to look over the contract, but I also took a copy to my dad. Our relationship had been strained by my decision to pursue a career in music, but my father was a trained accountant, so he was able to read the agreement and explain what it entailed. He was quite amazed at the size of the deal, which included a million-pound advance over three albums. I was knocked out that my dad could help me. I think it helped to mend some fences between us, as here was a side of rock 'n' roll he could fathom. Of course, based off what I'd read in all the rock books about the rip-offs that took place, it was likely that we would never see any of the money. But I wasn't in it for the personal wealth so long as we were able to pay for our albums and it gave us the freedom to pursue what we loved to do.

When the deal was done, every member of the band started receiving a weekly wage of eleven pounds. I used my share to lease a tiny, coffin-shaped room in a flat in Notting Hill Gate, across from Kensington Gardens. I shared it with two girls: Karen O'Connor, daughter of the singer Des O'Connor; and a black actress named Bukie. I would have to either walk through their rooms to get to the toilet and the kitchen, or, alternatively, walk across the public landing. There was nothing in the kitchen, not even a refrigerator, just an old stove that didn't work. In the morning, I would go next door to the newspaper shop to buy a can of Coke so I could wake up. But the important thing was that I was officially living in London.

To celebrate the signing, our managers took us to a Fulham restaurant. The clientele seemed a bit strange at first, until I was told that it was a place for cross-dressing men to meet.

The night we signed our record deal, we played a gig at the Marquee that Chrysalis filmed for promotional purposes. It was directed by David Mallet, who would go on to shoot a number of my '80s videos. The set started with a cover of Gary Glitter's "Rock On!," a song I suggested; then we followed up with a new song, "From the Heart," which would open the album. And then into "London Life," "Above Love," "New Order," "Listen," a song I wrote the lyrics and music for, and "Wild Youth," which would be our second single. Later that summer, we played a pair of shows at the Vortex on Monday, August 1, and Tuesday, August 2.

At this point, the band's creative method had started to crystalize into a partnership between Tony and myself. My writing process consisted of sitting hunched over the guitar singing into the voice box, serenading myself into a place of confidence. I would sing Lou Reed's "Sweet Jane," "Coney Island Baby," "White Light/White Heat," "Heroin," "Into the Sun," and "Rock and Roll"; Iggy's "Down on the Street," some Who, the Kinks' "Set Me Free," "All Day and All of the Night," and a few Roy Orbison tunes, "It's Over" and "Blue Bayou." These were all songs I liked to play on guitar to back my singing.

Then I would get inside Tony's lyrics and try to find a melody and guitar figure I could hang a song on. I really wanted the songs to be melodic, even if we were going to scream them out. I wanted them to work on both acoustic and electric guitars, loud or quiet, so the feelings could come through. Occasionally, I would write lyrics, as I did for "Trying for Kicks," "Prove It," and "Listen," but mainly I enjoyed the camaraderie and team spirit Tony and I shared. I knew I needed to learn quickly and not let ego get in the way. The punk ethos we followed was all about sublimating the will for the greater good.

Mick Jones wrote a lot of the Clash's early songs, and his approach helped us with our own. Songs like "From the Heart," a number Tony and I started to write at a crash pad where Mick lived with the Slits' lead guitarist, Viv Albertine, demonstrated our desire for our songs to speak about our true feelings. Also living in the same pad was Glen Matlock, who had left the Pistols in February and was now writing songs for his new band, the Rich Kids. Glen told me how he nicked the massive bass line hook to "Anarchy in the UK" from an Abba record, which I found amusing and creative. He did a bunch of writing in the Pistols, contributing catchy riffs, backing vocals, and melodies that carried over to their album, *Never Mind the Bollocks*, even though he didn't play on it. Glen continues to get a raw deal from Pistols fans, but I always thought his talent and contributions to the band were under- rated, as was his innovative sense of style. He introduced me to a girl- friend of his who made me some see-through black and multicolored patterned short- and long-sleeved singlets, one of which I'm wearing underneath my leather jacket in a famous picture of me with Keith Moon in '78. We were all having fun being part of a movement; we felt like part of one big community.

Generation X played "From the Heart" at the Marquee; the song that distanced us from the Pistols, who had made the negative thing their own. We wanted to create a new optimism rather than continue to wallow in self-pity. We were young and idealistic! We believed in the healing power of music and its ability to challenge society. We felt this new world should express the full range of emotions. The Orwellian nightmare of *1984* and Aldous Huxley's *Brave New World* could not be allowed to take place. In "From the Heart," we described personal emotions of the moment with love, feelings that came from the heart. Even amidst the negative scene of punk, I was searching for love. The landscape of '70s England led us to look for it in the darkest corners of the mind and soul, and then value what we found there.

We wanted to express ourselves in every way possible. I was now wearing tight black jeans, some dirty Converse sneakers, and a dyed- black soldier's battle dress over my homemade Soviet constructivist T-shirts. I was influenced by the Russian propaganda poster BEAT THE WHITES WITH THE RED WEDGE. I couldn't draw, but I could create shapes and artfully place them on my T-shirts. Tony could draw really well, and he had made a T-shirt of Patty Hearst as SLA member Tanya. The home-designed and hand-drawn T-shirts gave us a unified, grassroots look, one our fans could easily re-create themselves if they wanted to. One of my design concepts ended up as the cover of the "Ready Steady Go" single the following year.

All of this was topped off by my spiky, bleached blond hair, which created quite an impact. Steve Strange and I bought a load of soldier gear at an army store and dyed it black. I would walk around in these fatigues, with my lyrics, tapes, and records in a plastic bag. That's how I looked in '77, captured in Julien Temple's aforementioned Sex Pistols documentary, *The Filth and the Fury*. It was a style that came out of having zero money, which forced us to transform secondhand clothes into something cool. It turned out to be well within our fans' ability and budget to take our ideas and use them to create their own style.

I loved mixing fashion eras—punk hair, Gene Vincent leather jacket, military chic. That was part of punk's magic, that it embraced the creation of new designs or just the mixing and matching of styles from the past. Tony had a pair of leather trousers I was quite envious of, and after we signed with Chrysalis, I persuaded Jonh Ingham to give me some extra money from our record deal so I could buy my own. I wore those pants for six months nonstop to break them in, gig in, gig out, night and day. Channeling the power of leather pants gave me a great feeling. They were something I'd wanted ever since I saw pictures of Gene Vincent, the Beatles, Jim Morrison, and Lou Reed in leather, and now I had my own! My rock 'n' roll dream of fronting a punk band in leather pants had come true.

Soon after that, I added a box-shaped secondhand thigh-length leather jacket, the one I'm wearing in that picture with Keith Moon. To me, leather somehow stood for freedom. Because of the hippie rule of denim, people had stopped wearing leather, at least until the Ramones donned their motorcycle jackets. Black performers like Smokey Robinson wore leather, as Robinson did when I saw him perform in 1974. While Elvis Presley had worn all black leather in his '68 comeback special, by the '70s, there was definitely an unspoken sexual thing about leather because of the leather-boy look in the gay world. But we brought a youthful innocence to it that somehow spoke volumes. It was definitely an outsider fashion, since most people didn't go to work dressed in it. Leather for me was no longer about sexual repression or bondage but about a birth of freedom, at least for my heroes, like Morrison, Lou Reed, the Ramones, and the like.

It was during this "white light, white heat" summer of '77 that we started to think about recording our first single. We considered working with Phil Wainman, who had produced the Sweet. I liked Mick Tucker's drumming on those records. Drumming and groove was always important to me. If the groove isn't there, you might as well go home—nothing is adding weight to the words or the guitar playing. The Sweet records had an energy and excitement. No matter what you thought of the songs, the tracks all sounded good. We also used the fast eighth-note grooves that I was beginning to incorporate into "Ready Steady Go" and other Generation X song ideas, which would soon become a Billy Idol trademark.

Wainman was not the coolest choice as a producer, but he was an instinctual one for me, and Tony went along with it. We were a fast-paced, energy-infused three-piece who used speed and dynamics to make up for what we lacked in musicianship. We weren't a pop band, but I loved all kinds of rock 'n' roll and refused to cut myself off from a pop producer just because some bloody revolution was going on. No one's taking "Be-Bop-a-Lula" away from me—I don't care who the fuck you are. The punk credo was to stand up for your own beliefs and tastes, not bow down to yet another new set of rules. Meet the new boss, same as the old boss, indeed.

We felt that it was up to us to come up with the song concept and ideas and then bring in a producer to help record those ideas. For all his hit pop records, Wainman was actually a talented drummer and musician who expected a certain level of playing. Unfortunately, we didn't quite have that down yet. Our punk-rock attitude couldn't always make up for our lack of experience.

The recording of our first single, "Your Generation," went well regardless, as we'd been playing the song for nearly nine months. There were no major differences with Phil on that one. He let us play and recorded it as is. "Day by Day" was the B-side. Tony seemed to know more about the recording process than I did, but I had good instincts—I knew what I liked—and I think we made a good team, as Phil produced the songs and we got on with playing them. Some of the other members, however, were not happy with his criticism of their abilities.

For the single cover, Jonh Ingham took my Russian constructivist ideas to Barney Bubbles, an artist who made a great cover out of circles and rectangles in red, black, and white, which still looks good today. I was knocked out.

Tony picked out a font for Generation X, which we stenciled with red, diagonal stripes on all our gear and guitar cases. This same font was used on the lettering on the single sleeve. Characteristic of our punk ethos, we were as involved in our artistic image as we were in the music.

Our first single, "Your Generation," came out on September 1, 1977. Elton John, writing as a guest reviewer in the *Record Mirror*, panned it: "This is really dreadful garbage . . . hideously recorded." Of course, we were singing precisely about not having to listen to old farts like him, so we actually took the review as a compliment. (Ironically, years later, I did a guest spot with Elton for the Who's *Tommy* charity show at Universal Amphitheatre in 1988 as Cousin Kevin, and he came to a London gig on my 1990 *Charmed Life* tour, where he told me he liked my song "Lovechild," the B-side to the "L.A. Woman" single.)

The single cracked the Top 30, and we were invited to perform it on the BBC's *Top of the Pops*, a decision for which the punks mercilessly criticized us. Still, the Pistols had appeared doing "Pretty Vacant" on a video for that same show, so I thought, *Bollocks, we need to get through to as many people as possible. Who gives a fuck about the medium—the music is the message!*

We celebrated the single release by playing the Marquee with the Jolt on Tuesday, September 6, and later that week, with two nights at Barbarella's in Birmingham. We returned to the Marquee again on Tuesday, September 20. Tuesday nights at the Marquee were the slowest of the week, so if you could sell one out, it was quite an achievement, something the Who had done in the early '60s. When we attracted lines around the block, the weekly music magazines suddenly began to take notice.

One of the first stars we met was Marc Bolan. He had a weekly kids' TV show, *Marc*, featuring live bands. We were invited to Manchester to appear on what would be the show's final episode. Previously, he had debuted his album *Dandy in the Underworld* at the Roxy, where we met him first. We drove up from London and arrived, to be greeted by Marc with wine bottle in hand. Unfortunately, our gear, which was also coming from London, had got stuck somewhere along the way and wouldn't arrive in time for us to play. The producer of the show wanted to cancel our slot, as she had David Bowie coming from Switzerland to debut "Heroes," and couldn't be bothered to find a way to accommodate this "little punk band from London." We were mortified, but Marc came to the rescue. "I won't do the show if you can't find a way to make this work," he said. When the producer freaked, Bolan calmed her down by offering to let us use his Les Paul guitar and amp. The other scheduled band, Eddie and the Hot Rods, lent us their bass rig and drum kit so the show could go on. We played what would be our first television appearance. A week before it aired, Marc died tragically in a car accident. Everyone in Britain watched the show, which featured Bowie, and what turned out to be Bolan's last performance. I will always remember Marc for standing up for us. He had true rock 'n' roll spirit and is today regarded as one of the pioneers of punk.

The recording of our second single, "Wild Youth," proved more problematic. After three days in the studio, we still hadn't laid down a drum track, which was very disheartening. Everyone had gone home, and I found myself alone with Wainman, who said to me, "This lot is useless. You're the star. Why don't you just leave them?" Quite taken aback, I said, "I can't just leave a punk band. It has to first disintegrate." He just shook his head and sadly walked away. But his comment planted a seed of thought in my mind, the idea of being a solo artist. In any case, I had to continue with Generation X, as the punk ideal was not just about music, but an experiment that had to be seen through to its bitter end.

We eventually began tracking over one of the takes. "Wild Youth" had tons of energy, and boots stomping on orange crates gave it some sound effects, adding to the chanted background vocals over the roller-coaster backing. Derwood plays some great guitar on the record, but the real experiment came with doing a dub remix for the B-side. Phil wasn't interested in this at all, so we produced it with the engineer. We broke down the backing track to drum and bass, setting up many spin-and-echo effects aping dub reggae, but in the context of a rock 'n' roll track. Then we all took turns manning different faders on the control board, as we brought in the guitar tracks and small slices of the vocal at certain moments to catch the music of the track and send individual or grouped notes into an echoed dub or repeat, which eventually dissolved into distortion. It was a blend of punk-rock aggression and the dance-hall, dub-wise beats of the Jamaican sound, and a forerunner of the world beat that would later mark the music of the Clash and two-tone bands like the Specials, the Selecter, and Madness.

In a way, it was good that Phil left us to do the dub mix, as we were able to actually be hands-on in delivering the concept in sound, and I think it still stands up today. When I heard it in a club, it sounded great as an example of punk's ability to expand beyond three-chord thrash. I was always proud we did it.

Phil was a great drummer, and I can understand why he was so critical about the drum tracks. But we were a band learning and honing our act in public. I was beginning to see the validity of his suggestion about going solo, but I knew I had committed to the band when I signed the record deal. Anything else was out of the question, since we were just starting out. The plans Tony and I had made couldn't be easily cast aside. I also felt a strong sense of loyalty to these blokes who were sticking with me; and I knew I had a long way to go if I was ever to do it on my own. In 1977 it wasn't possible, but I could see that when Phil sat behind Mark's kit, the groove picked up immediately. It was something to think about.

"Wild Youth" came out on Friday, November 18, followed by another *Top of the Pops* performance, for which I wore a black leather motorcycle jacket with a red lining, leather trousers, and black leather gloves, bleached white spiked hair, and some facial acne for good measure! It was a strong look, for everyone from Gene Vincent and the Beatles in Hamburg to Billy Idol on *Top of the Pops*.

My rock 'n' roll punk-rock style was all attitude and a belief that somewhere way deep inside I'd find a way to exorcise the demons—my inferiority complex, the emptiness that couldn't be satisfied; that possibility fueled my tireless drive to succeed. It was about never sleeping and never being completely clean, either. The battle is both inside and outside. I was just a bloke fronting a punk-rock group and having a whale of a time. I was writing and singing my own music, and now performing for the nation I came from.

CHAPTER THIRTEEN

BANDS ACROSS THE OCEAN

Fulham Palace Road rehearsal studio, London

As WINTER ARRIVED, I WAS CAUGHT up in a movement that was truly inspiring Britain. But I loved the Velvet Underground and the New York Dolls, so it would certainly be a dream come true, and a career milestone, for Generation X to play in New York one day. I always envisioned New York as rock 'n' roll heaven. I sang with a slight American accent underneath my native British one, a Yank inflection from my childhood in the U.S. I was still British, but wanting to be rock 'n' roll, which, in my mind, was American. Many punks were anti-American and proudly Anglophilic, but I knew that music's impact was international. There were scenes breaking out in New York, Chicago, Cleveland, L.A., and San Francisco. It wasn't just the UK— punk was a rock 'n' roll world war!

That battle was reflected, for me, by the sound of Bob Marley and the Wailers' revolutionary album *Exodus*, which seemed to be coming out of every boom box. "Get up, stand up / Don't give up the fight." The reggae we listened to told of other people and races denied a true and free future. The Rastafarians talked of themselves as taking part in a spiritual rebellion. Were we sainted, too? Were we on some holy mission, or just rude-boy rebels? We were young and idealistic and set to conquer the world, our enthusiasm often overtaking our common sense in the year of the two sevens' clash.

Meanwhile, we continued to work on writing for the first album. Tony played me Bruce Springsteen's "Jungleland," which rocked but also had a gripping story line and several moving parts that built to a crescendo. I dug the idea of a narrative culled from his personal history; it inspired me to dig deep and come up with my own equivalent out of the raw materials of my life. Tony had a set of lyrics for a song called "Kiss Me Deadly," which we decided wouldn't be a three-chord bash, but a sequence of chords building dynamically from quiet to loud, emphasizing the narrative. It was what the Who did in their mini-operas. We thought about doing the same thing except with the speed and roller-coaster aggression of punk and our own street-smart attitude.

The setting for "Kiss Me Deadly" was Fulham. London, SW6, where Tony lived and we now rehearsed in a basement. I strung some picked chords together and spoke/sang the lyrics so the song would start very quietly. Then we added bass and drums to kick it into gear at the end of the first verse. We came up with an explosive middle section of wild drumming, with a guitar break leading into a full-on 4/4 final verse, with the recorded version running 4:24 in length. It told the story of two punks facing the turbulent violence, sexual exploration, and drug experimentation of the time. It could have been about Tony and me or you and your best girlfriend or any two people facing the politically and violently unsafe world in 1977. We were trying to communicate our experiences in a romantic but still realistic way, instead of just shouting grievances, as was the fashion at the time. This new direction pulled us away from the old punk, allowing us to maintain its aggression and attitude while advancing musically by exploring other, more complicated emotions and feelings.

The Ramones were touring England on their album *Rocket to Russia* and asked us to support them at their gig at the Rainbow, the biggest venue in Central London. We ended the year on New Year's Eve '77 by seeing what it was like to play a big hall. It was the same big hall where I had seen Captain Beefheart back in 1970, and Roxy Music in '73 with Sparks. Now I was treading those same boards myself!

The English crowd anointed us in a hail of gob. We loved playing with the Ramones. It was great to open for a group that was so influential to us, and to the whole punk scene. The Ramones were un-abashed about their love for early-'60s groups and Phil Spector, which was something we had in common. "Blitzkrieg Bop" and "Sheena Is a Punk Rocker" blasted us into 1978.

Meanwhile, while we'd been writing songs and working on what we hoped would be our own unique style, the Sex Pistols had been finishing a small tour of Britain to prepare for a U.S. tour in the New Year. We all had high hopes they'd be successful there. They'd had a fourth hit single in October with "Holidays in the Sun" to launch them across the water. We thought the Pistols would spearhead the way, even clear the path for us other punk bands, much as they had in England.

So it was really dumbfounding when they arrived back in England in February, having broken up in San Francisco at the end of a tour where they didn't even play New York, the mecca of punk! Their manager, Malcolm McLaren, seemed to grossly misunderstand the process of breaking a band in America. Everything that's big surely goes through New York. If you don't make it there, you won't make it anywhere. The U.S. brought out the Pistols' weaknesses, both personal and professional, and they were over as a band, at least as far as Johnny Rotten was concerned.

I saw Steve Jones at the Speakeasy in London when they had just returned, and he was moaning, "What can I do, Bill? I've lost my band." I was torn up to see him look so lost and vulnerable—I know that's how you can feel without the security of those once-strong ties with your bandmates. You get used to being a part of something like that. They had gone to America in triumph. I had seen one of their gigs at a college outside London just before they left, and they were great. I guessed America's vast spaces could eat you whole. Or was it our inner demons? Whatever had happened to the Sex Pistols, I vowed not to let it happen to me.

Blimey! If the Pistols couldn't make it, what did that say about Generation X's chances? John would quickly drop the Rotten and go on by his real name, Lydon, emerging after the breakup of the Sex Pistols to launch a great new group, Public Image Ltd., or PiL. His new band had a more experimental sound, a droning, slow-tempo, bass-heavy noise rock, overlaid by John's distinctive, castigating rant.

But we had our own album to worry about. The first item on the agenda was to record a third single to accompany the album's release. We picked "Ready Steady Go," which by this time was a Generation X standard. Full of excitement, we returned to the studio with Phil and began to lay the track down, but when we left the studio at the end of the first day, we were still unsure about the drums. We were somewhat surprised, therefore, when we returned the next day and listened. Mark's beats were much tighter and more rhythmically sound than we remembered and yet, some of his energy was siphoned from the track. Tony and I always wondered if Phil took matters into his own hands and got on the drum kit after we left.

Cracks had begun to form in our relationship with Phil; he didn't understand punk or how it was springing up from a nonprofessional ideology—he really had no time for that—so we weren't surprised when he decided he didn't want to do the rest of the album. At that point, we turned to Martin Rushent, who was already known for his work with the Stranglers and would later become an '80s pioneer of the influential Brit techno-pop sound when he produced Human League. We decamped to TW, a small studio that was a converted garage in Fulham, near the Hammersmith Odeon. Martin just let us play while he recorded. We bashed through some of our stage songs and worked on some new ones. Then we rerecorded "Ready Steady Go," retaining Laff's beats the way they were meant to be heard. It all went quite fast because it had to be done in two weeks, including mixing. Rushent's young engineer, Alan Winstanley, who prepared the board mixes of the whole album, was great. We loved what he'd done, but Martin remixed the songs. We always thought Alan's mics were better. Winstanley, often with his partner Clive Langer, went on to become a huge power in British rock and pop, producing the likes of Elvis Costello, Morrissey, Bush, and Madness.

This first Generation X album was essentially our stage show with a few overdubs. Recording it in a converted garage made it garage-rock, which was perfect for punk and our musical abilities at the time. Derwood shines on this stuff more than the rest of us, because he really is a great guitar player. As lead singer, I simply let loose, relying on my own instincts to lead the way. *Who gives a shit? It's not jazz. It's punk. I only have to be me*, which was what I did onstage. I had to work from those feelings and remember to have fun. What else did I have to depend on? The other lads were all supportive. In the 1970 Rod Steiger film *Waterloo*, Napoléon's Imperial Guard, when faced with a challenge, declared, "We can't go around, so the way is forward!"

Now, working with Martin, we felt that we weren't quite under the same scrutiny as we were with Phil Wainman, and this seemed to put everyone in a better mood. Phil was too much the professional journeyman to appreciate that Tony and I had a concept for a punk band, not a run-of-the-mill pop group.

Chrysalis had drafted Martin at the last moment to get an album out of us. Whatever his true feelings about our music were, he was a professional, and we worked well together. Every now and then, he'd give me a pointer on singing, but mostly, I was on my own, doing it my way, because I realized that I would have to live with it. You have to believe in yourself even when others don't, or you won't achieve anything. When you see people wavering in their belief, you have to be twice as strong to hold them in place. That's what I felt at the time. It's like being on the battlefront in wartime. Some will break and run when the shooting starts.

The first song on the American version of our album was a cover of "Gimme Some Truth." I loved John Lennon and wanted to do one of his songs. We originally performed this for a BBC session in '77, and that's the version on the 1991 Generation X compilation *Perfect Hits 1975–81*. I loved that Lennon basically excoriated everyone in this song, and we included "punk rockers" in the lyrics to update it a bit. I have always felt that Lennon was right up there with Dylan at fitting in those rolling, spat-out lyrics. He always did have a bee in his bonnet, lashing out against politics, or art, or sociology, or religion. There was something very punk rock about that attitude. We sped it up by playing eighth notes, added a ska guitar offbeat, and presto, it was a punk song. The American record company loved the idea of a Lennon cover, removing "The Invisible Man" from the U.S. version of the album. I loved our version, so that was all right by me.

"From the Heart" was a song we usually opened our live shows with. You might look at it as our response to the Pistols wanting to "destroy the passerby" in "Anarchy in the UK," our proof that we could write a punk love song.

"Promises Promises" was a song about how the vows you make sometimes get forgotten with the distortion of time. Perhaps it was a dig at our own heroes, who seemed to have left their youthful ideals behind. Today I understand how life can take the idealist and wreck him on the rocks of his own words.

We had read that in the '60s, the Who had a hundred core fans who networked through the phone system to help build the band's audience. In "One Hundred Punks," we thought of ourselves as Jimmy in *Quadrophenia*, the wannabe who self-destructs at the end, number 101. We created a way of drawing fans out to the shows with an early stab at viral marketing involving phone trees. We called them the Hundred Punks, and this was our song about them.

"Prove It" was another song for which I wrote the lyrics. I felt I had a lot to prove at this time in my life, that I needed to put my money where my mouth was, and that meant getting up onstage and performing as if our lives depended on it.

At first I wasn't confident in my own lyrical skills, and the work was always a joint effort. In those days, Tony would quite often arrive with finished lyrics, and then I would work on those. We needed songs, and we used most of the ideas that popped fresh into our minds. It turned out to be a fantastic learning experience, first making some singles, and then, quickly, an entire album of songs. The first Generation X album was now complete.

CHAPTER FOURTEEN

READY STEADY GO

Notting Hill Gate, London

THE SINGLE "READY STEADY GO" B/W "No No No" came out on February 7, 1978, with a cover Jonh Ingham copied from one of my T-shirt designs. Once again, we appeared on *Top of the Pops* to perform our new single, and this time we had an album to support. I also started to develop a feel for my own fashion as distinct from the prevailing punk style. I worked with a girl to create my own look, one that I would be comfortable in, and advanced the idea of punk fashion from ripped T-shirts and bondage clothes. For this show, I wore a light blue jacket with black lining and collar over a two-tone shirt that was pink on one side and yellow on the other. I had dyed it myself in the bathtub at Notting Hill Gate—I'm sure the girls at the flat loved that! I also had some white shoes with black piping made and I wore them with my leather trousers. I looked pretty colorful and, with my bleached hair, the look perfectly fit the song's lighter subject. The usual punk uniform of leather and denim had become too limiting for me. I wanted to stay one step ahead of the people who were copying us. I strapped on my Epiphone semi-acoustic, which I still used when I wrote, since I didn't own an acoustic guitar.

My status as an up-and-coming rock star led to some new and intriguing romantic possibilities. I began to meet a variety of interesting women. One was a makeup artist who taught me a little bit about her craft. We'd go to the art-house movie theaters when I had an off night. I also enjoyed the company of a thirty-five-year-old woman who worked at Chrysalis and lived near Notting Hill. She wore all these sexy stockings and garter belts. I could also take a bath at her flat. The photographer Sheila Rock was another friend of mine. And I was meeting plenty of birds on the road. One was a punk-rock chick with blue hair who styled my hair and screwed me until her boyfriend found out. With the avalanche of birds, I became a quick learner in the sack, as I hadn't had a ton of sex before this.

The band played up and down Britain as we traveled in a rented transit van, sitting on top of the gear. It was a nonstop blur of gigs, chicks, sweat, spit, bleach, more sweat, noise, screaming horrors, chicks, chicks, and more chicks. One good thing about being in Generation X was we were a fun band, without the political posturing of some of the other punk groups. The younger crowd loved our punk-rock hybrid. When we heard that our show in Glasgow was to be canceled because of the ban on punk bands within the city limits, we bused three hundred kids to a venue outside town and watched as they, in their excitement, pogoed their way from the bus to the ballroom floor. It was worth going the extra mile for our Scottish fans.

That July, Tony and I traveled up to Birmingham to see the Clash. They were great, but I was even more blown away by Suicide, the opening act from New York. The "band" was composed of two members, Alan Vega on vocals and Marty Rev on keyboard and drum machine. Wow! What an anarchic duo. Their electronic rock 'n' roll was a bit outside the scope of Clash fans, who proceeded to throw stuff at them. Alan was a menacing presence onstage, a Puerto Rican/Jewish Elvis by way of Iggy. The constant throb of "Ghost Rider," with its sixteenth-note bass lines and Marty's chord stabs, drove the dyed-in-the-wool Clash fans crazy with frustration. Alan antagonized the crowd and then smashed himself in the head with the microphone, drawing blood. This drove the audience over the top, and they bottled the band off the stage. As for me, I felt like Jon Landau seeing Bruce Springsteen: I had seen the future of rock, a future that would include not just guitar, bass, and drums, but electronics as well. Suicide were ahead of their time, but this crowd was not ready for it.

Chrysalis sent me to the States in the spring of '78 to do publicity for the album. Because the label wouldn't spring for two members for budgetary reasons, I went without Tony, which probably began an erosion of solidarity in the band. This was the beginning of me doing interviews and promotion on my own.

It was fantastic to be in New York. I stayed at the Warwick Hotel on 54th, the strange, steamy subway currents blowing my dreams into the night. I hung out with Blondie, and Debbie Harry took me to meet the New York Dolls' David Johansen and Syl Sylvain at their rehearsal space. I hung out at the Mudd Club and Max's Kansas City, where I saw Patti Smith showcase her *Easter* album, and met her back-stage. I was a big fan of her *Horses* album. At one point, she turned to her mother, and said, "Look, Ma, it's the face of the next generation!" I don't know exactly what she meant by that—maybe it was her way of referring to the band Generation X, but I was glad to be there digging on the scene and hanging out with someone who was a hero to us. Patti and her guitarist Lenny Kaye gave us hope that punk could be huge in the U.S. for the right reasons.

I was knocked out to meet some of the American punk bands we dug in England. At CBGB's, I saw Lux Interior and the Cramps. I met Bleecker Bob, who owned a popular Lower East Side record store of the same name that doubled as a hangout for many of New York's fin-est punk bands. Roberta Bayley, who shot the cover of the Ramones' first album, took my picture. If punk was a movement in England, it was still in its nascent stages in America, but these groups were my idols.

After a few days in New York, we flew to L.A., where I spent time with Joan Jett and about twenty of her very girlish lipstick lezzies in cute punk go-go boots. Then I saw the Germs and Darby Crash at the Whisky a Go Go. I went on Rodney Bingenheimer's KROQ show to debut some tracks from the album. He was using the "Wild Dub" instrumental remix as his theme music. I visited Licorice Pizza, a hip record store, and hung with local scribe and scenester Pleasant

Gehman. Sunset Strip seemed to wind its way like a snake through the bowels of West Hollywood. I crawled along the scales of its back as it took me toward the heart of the music world where, after the '60s and early '70s hippies, the punks had taken root. I stayed at a small motel just across from Tower Records. Compared to the fast pace of central London or New York, L.A. seemed to be very slow. That hippie laid-back vibe was still prevalent in Hollywood, which is really quite a small town, but punk was the new interloper. Over time, the two cults morphed together and became the edgy alternative scene we have today, with its focus on modern primitivism, scarification, tattooing, and piercing. Back then, the peace-and-love scene, which had saved people from Vietnam, was fading: with the war's end, its purpose had become thwarted. Punk had come in to express some of that angst toward society, with the economic depression hitting both the U.S. and UK. America hadn't seen a downturn since World War II, which had helped lift the depression of the '30s. While the '60s had seemed quite forward-looking and optimistic about the future, by the mid-'70s, those rose-tinted glasses had been removed.

Punk had enlivened the Strip with its burst of energy. Seeing Darby Crash sing that night gave his later death particular meaning for me, making it seem as tragic as the demise of Sid Vicious, both in their early twenties.

After two nights in L.A., we were off to San Francisco. I had quite a wild time in the Bay Area, where I hung out with the Avengers, a local punk band, and visited the legendary local FM station KSAN. At Mabuhay Gardens, a former transsexual bar turned premier punk venue, I jammed on "Johnny Too Bad" with San Francisco punk/ska band the Offs. It was my American onstage debut! I took a girl in the audience back to the hotel with me, where she insisted I put my fist in her pussy. She was pretty wet and I gradually got it in. As soon as I did, it was as if I set off an electric current in her body. She started rolling around on the bed and then onto the floor in a kind of ecstasy, eyes pinned to the back of her head. After about an hour of me having to follow her rolling around the room, she instructed me to "pull it out now." At this point, her pussy had already started to close up, trapping my fist inside. Wherever she went, I had no choice but to follow, lest I break my arm. I finally got it out, but my hand blew up to twice its normal size, so I had to sleep with it in a bucket of ice. By morning, it had gone down. At that point, I kissed her and America goodbye and was soon on a plane back to the UK. What a wild week, meeting punk-rock heroes and fist-fucking. The Clash may have been bored with it, but I was in love with the USA.

Upon my return to the UK, we began writing our second album, *Valley of the Dolls*, in between gigs, during any spare time we had. The Clash's second album, *Give 'Em Enough Rope*, came out around this time, and it was a lot more rock than punk. This seemed to encourage Tony, who wanted us to move in a similar direction, like his heroes, Mott the Hoople. I had chosen the producer of the first album, so I let Tony do the honors for this one, and he wanted Mott the Hoople's lead singer, Ian Hunter.

Tony was a bigger fan of Mott the Hoople than I was, though I remembered waking up to them doing "Thunderbuck Ram" at the three-day, twenty-four-hour outdoor music festival in Weeley back in August '71, and I liked the stuff they'd done with Bowie. We needed someone who understood what we had to do as a band, who would work with us on making the next step. Our eye was on making an album that would break us in America.

Along with Ian, we got Bill Price, who was a top engineer. The sound and quality of his work still hold up today. Ian had a young, in-experienced singer to work with, a little out of his depth; I had to reach beyond myself. We weren't going to be pigeonholed as just another Anglophile punk band. We had to change and grow or wither and die.

When we got to Wessex Studios to record the second album, we were a different band, at least in the sense that we were stepping be-yond punk musically but keeping it as an attitude. It was strange to be in such a high-class studio after the converted garage where we made our first album. But we set up the gear and got down to business. The budget was small, so we worked as hard and fast as we could, but the luxury of the technology now within our grasp meant that there was a lot to learn, and quickly.

At first, I found it difficult to write for the second album. Tony had penned a load of lyrics that he gave me to work on, but I didn't feel the same connection to them as I had our initial stuff. I could feel the lyrical direction getting less punk, but Tony's enthusiasm and the success of "Kiss Me Deadly" drove me to contribute, as I had to the first album. We took a risk in order to develop our own style, and though we didn't realize it at the time, we began to create our new sound.

While writing, I thought of all the ringing guitar-picking I loved and put a lot of chiming, revolving "flags" in songs like "Paradise West" and "Valley of the Dolls." "Kenny Silvers" is almost an acoustic strum-along with a rock arrangement. I also tried to employ curb-crawling riffs, which we hadn't tried much on the first album, such as in "Night of the Cadillacs," and "Love like Fire." It was rock informed by punk. A band had to be adventurous. You had to expose yourself and bare your soul to find out what you were all about. All or nothing was the spirit that prevailed back then.

Tony was deeply involved with a girl named Katy, so it wasn't so foreign to start singing about love or sex. We were one of the few punk bands to have females in our audience. Most punk bands really played primarily to guys, so it was liberating to have another subject to write about, one that was taboo for other punk bands, as their manifestos precluded presenting love in a positive way. "Valley of the Dolls" was about the sincere love we got from these dedicated female fans and the genuine excitement they brought. That factor changed the group's dynamic in the sense that it encouraged female participation. We also sang about our love for rock 'n' roll, such as in the fictitious fight for supremacy between Elvis and the Beatles in "King Rocker," or just sticking to our punk guns in "Running with the Boss Sound," about the time I was attacked by a teddy boy at Charing Cross station.

In "Paradise West," I sang: "And I thought it must be me who's crazy / The things I do for fun / Choosing poison to get to paradise / Paradise west one."

I had to pour myself into the songs to sing them. We were focusing on our own obsessions, problems, and frustrations, but also adding in romance instead of just negativity. It was a time of no hope in society, so you had to get positive to even have a chance of overcoming life's difficulties, or wallow in endless self-pity. We started recording our second album in the autumn of '78 and didn't have the luxury of a ton of time, so we kept up a certain momentum and worked hard.

When *Valley of the Dolls* came out in January 1979, the leap we had taken was hard to follow for some of the music critics and our punk fans, although on the positive side, with our slightly more straight-ahead rock 'n' roll direction, we picked up an audience that wasn't exclusively punk. So we outraged some purists but drew in music lovers and started creating the larger-than-life images that went beyond punk and into the '80s. Though it was horrible to be criticized so harshly by several critics and some of our fanbase, it was fun running into the dark, seeking light to illuminate our own expression.

We went on a short tour of England when "King Rocker" came out, performing twice on *Top of the Pops*. We had a hit with this single, and my glam outfit on *TOTP* signaled we weren't gonna wear "no uniform," as we stated on the first album. On tour one morning, I went down for breakfast and the chef was singing "King Rocker"—it was the first time I'd overheard someone singing one of our songs. The fact was, we were getting played on the radio quite a bit, and this brought in a whole new audience: not just punks, but fans of straight rock.

We played most of *Valley of the Dolls* on this UK tour, which was barely three weeks long. We basically owned nothing but the clothes on our backs, but our bid for rock stardom did fly a bit in the face of the punk purists' "no more heroes" theme. We had already sung about our love for rock 'n' roll on the first album, so I didn't think we were doing anything so wrong. This was two years after 1977. Was life quite so hopeless now that punk itself had brought back an aura of positivity to English dreams? We felt we had helped each other, band and audience alike, to break through the barrier of boredom. The political situation was just as bleak, but the grip of nothing happening had been finished, and people had polarized into separate groups.

AFTER "VALLEY OF THE DOLLS," THE single, came out in March 1979, we started to appear in some teenybopper magazines. Our more girl-friendly image made us popular, and that was another thing that wasn't kosher with hard-core critics and fans, who believed punk was the revenge of the rotten and the ugly. Fuck them! Punk shouldn't be just one thing, but that was what some fans wanted. I had to experiment with my image, keep evolving or perish. My hair was longer and not just spiky, but almost in a long quiff. I experimented with baggy pants, high heels, pink "Elvis" sport coats, waistcoats, and diamanté jewelry, but I mixed it in with my leather pants and boots. We were attempting to find a style beyond punk, mixing images we loved. Derwood wore a red soldier's dress coat. Mark got a big shiny metallic kit and he used his tom-toms on certain drum breaks. We drove around in a rented station wagon on yet another quick three-week tour. This time we hired a road manager and a couple roadies. Generation X was expanding fast.

With Jonh Ingham gone, Stuart Joseph was now managing us alone. We were young, brash, and had to move forward. While *Valley of the Dolls* was a relative commercial success, the criticism of its musical direction by our punk fans, as well as other factors both creative and personal, had begun to eat away at the band. Tony and I were starting to drift apart, and all sorts of dissension followed. Our well-oiled democracy was dissolving into fighting and unspoken dark thoughts.

Doubts about the prevailing group dynamic had begun to arise amongst all band members. It seemed to me that Tony had begun to suffer anxiety issues, and as an unwelcome result, I was doing the lion's share of the interviews. This was certainly not my choice—at the time, doing major press interviews put me well out of my comfort zone. And while I've never shied away from pressing my limits, I found myself answering questions on the meaning of our lyrics. That begged the question, if I was the singer and the press spokesman, shouldn't I write my own lyrics? Derwood and Laff wanted to write songs, too, but where were their ideas?

We rented a house out in the Oxfordshire countryside to write songs for our third album. That might have worked for Led Zeppelin, but it didn't for me. I was an urbanite. I didn't want to write songs about cows. Some really shitty songs came out of those sessions that should never have seen the light of day (but that didn't stop our record company from later exercising their rights to release them without our approval under the original Generation X contract we naively signed).

By now, we were all influenced by different music. I was still friends with Steve Strange, and he was getting involved in the New Romantic movement. I found it hard to ignore some of the synthesizer and drum-machine groove records by the likes of Kraftwerk and Human League. I have never only listened to rock 'n' roll. The way an endless disco groove turned into a soundscape intrigued me. I was also listening to Joy Division, who used straight-eighth pumping bass notes and constant rhythmic drumming.

I have always loved dance music. To this day, "Land of a Thousand Dances" is a favorite of mine. I was intrigued by Giorgio Moroder's electronic disco productions for Donna Summer, like "I Feel Love," with its classic four-on-the-floor beat and every instrument playing eighth or sixteenth notes in syncopation. The European avant-garde element was a direct outgrowth of Kraftwerk. The constant repetition of the groove has always appealed to me. It's what I have always loved about early rock 'n' roll, the forward momentum of music that is meant to be danced to. Nothing lets up; the groove won't let go. You are drawn inside it and released with abandon because of its certainty of purpose. Exemplified by the Rolling Stones' "Jumpin' Jack Flash," it's relentless in its simplicity, sexy and omniscient, godlike.

WE TRIED TO RECORD SOME NEW demos at Olympic Studios in Barnes, London, a fantastic place from which to draw inspiration, as everyone from the Rolling Stones to the Beatles, B.B. King to Jimi Hendrix, David Bowie to Led Zeppelin could all at some point be found laying down tracks there. We'd been stationed in the legendary studios for some time now working toward what was to have been the third Generation X album with the original lineup. It was May 1979, and things were beginning to come apart at the seams. Blow as we might on the faint embers, the original flame seemed to have burned out. Derwood had already threatened more than once that he was going to leave, and we were struggling to find a direction. We were all a bit on edge, and the sense was that this dream was beginning to come to a close.

After going out on a bender one night, meeting a girl, and ending up back at her flat, I woke up with a never-again hangover. First to arrive at the studio that morning, I started to play my guitar to see if I could come up with anything, or at the very least take my mind off the hangover. At some point, I remembered how a few weeks earlier, while playing in Tokyo on a promotional tour, we had gone to a couple of discos, where the kids were still in *Saturday Night Fever* mode, dancing with their own reflections in the mirror, and I remarked to Tony, "Hey, they're dancing with themselves." He said, "That could be a song title!"

Going on that memory, I worked out a bit of a chorus over E-A-B, four to the bar repeating, and I began to wonder if a verse wouldn't work over that same chord sequence. When Tony arrived, I showed him what I had, and we started to work on some lyrics, detailing a night on any club floor in the world, where a lonely dancer fills the mirror with his or her own sensual movements.

ON THE FLOORS OF TOKYO / DOWN IN LONDON TOWNS A GO, GO / WITH THE RECORD
SELECTION / AND THE MIRROR'S REFLECTION / I'M DANCING WITH MYSELF.
—"DANCING WITH MYSELF"

There was magic in the air. We sat on the back fire escape, and I leaned against the iron rails and played the same driving E-A-B chord sequence on my unplugged Epiphone guitar, singing *da daaa da da da da da*. In moments like this the muse would grab me by the balls, and I'd feel the teenage thrill, amazed at my great luck of plucking a tune out of thin air.

Tom Waits has said that every song has a distinct identity by which it's born into the world, and each song needs to be taken down on its own terms. There are songs that you have to sneak up on, like you're hunting for a rare bird. And there are songs that need to be bullied into existence; they need a shakedown. And then there are songs that come fully intact, like a dream sucked through a straw. "Dancing with Myself" was the latter, and Tony and I got caught up in the frantic buzz of its sorcery.

That day the words and arrangement just flowed out of us both, and we scribbled them down as fast as we could, pencil to paper scrap. I know the difference between something I thought of and something I was given. My hangover melted away, and all was right in the world for those moments—the words seemed like they were already hanging there, ready to be gloved from the ether. We couldn't help but laugh, giddy at the symmetry and the fit of the words and melody.

It's incredibly difficult to sit down to write a simple song about a simple idea with words that the listener will somehow feel they know upon first hearing. If it were easy, we'd do it every day.

We made the song all about the longing to find a partner in this life: "If I looked all over the world / And there's every type of girl / But their empty eyes seem to pass me by / And leave me dancing with myself."

And then, we made it a little more inclusive: "If I had the chance / I'd ask one to dance."

When the band arrived, we tried out this new song. I asked Mark to play a sort of reverse "twist" beat to try to get a momentum thing going, with the same repeating chords and beat all the way through. For an interlude, we chugged on B to E and, for a guitar break, we just picked out the individual notes of the chords and then went back to the verse/chorus. We recorded a version, and there seemed to be something there. What I wanted to do was put some of the punk energy back into our music, but keep it constant and sexual by making it great to dance to. You could pogo or slam dance to punk, but it wasn't primarily for fucking, like this would be.

What we had at this point was nothing more than a rough demo, but this was something altogether new; "Dancing with Myself" was a different kind of idea for us, and quite exciting. It was the song that would change everything.

IN THE MIDDLE OF EVERYTHING THAT was going on, manager Stuart Joseph's divisive machinations were making frictions in the band grow worse. In an effort to alleviate the tension, we made the decision to get rid of him. This would not be easy, and we'd end up walking through rock 'n' roll fire. Stuart responded with a lawsuit and secured a high court injunction to stop us from playing and recording under the name Generation X. Until it was all sorted out legally, we were in a bit of a limbo, so we went out and played several gigs as Wild Youth.

Chrysalis couldn't be seen overtly helping us, but they did anyway. We needed a new manager, and one of the people Tony mentioned to Chrysalis as a possibility was "whoever works with Kiss." I think he said it almost as a joke, but coincidentally one of the Chrysalis owners did actually know the manager in question, Bill Aucoin, and contacted him.

Bill came from New York to see one of our clandestine Wild Youth gigs. He seemed wild but cool, and he did give the last glimmer of hope to the slowly dying Generation X by saying he would manage us. At first we hardly knew him, but he soon set up a plan with the record company that would provide us with a weekly wage until the court action was over. Unfortunately, the court case stretched on for over six months, which seemed an interminable amount of time.

Surely, things should have been on the upswing. We had a powerful new manager, the record company was with us, and we thought we had time to iron out any problems. Nonetheless, the songwriting issues with Derwood and Mark meant that nothing would be resolved. Over the next few months, Tony and I drifted apart from our two other bandmates. With the lawsuit still hanging over our heads, Derwood and Mark decided to leave the group to start their own band, Empire. The different needs of the individuals, questions about who should be writing the songs, and what they would sound like had all made reconciliation difficult.

Looking back, we should've let Derwood in on the songwriting: he is such a great guitarist. Doing so might well have solved the temporary disagreements in the band, but I am afraid hindsight is 20/20.

Questions about songwriters weren't the only problem we had within the band, and soon I was about to add a substance into the mix that would outdo any problem we'd had to date and isolate me in a world of womblike ignorance.

CHAPTER FIFTEEN

AND I GUESS THAT I JUST DON'T KNOW

London

LIKE THOSE TOKYO DANCERS IN LOVE with their own vaporous images, I entered my own twilight world, where no one could see my thoughts and expressions—only I was privy to those. The deep inner sanctuary I had found kept me from feeling reality's sting. The shroud of death came close and blew on me, but with a warm, comforting breath. I was alive, but in a far-off trance. The shadow forms that populated this world didn't bother me. I was oblivious. I had a lover, a brown, dark substance you know by its names: Mr. Brown, H, horse, skag, smack, or Henry. I had fallen deeply in love, and nothing was quite so easy. Just let go, deeper, deeper, deeper, deeper, relax, all the way down. . . .

My new drug addiction meant I would be in a state where I couldn't function 100 percent in any environment other than a drug space. With drugs, I could have life on my terms. I was a junkie, and this was the honeymoon period. With the 24/7 rock 'n' roll lifestyle, heroin was an easy way to fly. Cocooned within a tomblike silence, I could slip far away.

The first time I did heroin was at the house of Thin Lizzy's Phil Lynott after a night at the Blitz. He laid out a line of what I thought was coke, but ten minutes later, I was sick. He laughed and told me it was smack. We then snorted heroin and coke all night long, chatting about music while alternately throwing up into a wastepaper basket, our rapid-fire conversation punctuated by the sound of vomiting. I didn't touch the stuff again for weeks, but it wouldn't be long before heroin and I reencountered each other.

One night, Tony and I decided to see a show by a dance group, Hot Gossip, who had a regular slot on the weekly *Kenny Everett Video Show*, where they danced to a set number, accompanying any band that was on the show. David Mallet was the show's director. Everett had been on the radio for years, playing music and doing humorous skits with a wacky brand of humor that he had taken to TV in 1979. The show was a huge hit, and Hot Gossip were all the rage. They wore up-to-the-moment styles of clothing and were very brazen. That night, I was struck by one of the female dancers with long, teased-up, crazy red hair.

I immediately fell for this thin, shapely, long-legged, crazy-haired redhead dancer, the "Stony-Eyed Medusa." We met after the show, and my attraction to her grew. Her name was Perri Lister. We went to another club, where she danced with one of her mates, sexily and suggestively and with abandon. The formfitting matching patent leather outfits they wore showed off their glistening bodies as they twisted and flowed and dipped through the night. I was smitten, but was she?

I tried dancing with her, but I'm terrible at one-on-one moves, so I got embarrassed. We momentarily lost contact at the club, but then the stony-green-eyed girl pinched me on the bum, and when I looked round, she smiled at me. *She's great*, I thought to myself, *a female version of me, or even wilder*. I was soon to discover I'd met my match.

Perri had grown up being tutored in the theater. Before Hot Gossip, she attended the renowned Italia Conti Academy of Theatre Arts in London, the world's oldest theater training school. Perri's mum and dad had both been in the theater—her father, Bert, worked as a personal assistant for Noël Coward for a time, while Perri's mum appeared in Coward's plays. They lived on Victoria Street in London. It was fascinating to sit with Bert and hear his tales of London in the '30s and '40s.

Soon, Perri and I were head over heels in love in a way I'd never been before. We started to spend all our time together. The dancers were paid fairly well; they worked hard and partied hard, too. One of their friends was a chap who worked for a Persian prince and had access to great weed, coke, and smack. I hadn't been doing a lot of drugs during our initial years in Generation X, as we had no money, except for the occasional English spliff with hash and tobacco. I started to get offered exotic drugs that had been used by many of the bands I admired. Perri and I had fallen in love, and heroin is the ultimate relationship drug, so the two went hand in hand. I was hooked on both lovers.

At some point, Tony's anxiety worsened. Before one show, he almost couldn't go onstage. He told us his doctor told him to avoid more pressure than necessary. He also said his doctor prescribed Valium and told him to exercise, run, and meditate.

Tony turned to jogging regularly to combat further attacks, and we began to grow further apart, even though we lived in the same house. He loved rock 'n' roll heroin chic, but not when it was close up. Tony saw through the glamour of drugs, while it blinded me. Despite the rifts between us, we began working on some new songs and looking for replacements for Derwood and Mark. We hired ex-Clash drummer Terry Chimes to play so we could rehearse and entered the studio to begin working on new songs, changing our name to Gen X as a way of telling people it was some form of continuation from Generation X, with similar core members, for instance, but at the same time updated or renewed. Shortening the name to four letters meant it could be that much larger on posters, bags, album jackets, or twelve-inch-record covers.

Drugs did prompt some ideas for new material. A newspaper article referred to Valium takers in Britain as the "happy people." So we wrote a dubbed-out deep-bass song of that same name. I wrote the lyrics and music for a song called "Poison," about being on smack and the state of mind that came with it. Even though I was diving headlong down a slippery path, something inside me was telling me it was dangerous and wrong. It was weighing heavily on me. With the glare of

the stage lights dimmed, we turned to the question of what to do with
the rest of our lives.

WHY DID YOU CHANGE YOUR NAME / IN A SEARCH FOR FAME /
NOW ALL THE LIGHTS HAVE GONE / WHAT IS YOUR POISON?
—"POISON"

By the time 1980 rolled around, I was looking for inspiration in the
ennui. I wrote all the lyrics and music for "Untouchables," about my
school days and growing up in the rock 'n' roll lifestyle, dreaming of a
world beyond the regular nine-to-five existence. But the song also dealt
with how people's dreams can be crushed by disappointment, forcing
them to give up and accept the norm. For me, fortunately, dreams had
set me free. These songs would be a turning point for me in spotlight-
ing my own voice and showing I had something to say, lyrically as well
as musically.

CHAPTER SIXTEEN

YOU BETTER HANG ON TO YOURSELF

London

CHRYSALIS ALMOST DIDN'T LET US MAKE a third album. I had to persuade Doug D'Arcy of my belief in "Dancing with Myself" and its possibilities, even the chance it might just launch my solo career. My persistence paid off, and the label finally relented. I told Bill Aucoin I felt we needed a producer who could do both rock 'n' roll and groove-driven dance music, so he got in touch with Giorgio Moroder, the disco pioneer whom he knew from his Kiss days when they and Moroder client Donna Summer were both on Casablanca Records. Giorgio passed. It was the height of the disco era, and he was the king of the genre: perhaps our music was outside his comfort zone. Nevertheless, Giorgio recommended Keith Forsey, a young producer/songwriter who had written with Moroder and worked at his studio in Germany.

Keith had met Giorgio Moroder when he was hired to play drums on some of the songs Giorgio was producing. Giorgio encouraged him to write lyrics and songs, which he did, before following Moroder to L.A., where he worked with Donna Summer. Forsey wrote "Hot Stuff" for the disco diva, named after a pizza they had delivered to the studio when they were writing. Three years later, when Giorgio went on to compose the music for *Flashdance*, Keith wrote the lyrics for Irene Cara's "What a Feeling," winning an Oscar for it.

Up until then, Keith's main success had been as a songwriter. He had something to prove as a producer in his own right, and so did we. He wasn't a "name" producer, but we were a band that was trying to reinvent itself, and we needed a fresh start and a fresh perspective.

It was a hot spring day in 1980 when I first met Keith, and he arrived to our meeting togged out in a SEX T-shirt and leather pants. I loved that he was trying to be on the same page as us, even if in a humorous way (especially in a humorous way). Tony didn't seem so hot on Keith initially, but we carried on and gave the plan the chance it needed to work. And when he picked "Dancing with Myself" as the song he wanted to work on first, I knew he was our guy, so we hired him to begin work on the album.

We set up in George Martin's Air Studios on Oxford Street, London's busiest shopping street. Right away, Keith really started to home in on the relationship of sound between the kick, snare, and hi-hat, the motor we would ride on, if you will. He was hands-on as a producer. Being a drummer, he could have played the parts he was asking for, but I could see he wanted the performance from us. He certainly pulled a great one out of the "Chimer" (Terry Chimes) on "Dancing."

Next, Tony laid down his bass with Terry and I was on guide vocal. Once we had that, we brought in Rich Kids guitarist Steve New. Here's the scene: Steve on his back, lying on the studio floor, off his face, working his guitar, surrounded by a screaming blockade of Marshall and Fender amplifiers, bottles of methadone lined up on the mixing desk. But still, he produced magic, the way mercurial geniuses do, adding that indefinable sound to the lead guitars that helps make the record what it is. Keith was freaking out, not used to dealing with such scenes of madness. And when the tape ran out, New, completely unaware, played on. We got what we needed—genius requires only one take, you just have to be lucky enough to capture it.

Then we asked Steve Jones of the Sex Pistols to come in and lay down his guitar "wall of sound." He filled four tracks playing slightly different rhythms, and they somehow melded together terrifically. Jonesy has a muscular sound, and over all the years I've played with him, he always gets that sound no matter what guitar or amp he's on. It's all him; it's in his fingers!

Danny Kustow from Tom Robinson Band came in and added a different flavor of rhythm and did a few really exciting takes. Keith and I spent a while on my vocal doing three different takes, and then Keith would pull the best lines from each and construct a performance that was better than any one single take. Then I would do three more takes and he would switch different lines from each, seeing if they beat what we already had on the main master he was compiling.

The next day, Keith started to mix. He spent two days doing it, and finally felt he had what he was looking for. He and I stepped into the main studio, put on the big speakers, and cranked the volume to see what it would sound like live in a club. I was knocked out! Somehow he had sonically and rhythmically made everything work. The song was unstoppable in terms of holding the groove all the way through. Here was our new musical direction, loud and proud!

Tony has an enduring vision of listening to the playback and realizing Jonesy had somehow managed to climb out a window of the studio's soundproof glass and onto the narrow window ledge, inches from plummeting to his death. He gestured to the shoppers six floors below, silently mouthing the words to the song's chorus through the glass as he windmilled his Les Paul, legs defiantly apart. He said afterward, "I was trying it out. You know . . . Dancing with Myself." And having a fucking hell of a time, evidently!

We also asked Magazine's John McGeoch, who went on to join the Banshees and later PiL, to play guitar on the album, adding some of his own ideas to my figures. I played my Epiphone guitar through an HH amp on songs like "Poison," "Happy People," and "Ugly Rash," the B-side to "Dancing with Myself."

At the same time, in the lyrics to songs like "Dancing with Myself" and "Heavens Inside," the street-romantic-with-a-bittersweet-undertone side of Billy Idol was beginning to emerge. With his new band PiL, Johnny Rotten was tackling the big issues with songs like "Religion," while the Clash had politicized their lyrics from the start. I was intrigued with the very large subject of our human emotions, like the need for love. That subject would later come to define my writing style. While other acts were addressing larger social problems, I was focusing on the more personal.

HE'S IN LOVE WITH HIS LONELY LIFE / TO THE PICKUP GIRLS /
HE'S A SWITCHBLADE KNIFE / HE DON'T WANT NOTHING / BUT HE TAKES IT ALRIGHT.
—"HEAVENS INSIDE"

I was also beginning to write and perform autobiographical songs about the paucity of spirituality within myself and the revolution I was caught up in. Despite the drugs that were increasingly becoming part of my life, or perhaps because of them, I was starting to examine my own feelings of emptiness that had led me to seek comfort in heroin. Until I met Perri, I'd really been starting to feel like a lone wolf. I was questioning my desire to be a rock star and was concerned with the possibility of becoming someone—if I wasn't careful—who would lose his soul in the process. These were not gang chants but increasingly personal observations. I had begun to carve out my own lyrical niche.

I had learned a great deal from Tony—we still wrote songs like "Stars Look Down," "Revenge," and "Oh Mother" for the new album together—but I was increasingly beginning to find my own voice.

Recording with Keith Forsey was exciting for me, though Tony didn't really get on too well with him. They would bicker all the time, and I could see the two of them might not want to continue together after the record was finished. I thought Keith was doing a great job. It was the best-sounding album we'd made so far. He didn't let events rattle him, and he could shake himself from an unhappy to a happy mood easily.

When we finished the album, I was the only one to seek him out at his hotel on his last night in the UK. I had dinner with him and his wife, Karen. I told him I liked how he worked and hoped we might do more, if I was ever given the chance to make another record. After all, my future was certainly up in the air at that moment. Keith had really tried to make my concept for the record work, and I appreciated that a great deal. Most important, we had a finished version of "Dancing with Myself" in the can. Would it be my bridge to the future?

During the recording of the album, Perri and I had been on a non-stop, twenty-four-hour binge without sleep. We made love in bed all day and night, while I was high on heroin, grass, and hash. With that particular cocktail, as orgasm boiled over, I would pop an amyl nitrate (commonly known as poppers) and soar to the sweet spot that intensifies the growing explosion of chemistry between two lovers entwined like vines, curling together, disappearing into each other . . . writhing, sighing, and groaning, soaring into heaven, only to slowly burn out and return to earth, spent but somehow wanting more.

Heroin is a dangerous and addictive drug. If you take it enough, it returns you to the place that is as comfortable and all-encompassing as your mother's womb. After three days, you're hooked. When you come off, you're debilitated, to the point where you feel like your skeleton is trying to get out of your body; you're dying for more. And unless you want to go on feeling bad, you need a continuous supply. If you take enough to not get sick, you can maintain a semi-regular lifestyle. Thanks to Bill Aucoin's renegotiation with Chrysalis, I now had enough money to fund my habits . . . and he, unbeknownst to me at the time, had enough to fund his.

The Stony-Eyed Medusa and I lived in a twilight world of drugs, sex, and rock 'n' roll friends. We roamed the London night in a small tools minivan I bought from my dad, dubbed "Power Tool the People." The slow-burning nights spun into a web that trapped me in its embrace until unconsciousness delivered me back to a moment of enforced sleep. Waking up on different floors and beds, I was surrounded by the ubiquitous reggae music, which we always played while we were "block up," a phrase we used for getting stoned. There had to be guardian angels looking silently through the hash fumes just above our heads. Why else would I still be here today, alive and well, to tell the story?

On one occasion, Perri and I took acid and went to see *Apocalypse Now*, then made love all night to George Faith's Lee "Scratch" Perry–produced album, *To Be a Lover*. It was amazing I was able to get out of bed long enough to record our album, but I was.

I continued going to Perri's gigs, where I ran into David Mallet, the director who shot Generation X's '77 Marquee performance. This meeting would prove fortuitous for the future.

Living twenty-four hours every day with Perri back then was quite the experience. We had a connection that was deeper than any I had ever known. It was a great trip for me to have a counterpart with whom I had so many interests in common, including fashion, music, movies, and the like. Perri had become my constant companion throughout this life of love, lust, and insanity. Only later did I realize that I had not paused to consider that my intense love affair with her, the heroin, hash, and other drugs were unraveling the constraints of my punk past and helping to further widen the gulf between me and Tony James.

The last nail in the coffin for Tony and me was the relative lack of success of our final album together, *Kiss Me Deadly*. The album was released in early 1981, and "Dancing with Myself" came out as a single in the UK, only reaching number 60 on the British charts. I suppose our new direction was mystifying a lot of people, as the album was of quite a different nature than *Valley of the Dolls*.

England moves quickly through different fashions and musical styles, and it occurred to me that the long break between the second and third albums meant that some of our fans might have moved on.

The record company started to say to me, "Well, you've done it here. It might be a good idea to go somewhere else, such as the USA and try again?" At this point, Tony and I had been on different pages for a while, so this time I seriously considered moving on from our partnership. Bill Aucoin agreed, and it seemed that he, too, wanted to concentrate on me as a solo artist, which I had begun to see as a good way to start afresh. I had worked with Tony for five years and had learned a lot from our collaboration, but maybe I had to gamble on myself once again. I had always dreamt about being in a group, but I now saw how fragile group harmony could be. If Tony and I were each in a different headspace and Gen X was fizzling, the only thing to do was to forge ahead and go solo.

Following the disastrous critical lashing we got for *Valley of the Dolls*, the terribly unproductive time spent writing in the country for a third album, and *Kiss Me Deadly*'s lack of success, my musical tastes continued to evolve. Perri being in a dance group made me think more about making music that was good for choreographed moves in a club. Dance and music represented an interesting opportunity, a new sense of place. I was listening to more techno and groups like Kraftwerk. I liked Joy Division, and noticed a small number of bands, like PiL, Simple Minds, Human League, Daniel Miller's Soft Cell, and Cowboys International, were all finding ways to go forward with a post-punk hybrid, often incorporating other forms of music. The steady drum patterns were kept simple and direct, without too many Keith Moon roller-coaster fills or time changes. I thought it reflected the influence of disco, like Giorgio Moroder's work with Donna Summer, that was being heard everywhere on the New York club scene. I began to think the way forward was to combine dance music with rock 'n' roll, keeping the punk energy but streamlining the music so that the groove was consistent throughout the song, without too many fills that distracted from the central idea.

I didn't really know what the others truly thought about this, although Tony seemed to grasp the idea when we wrote "Dancing with Myself" to test this new concept. I got really excited about the idea, as I felt it might help us to survive the now-collapsing first wave of punk and move into the future. If we didn't take this new direction, I honestly wasn't interested in continuing. I had to follow what was in my heart.

We didn't believe in a future with punk, which colored my actions as well as the band's. Punk rock had become a parody of itself. What we'd stood for in the beginning was already over. If there was "no future," what we decided to do now really counted. There was no time for fussing and fighting, my friend.

I had to write and sing my own lyrics if I was going to survive and thrive. I had to put myself in a position where I didn't have Tony to rely on, or I'd never have done it. He was a really good songwriter, much better than I was, but it was sink-or-swim time. Being hooked on heroin during that period made me more isolated from Tony and the rest of the band. It also filled me with the confidence that I could do anything I wanted.

I had begun to see the light. That light was my chance to go to New York. That light was also the love I felt for Perri, for rock 'n' roll, and for the possibilities of my own life, for forging onward and being unbounded by the pull of gravity.

I did have a sense of apprehension that leaving England would hurt my friends and family. But then, I thought it couldn't be any worse than all the other separations I had endured during my life. The traveling salesman goes where the work is. It could be lonely at first, I could fail, but nothing could be as lonely as being a has-been in the UK. I had to pursue my dreams. "Dream, baby, dream," Alan Vega sang. He was in New York, and now I would be there too.

Leaving Perri was another matter altogether, but I decided I should test the waters alone, because it was all so uncertain, and I convinced myself that heroin would dull my pain. I loved her more than my life, but not more than the possibilities the future held, if pressed. "Let the *thing* be pressed." I felt that our love would not fade and that we would find a way to reunite after I had settled in New York and had taken a few steps toward establishing a new career in America. I might suffer some personal discomfort at first, but a new stomping ground could make that easier to absorb and allow me to find myself musically and lyrically without feeling pressured. And so I was off to the city that never sleeps to seek my destiny.

PART II
NEW YORK CITY

CHAPTER SEVENTEEN

A ROCK 'N' ROLL CONQUISTADOR INVADES AMERICA AND BURNS HIS BOATS UPON ARRIVAL

New York City

With my Gretsch Country Gentleman guitar in one hand, a suitcase in the other, the trunk with my pink Elvis '50s-style jacket and effects on my back, I made my return to the wildest city in the world.

There are eight million stories in the naked city, I remembered as I ventured into the customs area at JFK, which had been Idlewild Airport when I flew back to England as a six-year-old. Now, here I was nearly twenty years later, in the spring of '81, striking out into the unknown with no certainty of success, just like every other immigrant has done over the centuries. Most of the Irish side of my own family had arrived here just twenty years before, settling in and around the bowels of the city.

The New York sky was deep and dark, its tall skyscrapers reaching shockingly into the ozone, touching hitherto unknown heights, thanks to the hard bedrock at the island's core. I was an Englishman now, but my memories of New York as a child gave me a leg up over other transplanted Brits. Surely this city might welcome yet another stranger in a strange land, one more explorer doing his damndest to act unafraid in the face of his exceedingly uncertain future.

The storm clouds that hovered above the skyscrapers cleared on the day I arrived to reveal a blue sky that was out of sight except for the sliver directly above one's head. The heavens blazed my coming to America that first night with shooting stars and a strange halo effect that might well have been the man in the moon laughing at my audacity.

I first tried to become acclimated to this gigantic metropolis's sights and sounds, which were, to say the least, a trip. In comparison, London was a quaint village! That first night I arrived, Brendan Bourke, an A&R exec from Chrysalis, took me to a hotel. It had a small kettle and cup so I could make something to drink. Alone now, I went to the corner deli for some coffee and milk. Well, the corner deli was huge and didn't have one type of milk, like in England, but vitamin A, A and D, E, skim, and what seemed like twenty-five other types of milk! So I thought I'd try the coffee, but the aisle with the coffee held just as many choices. So I tried the bread aisle—Jesus wept!

The speed I inhaled that next brisk March morning stung in my nostrils. This was my own personal preparation for going out into the strangeness of New York City, with its hustle and bustle and pimps and whores of all kinds. The delis on every corner, the cars, trucks, and yellow cabs on the gridlocked streets, the junkies/drunks lying in their own excretions on the sidewalks, ignored by passersby. The police didn't even bother kids who looked like me, because they had real criminals to chase after.

The sky glowed orange with pollution, and the stench of sewage colored the senses, the sheer volume of people giving one the feeling of how easily a person could be swallowed up and forgotten. I liked the twenty-four-hour nonstop feeling the city had, and decided to be one with it. The pain in my nostrils retreated as I ventured out into the chilly air, the speed giving me an otherworldly look at the town I would embrace as home. New York, with its different complexions, accents, and customs, was a huge melting pot, and I was ready to melt with it, mind-melding to become less of a stranger with each passing moment.

On every corner, large boom boxes blared out rap music, the new soul. Kids were holding break-dance competitions with each other instead of fighting. It reminded me of how we created punk as a way out of our depression. Their spoken-word raps addressed everything from their own disenchantment with Reaganomics to sexual boasting to the dangers of drugs. My arrival in New York had coincided with the birth of this new art form. The whirling and swirling dance moves reflected the energy on the streets, as kids twisted their rubberized bodies, going from doing the robot to spinning on the cardboard-covered pavement.

Although I knew that rap music had its roots in the reggae toasters and dance-hall music of the early '70s, it was not until the early '80s, after the Sugarhill Gang's "Rapper's Delight" and Kurtis Blow's "The Breaks," that the movement exploded, just as I got to town. This new soul power invigorated me, but I wasn't ready to create my own music. Not yet, anyway. The move had taken up all my time and energy.

With the aid of Brendan Bourke, I found a small room to live in on Seventy-First Street by the Hudson River. The apartment was completely empty except for a small mattress that lay on the bare boards of the floor, a tiny black-and-white TV that Brendan lent me, and a radio permanently tuned to New York's only country station.

I had an early opportunity to begin to familiarize myself with American media thanks to that tiny TV. I was shocked when one day soon after my arrival, the news was filled with reports that President Reagan had been shot. While the TV commentators were discussing the shooting, the screen showed a picture of Reagan with a sniper sight on him.

Once I was moved in, I needed bedding for the mattress. After visiting what to me was an enormous store, I got a set of sheets folded up in some brown paper wrapping. The streets looked empty, and the sky darkened as I made my way back to the apartment. Suddenly it started to pour, and I was drowned like a rat in a matter of minutes. I took shelter in an empty restaurant. I walked away from the door and sat down at a distance. Suddenly a man and his daughter came in. I was bedraggled, hair down, completely soaked, but the man and daughter came right up to me and said, "You're Billy Idol, aren't you?" They were from England, on holiday, but in my soaked state I wouldn't have even recognized myself. This was the first autograph that I gave after coming to live in New York, and it gave me some confidence as I began to plot my next career move.

Confident or not, I knew New York City was a place that can chew you up and spit you out as easily as a bullfrog catches a fly with its long, unfurled tongue, digesting it quickly before shitting out the unwanted part. Would I end up so callously disposed of? It was definitely a possibility. Just because I had a couple of hits in England didn't mean the teeming masses of America would see anything in me. Given what happened on these shores to the Sex Pistols, the likelihood of this English punk being embraced stateside seemed pretty remote. I'd thought Johnny Rotten and company would blaze a trail, but they'd come back in tatters. Nobody else had really made a dent, though the Clash were still trying.

Despite being aware of this ominous history, I felt I had a strong team around me. Chrysalis Records had found some success with Blondie in the U.S. and seemed to know their business. My manager, Bill Aucoin, had achieved massive success with Kiss, so I was with people who had a track record.

Bill Aucoin was a true maverick, a wild man of rock 'n' roll. He was a force of nature, and he became my mentor. When he got excited about an artist, he loved the *selling* part of the job. He could step into a meeting and take a room full of people with no interest in me and turn them around. He'd tell label executives what they needed to do by giving them a new vision. Then he would tell them how to use their standing in the industry to contribute to or even change popular culture in a positive way. He had them eating out of his hand. Then he would explain how I played into this vision. It was all going to be a guaranteed success, and fun to boot! He would become more animated until they were infected by his wild enthusiasm. "You can't be afraid," he'd tell them. "You've got to step up. Billy is the real deal." By the time he was finished, they were true believers, lit up like Christmas trees and promising Bill anything. The man's sales pitch was an incredible performance in and of itself, and I would have to go some distance to beat his energy in the boardroom with my own actions onstage. The execs in the room ended up raving too. That was Bill Aucoin—from zero to a hundred miles per hour in the span of a pitch meeting.

At the time, Bill was a slender man in his midthirties, about my height. His upper lip was adorned with a mustache, and he usually wore an amused look, especially when he was enthused about a subject. He would tell me Jim Morrison wasn't afraid to be himself. He told me about seeing the Doors in New York in the '60s when Jim let a member of the audience give him a blow job on stage. This was a defining and liberating moment in Bill's life, encouraging him to accept the fact he was gay and realizing he had to be true to his own inner being. Bill loved this wild bravado in an artist, and he would often talk to me about the kind of energy and feelings an audience would respond to. "Billy, you've gotta be wild and crazy," he would tell me, and I've never forgotten those words. I was already committed to being true to myself, but now I was feeling liberated as well. I was pushing a boundary both physical and mental, where the emotions were channeled to reach a positive, uplifting experience for the audience and for me. I knew what he meant, and I saw the truth in his words.

The next day, I jumped on a bus that took me near the Fifty-Seventh Street offices of Chrysalis Records, not far from where I was headed, Bill Aucoin's office. The stares of the people on the bus were quite amusing. I don't think even blasé New Yorkers were used to seeing somebody dressed in English-style punk-rock clothes, let alone someone clad as I was, in skintight leather pants and a ripped T-shirt that revealed my chest and body, along with a New Romantic tasseled cape slung around my shoulders over a leather jacket, bondage boots, and spiked, bleached-white hair. As I walked along Fifty-Seventh Street, the black guys on the corners would go, "Silky, baby," or "Where's the party?" or "Punk rock don't stop," which happened to be a key line in Blondie's "Rapture" but would also later give me the idea for the title of the EP I would record early the next year. These new greetings and sayings, and all the different accents, seemed very fresh to me.

Walking into Aucoin's office, I tried to act as normal as I could. The fact is, I had arrived in New York suffering from serious heroin withdrawal. I had taken so much before I left, I had a bad skin reaction. Scabs covered my face, and I had an extreme case of constipation. Bill was a bit shocked at how I looked, which was something, because he was a hard guy to shock.

I did have a three-week supply of DF 118s, a heroin substitute (like methadone) that was used for getting over the initial cold-turkey reaction. The DFs kept me functioning, and some booze quelled most of the clammy sweats and general discomfort. I took speed to counteract how sick I felt and to keep up with New York's quick pace.

I looked around Aucoin's giant office, which had Kiss doll puppets hanging from the walls, and met Bill's secretary, who suggested an enema. Bill's second-in-command was a guy named Ric Aliberte, who suggested that I brush my hair down like Rick Springfield, pointing out how well he was doing with his clean-cut image and hit *Working Class Dog* album. "I am not turning into David Cassidy," I said. I was sticking with the look I had. I wasn't starting all over to deny my style, but to make it stick. Punk was my roots, and I would celebrate those roots for the rest of my so-called career, I told myself. It was weird but fun to be challenged on my beliefs. Maybe I was being naïve, but I was confident that I knew what was right for me, and I wasn't going to let anybody else make decisions like that when it came to my career.

This attitude was further cemented in my mind when later that week I saw Bo Diddley playing at Tracks, a small club on the Upper East Side. Despite feeling like crap, I spent the evening enjoying one of the greats of early rock 'n' roll. Jesus, he was still playing that red, box-shaped guitar from the '50s with its built-in sound effects, which doubly empowered me to not change my own image. America would have to accept my style instead of that poodle-head look all the U.S. mainstream bands of the early '80s had back then.

Bill Aucoin kept telling me I should try out a guitarist named Steve Stevens, who was leaving a band, the Fine Malibus. I met Steve in Aucoin's office, and we had a heartfelt discussion about rock 'n' roll stardom, the meaning of punk, and what I wanted to do with my music. My idea was to incorporate the energy and spirit of punk into many different musical settings. Steve responded well, and said he'd help me put together a band. For the moment, we decided to take it one step at a time and see where it all would lead.

I now had a lead on an exciting new collaborator, but I was still feeling relatively unsure about which musical direction to focus on next. This would change after one particular night that summer. On the evening in question, I was missing Perri terribly. I decided to head out to the club Hurrah on West Sixty-Second Street to take my mind off her and drown my sorrows. I entered the club and stood by the crowded bar. The place was jammed with people listening to a DJ, several deep at the bar. It was hard to get a space. I was finally able to order a screwdriver and, once served, hung back with my drink to check out the not-so-bad-looking birds hanging around. The energy in the place was palpable, but nothing special.

Suddenly, the DJ played "Dancing with Myself"! I watched in amazement as the previously crowded bar area emptied and people literally threw themselves over tables, chairs, and couches to get to the dance floor. As the song continued, I was practically the only one left at the now-empty bar.

Jesus! That's it! I realized. I'd had the answer all the time. That dance beat we put into "Dancing" was right, and this place was going nuts for it. I left the club excited and confident. If I could just find something else with "beat-y" drums for Keith Forsey to produce . . .

CHAPTER EIGHTEEN

MAKING MONY MONY: A LEFT-COAST FUSION OF PUNK AND DISCO

From Bromley to New York City to Los Angeles

IN 1970, THE BACK OF THE *charity shop near Bromley South held many wonders.*

"Do you want to fuck?" I asked. And she said yes! I'd never had sex, so I was a bit nervous as she took me by the hand.

She must have sensed the situation. "You're a virgin aren't you?" she half asked, half declared. "No, I've done it before," I lied as we walked up the hill for a tumble in Church House Gardens. We went behind some bushes and she lay down. I got on top and got hard but was having a bit of trouble getting it in her, it being my first time. She rolled me over and said, "Oh, let me do it," and she stuck my dick inside her and really shagged me.

As we went at it, "Mony Mony" by Tommy James and the Shondells was playing on someone's transistor radio nearby. . . .

THAT SONG HAS ALWAYS HAD SPECIAL significance to me. I love its repetitive, we would say now machinated, groove. It really grabs me. From the first time I heard it, I liked Tommy James's voice, and always thought maybe I could get away with it too.

Eleven years after that tumble in Bromley, as I walked along the New York streets on the way to meet one of the Chrysalis Records promotion guys at his office, the traffic and movement of people became background noise for my own thoughts. When I arrived, I asked him about recording a cover song. I started out by asking a dummy question, wondering about "Shout," though what I really had in mind was doing a version of "Mony Mony" that would keep them dancing on the floors of the late-night New York clubs I had been frequenting. I wanted to be sure that he was not giving me lip service regarding "Shout," so I knew my strategy had worked when he was lukewarm to the idea but then got excited when I mentioned "Mony Mony" as another possibility.

I called Keith and told him about my idea to record "Mony Mony," which he seemed to like. He told me that if I came out to L.A., he could round up some musicians. He registered just the right level of enthusiasm I needed to hear. I told Aucoin and the record label, and they agreed that putting out a four-track EP, to be called *Don't Stop*, might be the way to stimulate the market. For me, it was a way to get out of the freezing East Coast winter.

After a couple of months I moved to a Jones Street apartment, which I shared with a girl I dubbed Fish, a junkie college student I met at a late-night club who had an upper room to let. She had a huge, nasty-looking scar on her arm where she had been injecting herself. One Sunday, she took me down to the Lower East Side around Avenue A or B, and we scored some dope called Toilet. I had heard that they didn't "beat" couples, so by going together, we were pretty much left alone. Another time we went to score with a black guy, who took a .38 snub nose out of a drawer and placed it in the back of his waistband before we left. That's the way it was. You went up to a hole in a door or wall and traded some money for some little white bags. We'd return to the apartment, divvy up the dope, and shoot up. Just shows how soon one can acclimate to the junkie life if you feel sick enough. I joined Fish "in the womb," where we slumbered like junkie babes in the woods, deep inner dreams playing in our subconsciouses as the din of New York traffic receded in our ears. Keith came to visit me at the apartment, and I played the beginning of what would be "Hot in the City" for him on my Gretsch Country Gentleman. "It's hot here at night, lonely black and quiet on a hot summer night." We had just been in the middle of a blazing summer and only the night brought any relief from the broiling sun and constant hum and drip of the air conditioners. Since we didn't own one, I had a fan next to my mattress on the floor, but it didn't help. I hate humidity.

I got the idea for "Hot in the City" from seeing Nick Gilder's gold record of "Hot Child in the City" in Chrysalis's UK offices and thinking, *Why do you need the child?* In fact, I hadn't even heard the song, but I continued by writing about my new life in New York, walking the streets and taking the subway, staying up all night feeling young and free, stomping out a kind of history of my time there and trying to soak up the excitement of the club scene, the Mudd Club, Max's, the Continental. The song was very simple, a midtempo ballad that wasn't like anything we did in Gen X. I was searching for what would really be Billy Idol music. I lowered my voice to sing. It was the beginning of finding another way of singing for me, a deeper side. Armed with "Mony Mony" and "Hot in the City," as well as a plan to rerecord "Untouchables," I flew out to L.A. to begin work on the debut Billy Idol solo EP.

THE SUN SHONE BRIGHTLY THROUGH THE palm trees at the side of the road as I made my way to Giorgio Moroder's house in Beverly Hills, where Keith was living. Keith had started out as a drummer in a '60s band, the Spectrum, best known for the end title theme for UK TV producer Gerry Anderson's puppet show *Captain Scarlet*. By the early '70s, he found his way to Germany, playing as a percussionist with Krautrock artists like Amon Düül, the acid-rock/jazz band that doubled as a cult with its own commune. He learned to speak German and became a much-in-demand session player.

Fresh from my tiny Village shithole, it was wild to arrive in the swanky part of L.A. Giorgio's house was all glass and marble, very '70s, and he had one of those big projector TVs, a far cry from the tiny black-and-white set Brendan Bourke had lent me in New York. I accompanied Keith to a session he was producing at Cherokee Studios in Hollywood. There was a ton of musicians set up in the studio, a mostly black band with horns, drums, and bass guitars at the ready. Keith went into a tiny booth separated from the rest and began playing a shaker for a couple of takes, hitting the groove immediately. "They weren't recording me," he explained later. "I was just playing for the musicians to keep time." That says it all about what a rhythm machine he is.

The plan was to work on the arrangements of the songs in a small rehearsal studio before recording them. We went through the arrangements of all the songs, but spent the most time on "Mony Mony." I came up with another song called "Baby Talk" in case we needed something else.

The next day, we went into Westlake Studios on Beverly Boulevard. The original Tommy James version of "Mony Mony" sounded like a tape loop, and we wanted that kind of rhythm from our drummer, but with a real guy playing it. In the end, we got it, and I was so happy, for in the process I had come to realize how important it is to be working with great musicians and talented people. Mick Smiley played bass, Quiet Riot's Frankie Banali played drums, and on guitar was Asley Otten.

Keith and I had agreed that "Mony Mony" should have an R&B feel, so we decided to add some black female background singers. We created a riff for the middle section, where we could put in a vocal arrangement later on. We also recorded versions of "Baby Talk" and "Untouchables." Not bad for a single day's work!

We then recorded "Hot in the City" at Giorgio's home demo studio, with Keith starting by laying the drums down himself, slowly building them from the ground up. The whole EP had a sound that was quite unlike Generation X. It was a new direction for me, combining the disco beats of the New York club scene with punk-rock guitars and choruses. It was an exhilarating breakthrough, a novel fusion, and took me far from my punk roots to a stylistic breakthrough.

I was taking chances and doing something very different with this music by including sexy soul vocal licks by Stephanie Spruill and her two singing partners. Even the synth pulse that drove "Hot in the City" was something I hadn't done before, but it did, in part, represent a musical direction that I had decided to pursue by embracing modern techniques while retaining an old-school vibe. Was it R&B? Disco? Techno? Rock? No, it was all of these ingredients combined into a single sound. It was something I enjoyed doing, and it was a new sound and feel that went together very well with the lyrics and music I was now writing.

Keith mixed the songs with the help of engineer Brian Reeves at Westlake Studio A. We stayed up all night until eight the next morning finishing "Mony Mony." Keith and Brian would check the mixes by playing them back in their cars as loudly as possible to find the correct balance. Keith had promised we'd have a blast creating the EP, and he did not disappoint. He had come to London for the final Gen X album, and now I had reciprocated by traveling to L.A. I had fresh ammo for the dance floor—now to take it back to New York and see what happened.

WHEN I RETURNED TO NEW YORK, I took my finished version of "Mony Mony" to the Ritz on a Tuesday for dance night to debut it. Hardly anyone was there. People were lining the wall, but very few were dancing. I talked to the DJ, a fan of "Dancing with Myself," and convinced him to give "Mony Mony" a spin.

He placed the needle to the vinyl and suddenly, the jaded dancers who had been hugging the wall came to life. Instantly, the dance floor was filled with bodies doing '60s moves like the Swim, the Donkey Trot, and the Mashed Potato. Everybody was into it! I had my follow-up to "Dancing with Myself," and any questions I'd had about my decision to move to America began to fade.

When it came to releasing the EP, Chrysalis Records' A&R exec Jeff "Buzz" Aldrich thought "Hot in the City" was too good just to release as part of the EP. He felt it could be a single and should be saved for the album we would make next. So instead we put the Gen X version of "Dancing with Myself" on the EP, as it had not yet been officially released in the States. My first solo effort was a cool little record. I was truly on my own, crossing over from one gig to another somehow, without too much of a bump. It didn't take long, and there it was in the

New York record bins. The divider label read like a command: BILLY IDOL: DON'T STOP.

I was asked to do some promotion, and I agreed to go to L.A. to perform on *Solid Gold*, the U.S. chart TV show hosted by Marilyn McCoo and Andy Gibb. I had been missing Perri a great deal, so I arranged for her to fly from London to join me for the trip to Los Angeles. Along with Bill Aucoin, we flew out for the show, on which I was to lip-synch the words to the recorded track. After doing so much TV in the UK, I was up for it.

When we arrived for the rehearsal, a choreographer had worked out all these '60s steps for me to perform with the Solid Gold Dancers, but I told him, "I sing, *they* dance," so he got them to perform their routine around me. My long, hard stare into the future at the end of my performance let everyone know, "I'm a punk rock 'n' roller."

When we returned to New York, my goal was to find my own band so we could work up new songs to record and play live. My mind went back to my meeting with Steve Stevens. The two of us had hit it off right away, and he had agreed to help me put a band together to see if we were compatible. We met, talked some more, and decided to go ahead and form a group. Steve knew a young, good-looking bass player named Phil Feit, who knew of a drummer, Steve Missal, and it was in Steve's room in the Eighth Avenue Music Building—a huge rehearsal facility located near Times Square—that we began to play together.

This graffiti-covered building was not soundproofed, and the cacophony of noises emanating from bands of all genres practicing their music reflected the past and present. Our small rehearsal space inspired the title of the song "Hole in the Wall," but the song was also loosely about the experience of scoring drugs. Then I came up with "Dead on Arrival," inspired by my belief that by the time punk, in the form of the Sex Pistols, came to America, it was stillborn. It later became the name of Lech Kowalski's punk film about the Sex Pistols' apocalyptic tour of the States, though the song wasn't included in the movie itself.

Patti Smith Group guitarist Lenny Kaye also had a room in the building, and I had a few good chats with him about the burgeoning NYC music scene exploding all around us. One night, after a rehearsal, we gave a young, punky disco girl named Madonna a lift somewhere. She seemed awfully confident for an as-yet unknown. I was beginning to feel comfortable in New York, and enjoyed being part of this community of musicians. I felt very much alive—not dead at all—but alive with a love for life, for music, for taking risks, for Perri. Alive with a love for New York.

Although we had only learned a few numbers, when I heard that Max's Kansas City was closing down, I went to see Steve Missal, who was in a band playing there that final night. Thinking it would be an honor to play there before it shuttered, I asked him if we could go on before they played. He agreed, and lo and behold, my first solo gig in the United States was playing the last night at the club where the Velvet Underground, Iggy and the Stooges, the New York Dolls, Suicide, and so many of my favorite bands had once performed.

Steve Stevens, Steve Missal, Phil Feit, and I played "Dancing with Myself," "Mony Mony," and the few other numbers we knew, which at the time amounted to our entire repertoire, but it was a kick to just get up there and play. It really helped make us feel like a functioning band, rocking in front of people in a legendary club that was about to close its doors. It was just our first gig, but Steve Stevens, even without the usual array of effects guitarists rely on for live performances, was outstanding. He can be blinding when he plays like that, raw, 100-watt straight through, slowly writhing in the night like a sleeping serpent curling its body against mine, slowly sighing.

CHAPTER NINETEEN

IF YOU CAN MAKE IT HERE

Fifth Avenue, Manhattan

"New York, New York" was playing through the Olympic Tower elevator speakers as I ascended to Bill Aucoin's high-rise apartment. It looked out over Fifth Avenue and was particularly spectacular at night, the passing car headlights illuminating the street below, turning it into a golden highway. New York lived and breathed like a pulsating animal, and it seemed, from this height, that it was possible to accomplish any dream or thought, no matter how high one's aim. Dreams could become reality: the very height of this skyscraper attested to that.

Bill and I would meet often at his apartment in the sky to plan our next move. One night, he took me down several flights to where the newscaster David Susskind was having a party. As Bill talked, the city's glittering magic began to take hold. "You can't be scared of anything," he would tell me. He would begin every telling phrase with "Lookit" and "I gotta tell ya." Bill seemed to be an expert on everything. He had been successful in both television and music, and this young, blond punk kid from London hung on his every word. He had a concept of freedom that went beyond the norm, and enjoyed an openly gay lifestyle at a time when it wasn't fully accepted. You must fight for your freedom but somehow have fun doing it; that was Bill's credo. "Celebrate your personality!" I took his advice.

Although he usually wore fine suits, Bill was probably the least "suit" person in the world. With an excited expression on his face denoting knowledge both moral and immoral accompanying his rapid-fire pronouncements and enlightened attitude, Aucoin bestrode the world like a colossus disguised as a businessman, flouting all laws and conventions. This is the man who literally made it snow one hot Christmas Eve in L.A. at a party he threw at the height of Kiss's hedonism years. Bill was a dreamer who brought other people's dreams to life. Had I become part of that dream? At the time I arrived in New York, Bill, who was then still managing Kiss, was looking for other art/music provocateurs to work with, Steve Stevens being one of those he found. He knew everyone on both coasts, and at the moment, those were the resources we were pulling on. From the windows of his high-rise, the horizon stretched to no end.

I met the guys from Kiss on one of my first visits to Aucoin's office. Paul Stanley and Gene Simmons were there doing last-minute work for the cover of the album *Music from "The Elder."* After the meeting, Gene very nicely invited me to lunch at a posh uptown restaurant, but instead of talking about the music scene, he talked about tax havens and how to organize money, which I found amusing, as I had only change in my pocket and nothing in my bank account.

I was taking in New York and enjoying the experience. I met quite a few fellow English people in the city during my first few months there. There was a mate of mine named Mark May, who sometimes crashed in my room or in the adjoining makeshift greenhouse. I'd wake up really hungover and hear him pounding on the door to be let in, as the sun had come up and poured through the glass windows, waking him up with a thirst that drove him to desperation.

There were so many clubs to go to, and it was great to have a pal to go with. Mark was really tall and had black, spiked hair, a little like Sid Vicious's, so the two of us together were quite a sight. The constant nightclubbing until dawn was the only way to stay out of the close confines of my tiny room. Places like Club Berlin were reverberating to the sounds of Soft Cell's "Tainted Love" or Depeche Mode's "I Just Can't Get Enough." The English dance-rock invasion was in full swing.

I had lucked into another scene that included the music I was already into. Clubs like the multifloor midtown Danceteria, the Lower East Side Brown's, or the Nursery were open all night, pumping out post-punk dance-rock to a crazy scene of gyrating dancers, while the less motivated were junked and passed out on the floor and the stairs. Amazingly enough, Mark and I got ourselves thrown out of the Nursery one morning, which was practically impossible.

In those days you could meet every class of person out at night in the New York clubs. The venues weren't segregated by the music they played, as they would be later in the '80s. The break-dance scene joined the uptown rappers with the downtown art denizens. I remember seeing Grandmaster Flash at the Ritz on Eleventh Street and hearing Afrika Bambaataa spin at the Roxy, a former roller rink on the West Side. You could see how the rap kids picked up style from the punk kids on Eighth Street in the Village, wearing cutoff fingerless gloves or leather wristbands.

Music, sex, drugs, nightlife, sleep, do it again was our mantra. Living as if there was no tomorrow was key, seeing as the Sex Pistols and others had told us that there was no future, and we were convinced we were living in some *Mad Max* postapocalyptic world. At this time, New York was pretty run-down; it seemed like a future world gone wrong. The city was struggling back from an economic depression, but the low rents and overlooked laws fertilized a breeding ground for clubs, boutiques, and art galleries.

Mark, who was over six feet tall, favored small girls with gigantic tits, so it was brilliant to see him contort hs long, lanky frame as he leaned forward drunkenly while ogling some NY punk chick with really big hooters late at night at the Peppermint Lounge. Bands like Johnny Thunders and the Heartbreakers played while we stood on the balcony above the general mob. We called ourselves the Chosen Scum because we could get into the Ritz balcony or past the velvet ropes of any club in town. At one party, they were handing out Special K, a hallucinogen that turned your world somewhat inside out for a time, letting you reside in an alternative universe before bringing you back. I'd usually sleep until two in the afternoon, wake up, rehearse, head out to eat, and then do drugs, which people gave out freely. Most of the time, I could get away with having zero money but still get fucked up on the free booze, free coke, and free pot, with all the broads I could take home. I still loved and missed Perri, but sometimes when opportunity stares you in the face, you take solace in somebody else's sheets. Sometimes it was a matter of going home to a different apartment or just hanging out to share drugs. Drugs have a way of making it easy to give in to temptation and, later on, to explain away transgressions without allowing reality to sink in.

One of the first gigs I went to at the Ritz was a Prince show. At that time, he was wearing a raincoat with thigh-high socks and a jock strap that squirted water during his guitar solos. There weren't many people in the audience—he was yet to be the superstar he would become—so I stood not far from the stage to watch him. I liked where Prince was trying to go. He was having fun with the music and at the same time being sexual and outrageous. His music's groove-driven sound, with its machinelike quality, was exactly what I had in mind. And even though I had my own unique take on it, I was starting to realize it wasn't just me who was traveling down this road. The mashing-up of rock, soul, rap, and pop marked a major change in music that would rule the '80s.

In 1981, New York City was a melting pot for all the different genres that were converging at that moment in time. From downtown punk and jazz to midtown disco to uptown rap and salsa—it was anything goes, as long as it had attitude. America was entering a new decade with a new president. The country was hungry for new fashions and fresh ideas. Just like in the UK in 1976, it was the outsiders, those on the fringe of society, who would come into their own as they led the way from the extreme to the mainstream. America had been safe inside its AM/FM radio walls of the '70s, but that system was not going to do it for the new generation hitting the nightspots. The bridge-and-tunnel people of the New York tristate area wanted a scene of their own. The gradual unification of musical styles from New York and around the world was beginning to propel that change.

CHAPTER TWENTY

HOT IN THE CITY: THE MAKING OF SOLO BILLY IDOL

One Sheridan Square, New York City

MTV LAUNCHED IN AUGUST 1981, THE same month I began re-cording my first solo album. I already had "Hot in the City" in the can as a first single, but we had to see what else we could come up with. I was scrambling for ideas, but I wanted to give Steve Stevens and my-self a chance to grow and possibly write together, as Tony and I had in Generation X, to capture that camaraderie, the back-and-forth of ideas, with the final goal of the song realized, recorded, and released. Life needs that kind of energy and connection. Fuck, *I* need it.

Steve had a song title, "Shooting Stars," that I liked. I felt that my experience with using drugs could be incorporated into the lyrics. I was also thinking about my roommate and landlady, Fish. "I think it's kinda sick, she thinks she's really hip . . . Well you wanna play the fool, you wanna be so cruel." I'm probably singing about myself and making it sound like it's about a girl. But really, it's about both sex and drugs. I was in thrall to drugs, but as yet they hadn't taken over completely. The real me still poked his head through, and so we had another song for this album.

Gary Cooper once remarked on the wild American West, "Well, we brought law and order to the territory; built railroads, homes, towns, and I guess you might call it civilization . . . but by damn,

wouldn't it be fun to tear it down and start all over again?" I suppose
that's what I was doing by going solo. I was trashing the old, tearing
it down to make way for the new and the necessary. Reworking my
music was stimulating, but it didn't come easy, especially as I was so
used to having Tony there. Still, I had to carry on into this new world
of discovery. This new Billy Idol band was a good bunch of guys. It was
time to play the songs we'd written, write more songs, and get them
down on record.

New York teemed with life lived at close quarters, in the raw, close
to the edge. Just off the end of Jones Street was 1 Sheridan Square,
where my mate Ace Penna lived, his first-floor window permanently
open in the summer so that you could shout up to him from the
street. Ace, a friend of Brendan Bourke's, had worked with some of
the up-and-coming New York bands, and I would sometimes hang
at his place before going out on the town. We used to watch *Saturday
Night Live* reruns every night, which was a great education about the
Blues Brothers, John Belushi and Dan Aykroyd, because we never saw
these early *SNL* shows in England. With that irreverence fresh in our
memory banks, Ace and I would hit the street. He turned me on to this
"new Irish band, U2" and played me their album, *Boy*. The group was
already making its mark in the States.

I really needed my own place, and when a room came free in Ace's
building, on the opposite side of his floor, I rented it. The extent of my
belongings at the time included a mattress, my guitar, a stereo, and the
small portable black-and-white TV on loan from Brendan Bourke.
The apartment was bare of furniture. I found a discarded couch on the
street one day and brought it back for something to sit on. My mate
Mark May had returned to England, but he planned on coming back
soon. Perri was also still back in England at this point, and I missed her
desperately. With the exception of my band, I was on my lonesome in
the middle of the wildest 24/7 city in the world.

We had a few new songs, plus some Generation X material, so we
played some "jump-up" gigs, where you get up semi-unexpectedly
and play mainly for the fun or hell of it, to create a buzz. These dance
and after-hours clubs didn't have many live bands, but they had big

audiences that were familiar with my music and me. They were great places to launch an indirect attack, kind of a "hit 'em when they ain't looking" strategy. Also, these gigs were another character-building and bonding activity for my bandmates and me.

One night, we played a 1:00 a.m. gig at AM/PM, an after-hours club, and the Sex Pistols' Steve Jones, who was also living in New York at the time, joined us on guitar for "Dancing with Myself." I don't think Jones thought too much of Steve Stevens at the time, but I thought he was great. I knew even then I would need every one of the many textures Steve Stevens's guitar playing would bring.

Another time, we did a show on Danceteria's tiny first-floor stage. The PA wasn't much, but it was the spirit that mattered. An added benefit that had not gone unnoticed was that all my bandmates could get into the club for free once we had played there. I don't know if we were any good, but it was all in the punk get-up-and-do-it-yourself spirit—just the way I had done everything else thus far in my rock 'n' roll life. I enjoyed bringing that sense of adventure to my solo endeavor. These ad hoc shows trained us to be ready for anything, including playing with unfamiliar gear or in unexpected circumstances. In such events, the energy is fraught with tension, but once it's released, the band plays with an abandon that is truer in nature to the rock 'n' roll spirit. The audience responds to that kind of spontaneity more so than to something that's been planned and worked to death. The band put that jump-up spirit and energy into every live performance we did.

Perri and I had managed to keep up a long-distance affair through letters and stolen phone cards. I met tons of girls in the clubs, but Perri is one of a kind. I loved her wild look, but I also dug the nutty person she was, with all the eccentricities that come with artistic people. Back in London, Perri had formed a spin-off dance troupe, Spinooch, after leaving Hot Gossip over a managerial rip-off, but that didn't work out, so she came back to New York to stay. We had a blast being together in this new world of love, kicks, and possibilities. We both had hopes that we could find our way to success in the States. So, for the moment, we had New York City to entertain us, and we had each other.

At Keith Forsey's suggestion, we made plans to record the album in L.A. in February '82. It would be a fun break from the icy chill of a New York winter that seemed to stretch into infinity. But I was conflicted about going. I was both excited and a little sad, as I knew I'd be missing Perri again once I got to L.A. But on a shoestring budget, and with a number of songs yet to be written, this disparate group of New York musicians and an Englishman needed to continue bonding—socially and musically—if my experiment was going to work. Perri and I would savor our time together before I had to leave. We sat before a glowing log in our small apartment, having the occasional bag of street H. Other times, our friend Bobby Belenchia from Yonkers, who worked at Famous Ray's Pizza nearby, brought a log with him. The label money barely covered the rent, so thank god Bobby also came with a pizza. That winter, we lived on air, weak heroin, and New York pizza slices.

Perri brought the best out in me. When it came to overindulgence in bad habits, however, she also brought out the worst. At the time, what I was doing seemed to be merely par for the rock 'n' roll course. Alcohol and drug addiction seemed requisite: that was how we were turning the world around. Up was down, and night was day. Looking back today, I can see I should have known there would be ramifications for being so ambivalent. But the drug's effects were so strong, they hypnotized me into thinking nothing would ever go wrong. I was dancing with the devil, all right; in fact, we were arm in arm, swinging each other around. I felt like I was in another dimension, my own private world, at once engaged with reality but somehow removed at the same time. A calm descended that nothing but the need for more could replace.

I was a functioning drug addict, if there is such a thing. I'd rarely shoot dope, just snort the weak NY street shit two or three times a week. I didn't have the money to do it every day, plus I had too much to do. I didn't want to be dope-sick all the time. Three days in a row and you could get quite dope-sick—nothing you couldn't shake off if you had to, but you still felt vile. I never wanted to get hooked on the needle. I didn't want to get too fucking serious about anything other than Perri and music, at least for the moment.

I was celebrating my first nine months in the States, and I had a
lot to show for it, with an EP, a great new guitarist, a new band, and a
fistful of new songs to record under my belt, songs that had appeared
seemingly out of nowhere in the chaos of the city that never sleeps.
At first it was hard to distinguish the good ideas from the bad ones.
Then, sometimes unexpectedly, one of the tunes, perhaps a melody
with half-formed words, would suddenly form a sentence that gave
me goose pimples or a warm flow of energy that told me I might have
found something special that could be developed into a song. I believed
that only by living life to the fullest could one ingest sufficient unique
experiences to gain something that could be regurgitated in the form of
a song.

We also had some great records to listen to in that West Village
apartment. We listened over and over to Alan Vega's solo album *Colli-
sion Drive*. He was doing club dates around the city with a pickup band
that looked like they probably played in a Holiday Inn, with black
flares and feathered haircuts. Still, they played Alan's forward-driven
machine beat just great, so looks can be deceiving. I had been hanging out with Vega, whether he was playing with Phil Hawk on guitar
or with Martin Rev in Suicide. I traveled up to Boston with him and
Marty for a gig at the Rat, and another time I took my first U.S. train
journey to Philadelphia to see Alan play a solo club gig.

He would stare straight at Perri and me while he sang the ballad
"Je T'Adore." There was our compadre, singing to us from the stage.
It was really romantic. "Je t'adore, Perri. I love you, I love you, baby."
I liked that Alan had a rep for both the performance side of his art and
also the soft "I love you" romantic side, like Suicide's "Cheree," or my
favorite, "Dream Baby Dream." "You gotta hold on tight . . . to life,"
he'd croon, twitching and smiling to himself. "That's all you got, baby."
A punk with a heart? What's wrong with that?

Alan was a wild man, punching himself with the microphone and
rolling around onstage, all the while punctuating the performance with
his soul-man grunts and howls. Suicide drove most people away, but
I loved them for the visionaries they were. Phil Hawk and I would be
the only ones smiling at those gigs amid the looks of horror and disgust
all around us. But I loved Suicide and Alan's solo gigs, and I started

to work with Phil to see if there was something we could do together. We decided to collaborate on a song, "It's So Cruel," for my first solo album.

Alan Vega was leading the way to the future. His band was playing this tight-groove, machine-rock blues that was old and new at the same time; he had a million influences, and wasn't afraid to show them. One minute he'd be a raging Otis Redding, and the next, a lizard-like lounge singer.

Perri and I also saw the great reggae artist Burning Spear at Bond International Casino in Times Square. He played for three hours to a half-empty room whose denizens included Perri, me, and the Go-Go's. We were stunned at how beautiful songs like "Marcus Garvey" were. We also got to see one of the Clash's '81 gigs at Bond's and Public Image's infamous Flowers of Romance show at the Ritz, where Johnny Lydon and company played behind a curtain, causing a riot in the enraged audience, who pelted the sheet with beer cans before the performance was cut short.

Perri and I were hooked on performance art, working on ours and watching others do theirs, then enthusing about it. Often, our discussions would get lost among the sensationalism and drugs.

Just before I was due to leave for L.A. to record with Keith Forsey, while in Bill Aucoin's office I noticed that Kiss had recorded a song with Lou Reed, one of my all-time heroes. He probably did it because Bob Ezrin, who also worked with Kiss, produced his album *Berlin*. Thinking he might write with me, the office set up a meeting with him at his favorite NY pizza place, John's on Bleecker Street near Seventh Avenue. I had seen him play four times: once at an outdoor festival in Dulwich in '72, then on the Rock 'n' roll Animal tour in '74, opening for the Who at Charlton football ground in '74, and in an intimate NYC setting in '78 for the Take No Prisoners tour.

Lou sat in the shadows. We made some small talk about New York and what I'd done since moving there. When I proposed we write together, he responded that I would have to pay him an inordinate sum for every half hour we collaborated. I knew Lou had been in the game a long time, and I could see his veteran scars showing, but this shocked me, with my punk egalitarian ways. The thought of paying to write with someone was almost funny. I wasn't after working with Lou for his name value. He was our King of Rock 'n' roll, the Rock 'n' roll Animal, the man fronting the Velvet Underground at Max's. I saw Berlin through his eyes—he was Metal Machine Music! Still, it was cool to meet him and he was great, but I got the punk message reaffirmed right there. Fuck heroes. Just write your own goddamn songs.

CHAPTER TWENTY-ONE

HOLLYWOOD DAZE AND TEQUILA NIGHTS

Sunset Strip, Los Angeles

THE NIGHT WAS DARK AT MIDNIGHT in Los Angeles, and the wail of a police siren followed me as the speeding car I was in careened down a side street and blasted into an intersection, barely missing another vehicle. With a screeching of brakes, the automobile in which I was riding slid just past the other car, missing it by inches. I clung tightly to the dashboard for dear life, certain I might die at any moment. Inexplicably, the driver made a mad dash on a parallel road, but then a police car began desperately trying to follow us in a wild chase. Its red beacon and flashing blue light reflected its rapid pace and echoed the crazed look of the nervous officers whose wide-eyed stares were practically pressed to the windshield in pursuit.

I was being driven by a washing machine salesman high on a couple of Percodans he'd taken after having four wisdom teeth removed earlier that day. The glazed look on his face told me the pills had kicked in and were influencing this mad behavior. "Why don't you just pull into a driveway and hope they pass us?" I asked in desperation. Amazingly, he did so, but managed to smash into a gatepost before backing up and careening down an alley just big enough for us to drive through. The police were right behind us, looking more agitated than ever, if that were possible. The grim scowls on their faces seemed to ask, *Why are they running?*

We pulled around a tight corner by some garages at the back of the alley, and the mad dash came to a grinding halt with a screech of the brakes just short of someone's backyard fence.

The bright headlights of the cop car with its harsh white beams shone into our car, the stillness punctuated by a voice crackling from a bullhorn: "Keep your hands on the dash where we can see them. We want to see those hands!" Slowly, out of the dark shadows of the back lot emerged the figures of two men, guns drawn. One moved to the passenger side, motioning with his snub-nosed .38 for me to get out of the car, keeping my hands in view. Another grabbed my black friend, G.A., who was sitting in the back of the car, dragging him roughly along the concrete on his knees, placing him in front of the piercing white beams, making him put his hands on his head. After I got out of the car, they put me alongside G.A. I noticed their treatment of the two white guys in the car was a lot different from the way they were treating G.A. *Land of the free?* I thought to myself.

When they demanded to know where the drugs were, I laughed. "If we had any money, we might have some." I explained the story of the washing machine salesman's dental problems. They didn't believe me—my calm answer seemed to leave them nonplussed. By now, a police helicopter was buzzing above us, illuminating us in the harshest spotlight I'd experienced in my still-fledgling career. More squad cars arrived on the scene, including the California Highway Patrol, the famed CHiPs I knew only from TV.

"Where are the drugs?" they demanded. I answered with the same tale. By now, they had learned that the driver was the car's rightful owner and that none of us had a record. They began to believe that my story was, in fact, the truth. The Percodan had caused our driver to flip out, and as none of us was holding anything incriminating, they finally let us go, giving the driver a small fine for crashing into the gatepost of the house and demanding that G.A. take the wheel. My first day in L.A. to record my first solo album had ended up in a police chase.

The next day, I headed to Westlake Studios for a writing session. We still didn't have the full complement of songs for the album. Keith Forsey set me up in the control room with my Epiphone semi-acoustic and a drum machine. "See what you can find," he said, and left the room to give me space to allow "Jah to come down" to invade my senses and infuse the session with some heavenly splendor.

Luckily for me, I didn't have to wait too long. Jah must've known I needed something special on this day. I stared at the blank piece of scrap paper in front of me. Taking the pen sitting alongside it in hand, I wrote *white wedding* at the top. What made me think of that? Well, my sister had recently gone to the altar pregnant. And while that fact was perfectly all right with everyone, seeing as how she loved the guy, I started thinking about how, in the more recent past, this would have been called a "shotgun wedding." I started to imagine an alternative reality, one in which I was pissed off at this violation of my sister and I arrive at the wedding hell-bent on revenge.

I started playing to the drum machine set to a standard 4/4 beat, and then chugging in B, my favorite key, the key of "Ready Steady Go," "Your Generation," etc., I started to sing this eerie first line:

HEY LITTLE SISTER WHAT HAVE YOU DONE / HEY LITTLE SISTER WHO'S THE ONLY ONE?

Is this guy in love with his sister in an incestuous way, hating the thought of anyone else having her? The lyrics imply it, but without spelling it out—they create an uneasy feel.

HEY LITTLE SISTER WHO'S YOUR SUPERMAN / HEY LITTLE SISTER SHOTGUN

Then I added a simple chord change, from D to E to B. "It's a nice day for a white wedding." E to D to B . . . "It's a nice day to start again."

This was probably me echoing my own experience of beginning again after the Gen X breakup. I circled around this verse/chorus idea for a few minutes before settling on a chugging B again.

THERE IS NOTHING FAIR IN THIS WORLD GIRL / THERE IS NOTHING
SURE IN THIS WORLD / AND THERE IS NOTHING PURE IN THIS WORLD /
I LOOK FOR SOMETHING LEFT IN THIS WORLD / START AGAIN!

That gave me a middle for the song. I continued to work around these ideas. I began to play a B-minor over the chugging B-D-E/B-E-D chord changes and simply picked up and down the strings, giving the music what sounded like a "spaghetti western" feel with which we could start the song.

Twenty minutes after I had started, I came out of the control room to find Keith sitting right outside the door, reading a magazine. "Teach," I said, "I've done my homework." At first he couldn't believe I had come up with something that quickly. Still, after he examined my work tape and heard a bit of explaining from me, we immediately started to construct a more coherent demo that we could play for the whole band. I played the bass and guitar, and we made a twenty-minute demo that incorporated all the pieces of the song. If overlong and repetitious, it still gave us a picture of the song and something we could edit with the whole band there.

I was pretty knocked out by my efforts and glad that I'd come up with something of the caliber of "Dancing with Myself." This time, I had written it on my own, without a collaborator. *So this is how this solo stuff works*, I thought to myself.

ONE NIGHT I'M KNEELING IN A back alley with two different California police forces training their guns on me, the next I'm in my second-floor room at the Sunset Marquis in a pissed-off mood, wondering whether I should dropkick the room phone over the balcony into the pool below like a rugby star attempting a field goal. While I was imagining the announcer intoning solemnly, "William Broad is about to make the winning kick," and was set to deliver a deathblow to the offending instrument, a security guard in the courtyard shouted, "Don't you dare kick that phone!"

Calling the manager on his walkie-talkie, he yelled out, "We've got a weird guy destroying hotel property—over." The hotel manager was angry when he arrived at my door, threatening to throw me out of the hotel, but he relented when he saw it was just a phone. Putting on my best English gentleman airs, I offered, "I'm so terribly sorry, but I've just heard the news my grandmother is dying in the UK, and I'm dreadfully upset."

It was a lie, but I offered it in my best clipped British accent, all apologies and charm. The manager seemed inclined to accept my explanation, subject to checking out what the other members of our party were up to. We proceeded to Steve's room, knocked on the door, and waited. It took a while for Steve to respond, so the manager knocked again even harder. Very slowly the door opened ever so slightly, revealing Steve's bleary eyes peering at us through a very small gap. It took a little persuasion, but when Steve grudgingly opened his door fully and allowed us to enter, no explanation was necessary for his initial reluctance to let us in. Certainly the manager did not ask for one. Instead he gave us an hour to check out of the hotel. Had he asked what Steve thought he was doing, he would have received a simple answer: he had decided to redecorate his room. Just the previous day, Steve had received a huge bag of personalized black guitar picks, and once he had decided the colors in his room were too bright, he'd taken matters into his own hands. With several tubes of superglue and a chair to help him reach the higher sections, he spent an entire night giving the room a more subdued feel by wallpapering an entire wall and half of another with his personalized picks. That was the best explanation I could get out of Steve, but I had to admit he'd impressed me with yet another flash of creativity. "Fuck my grandmother," I gleefully replied. "That's great, Steve!"

The next day, we began to work as a band on "White Wedding" in the studio with Keith, who played drums. We tracked to his beats, just as we had done with "Hot in the City" a few months before. Keith added his signature *bom-bom bom-bom* tom-tom overdubs, one of his undeniable drum hooks. For the video, we filmed nails being driven into a coffin synched to the beat of that tom-tom fill—that's how much of a hook it was. Keith tracked the dry, eighth-note guitar to the deep-rolling bass line à la "Dancing," and it once again knitted the track together, making the rhythm unstoppable. Steve added a lovely finishing flurry of notes to my plucked B-minor chord "flag," showing he could be both delicate and hard rocking. His droning guitar wail answers my vocal, rhythm and lead guitar brilliantly filling out the track.

"White Wedding" turned into a huge production number when we decided to add a second synthesized version to the rock version for the dance mix. The guitars fade into a doomy keyboard pad with electro-rock rhythms to give it that Giorgio Moroder disco thing I dug. I then intoned another vocal on top of it, enjoying the spare, dark vibe and the different feel. I wanted my music to be pliable, so individual songs could work in a number of different ways. When a song is good, the number of interpretations it accommodates grows, as do the instrumental possibilities.

After we recorded "White Wedding" and the session ended, we decided to do a jump-up gig at a small joint on Sunset Boulevard where L.A. musicians hung out. We debuted "White Wedding" there to a somewhat indifferent audience, but we didn't care. The song was a blast, and we felt great adding it to our repertoire. The joint was called the Central, which Johnny Depp would later reopen and name the Viper Room.

After getting kicked out of the Sunset Marquis, Steve and I moved across Sunset to the Chateau Marmont. I had one of those little bungalows off from the main hotel. I started drinking tequila in the dead of night since I was suffering some withdrawals from "chipping" the H, and I found it difficult to sleep. I would drink half a bottle of tequila, become comatose, and wake up a few hours later from having psychedelic nightmares.

One night I was put to sleep drunk and raving in the early evening by Brendan Bourke, who then took what remaining booze I had left. I woke up at two in the morning jonesing, knowing I couldn't get any more booze until six. I was pissed-off drunk and raging in an alcohol-induced nightmare. Incensed, I began to smash up the room, taking out the bungalow windows with my elbows, screaming. I destroyed the TV and whatever else was in my immediate vicinity that sounded good crashing to the floor. Soon, the place was in complete shambles. I was nude and covered in blood and sweat, going nuts.

The hotel manager was alerted. She came up, took one look at the mess, and ordered me out. Brendan was called and told of my destruction, but he got them to agree to let me stay until morning. After a short while I was able to get back to sleep. I awoke a few hours later on the floor, still naked, as daylight streamed into the room. I rolled

a joint and started to smoke it in front of the broken TV with shards
of glass all around me, the door hanging off its hinges and the windows shattered. The smell had to be discernible to anyone passing by,
and wouldn't you know it, pretty soon I heard some urgent-sounding
voices outside. Curious, I went to the window to take a look: my curiosity was rewarded when I saw some cops moving down the path-
way leading to my room. They seemed to be looking for something. I
quickly extinguished the joint and looked around frantically for any
illicit substances I might hide or destroy. I was sure that they would
soon be knocking at my door. "Billy, you've gone too far this time," I
said to myself as I waited for the knock that would inevitably lead to
something bad. But nothing happened, and yet I could still hear them.
I decided to take matters into my own hands and open the door, ready
to go quietly rather than make a scene and make matters worse for
myself. I opened the door and went outside, but the cops had moved on
from my bungalow and were searching farther away toward another
bungalow. They showed no interest in me as I stood there fully nude,
just outside my door, staring at them. They continued to comb the
ground, looking for . . . what? It wasn't until later that I learned that
John Belushi had OD'd in another bungalow the previous night. After
that, the hotel manager had forgotten all about me, and after sending
her a bouquet and promising no more destruction, I moved to another
bungalow.

It wasn't just drugs that were messing with my brain and causing me to act irrationally. I longed for Perri, and the thought of her
being in New York while I was alone once more, three thousand miles
away from her, was driving me crazy. Combine that with the pressure
of recording my first solo album, and it was all really difficult to deal
with.

Despite the fact we had "White Wedding" as a song we could hang
the album on, I still felt a little unsure of how it would be received. I
felt the weight of the world on my shoulders, and I was feeling insecure, which led to some irrational behavior. I should have trusted my
initial instincts about Keith and Steve Stevens, as I believed in both of

My maternal grandparents, Michael
and Anna O'Sullivan, who gifted me
my banjo when I was three, and my
Ringo Starr snare drum at seven.
Courtesy of Idol family archive

Dad in his Fleet Air Arm uniform,
atop his fighter plane, 1945. *Courtesy
of Idol family archive*

Mum, in Eire, on her honeymoon.
Courtesy of Idol family archive

Wedding day, through an archway of
"Handy Angle" slotted shelving, 1953.
Courtesy of Idol family archive

Off on their honeymoon.
Courtesy of Idol family archive

American summer, three or four years old, on Long Island
with my dad. *Courtesy of Idol family archive*

On a holiday drive to Niagara Falls
and the Great Lakes, with Mum,
1959. *Courtesy of Idol family archive*

Long Island, after a blizzard.
Courtesy of Idol family archive

Back to Dear Old Blighty, representing Goring Cub Scouts,
proudly carrying our troop flag. *Courtesy of Idol family archive*

At Goring Church of England School, fuck knows what year. *Courtesy of Idol family archive*

Frightening Mum and Dad with my hair length and nicotine-stained fingers at Christmas dinner. *Courtesy of Idol family archive*

In Bromley with my sister, Jane, and parents, 1974. Note short-cropped Lou Reed hairdo. *Courtesy of Idol family archive*

A classic Bromley Contingent photo.
Seated, left to right, Siouxsie Sioux,
Debbie Juvenile. *Standing, left to right,*
Simon Barker, me, Steve Severin.
© *Sheila Rock*

Waaaaah! I wanna be the singer! With
Gene October, in the band Chelsea.
© *Ray Stevenson*

Generation X, on the Roxy stage we built, in front
of the black backdrop I hung, 1977. © *Alain Bali*

At the Marquee, Wardour Street. Yes, we had chicks in the front row, thank god.
© *Adrian Boot*

The book that spawned the band.
© *Tandem Books*

In Paris, live at Le Gibus. © *Ray Stevenson*

My dad searched all of England for a black shirt for me, but they hadn't sold black shirts since World War II because of fascist implications. © *Ray Stevenson*

Backstage at the Marquee, a gig that was a huge break; most groups who played there already had records out—the power of punk! © *Ray Stevenson*

"You're nicked, Sunshine." With Tony James,
Bob "Derwood" Andrews, and Mark Laff. © *Ray Stevenson*

Marc Bolan, at his *Dandy in the Underworld*
launch party, Roxy Club, 1977. © *Steve
Emberton, Camera Press London*

Gen X: Terry "Chimer"
Chimes, James Stevenson,
Tony James, and moi.
© *Adrian Boot*

At the piano with Keith Moon at a charity event,
1978. © *Steve Emberton, Camera Press London*

Family portrait day, at my parents' house in Bromley, 1978. *Courtesy of Idol family archive*

New York City, 1978, Generation X press promo tour, with my pink Elvis '50s-style jacket. © *Roberta Bayley/Redferns/Getty Images*

The final night of the legendary Max's Kansas City and the very first Billy Idol solo show, 1978. © *Justina Davies*

Attacking Keith Forsey at Electric Lady
Studios, recording *Rebel Yell*, with Steve
Stevens and engineer Michael Frondelli.
Courtesy of Ellen Golden

The Cat Club, New York City, 1984.
With Perri, Ron and Jo Wood. © *Ron
Galella/Ron Galella Collection/WireImage*

With Perri, at an all-night rock 'n' roll
bowling club, New York City.
© *Ray Stevenson*

Getting dirty before we get clean, the Stony-Eyed Medusa and yours truly, Dortmund, Germany, 1984. © *Picture alliance/Fryderyk Gabowicz*

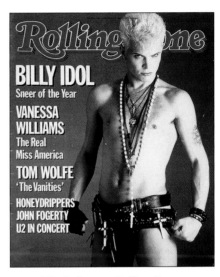

The infamous *Rolling Stone* cover issue, January 31, 1985, complete with leather loincloth and my "bible belt."
© *Wenner Media*

Appearing on *Saturday Night Live*, host: Don Rickles.
© *NBC/NBC Universal/Getty Images*

Whiplash Smile tour, with Steve Stevens, 1987. © *Daniel Gluskoter*

Clubbing with a very young Drew Barrymore, 1984. *Courtesy of Idol family archive*

Gold and platinum records galore, the Rebel Yell touring band. *From left to right:* Thommy Price, Steve Stevens, Bill Aucoin, me, Judi Dozier, and Steve Webster, 1984. © *Bob Gruen/www.bobgruen.com*

At Florida's mysterious Coral Castle, in the "moon for a rocking chair," from an unreleased "Sweet Sixteen" video shoot, 1987. © *R.J. Capak / Universal Music Group*

"Boots and Scarves," minus the scarf, Los Angeles. © *Johnny Rozsa*

With Sam Kinison, Madonna, and David Bowie, 1987.
Courtesy of Everett Collection

With Les Paul, holding my signed Les Paul Junior—extremely coked out (me, not Les). *Courtesy of Idol family archive*

At home, writing songs on my beloved Taylor acoustic—a gift from Steve Stevens, complete with mother-of-pearl *Whiplash Smile* logo inlay, and inscribed "To My Idol." *Courtesy of Idol family archive*

Charmed Life tour, with the aid of a walking stick, at Bercy in Paris, 1990. © *Alain Benainous/Gamma-Rapho/Getty Images*

With Bonnie and Will; the apple didn't fall far from this tree. *Courtesy of Idol family archive*

With Will at the *Batman Returns* premiere, June 1992. Note Will's Batman shoes. © *BEImages/RexUSA*

As "Cat," in the movie *The Doors*— I insisted on having the longest hair on set. © *Tristar Pictures*

Bonnie Blue's First Communion. This photo is what heaven looks like for my mum. *Courtesy of Idol family archive*

Locarno, Switzerland, at the Moon and Stars Festival. © *Charles Jischke*

Peace & Love Festival, Borlänge, Sweden. © *Charles Jischke*

them. The effects of withdrawal were probably preventing me from seeing things more clearly. After all, this was only the second album Keith and I had made together, and it was the first with the triumvirate of me, Keith, and Steve Stevens. We were beginning to embrace a more power-pop rock-dance direction, evolving away from Generation X's punk-rock approach. This was new for me. In a rock world populated by REO Speedwagon and Journey, did any of what I was doing make commercial sense?

The lyrics of this album would celebrate Perri and our love affair, which was now going global since we were no longer just living in London. I wanted my lyrics to reflect my personal experience over the last year since the final Gen X album. One thing I was certain of was that my lyrics were unlike Tony James's. Whether that was good or bad, I wasn't quite sure. They weren't about guns, fictional rock 'n' roll gangs, or science fiction. They were about me, struggling with a new life in a strange country, trying to forge some kind of future. They were also created simultaneously with a melody, which meant I was concentrating on the words, and "singing good" phonetically. I was more economical, trying to make sure each word and sentence was more meaningful. At least that was my intent. I was learning my craft and trying to grow lyrically.

Making the *Billy Idol* album wasn't all darkness. Despite my insecurities and missing Perri, much of it was a lot of fun, especially seeing Steve Stevens work his guitar and effects, dragging those tortured sounds from deep within his amp and speaker. After two weeks in the studio we had recorded almost all the songs we had written in New York. Everyone in the band really did his utmost to create the best backing tracks possible. Not all the songs were dance-rock numbers. "Hole in the Wall" and "Dead on Arrival" were straight-ahead rock songs infused with attitude, but Keith Forsey's sensibilities meant the production had a feel unlike the '70s rock most people were listening to on U.S. radio. We were not making predictable stadium rock but tight, four-minute, groove-based dance-pop tracks that just happened to feature great rock guitar. We would never have achieved the desired effect on "White Wedding" without Keith playing drums. I love his tight beat-keeping and will always be proud of what we achieved together on that song. The rest of the group departed for New York, leaving Steve and me to finish the album with Keith. Steve worked on guitar overdubs while I sang the final vocals.

At this point, everybody could see that, if I were to complete my vocals in a timely, non-fucked-up way, the best thing would be for Perri to come out to L.A. Once she arrived, the final vocals went well. I pulled myself together and stopped overdoing the tequila at night, relaxed, and enjoyed singing. It was magic to have Perri with me.

We did a dance mix version of "White Wedding" by joining the rock and electro versions together, and when Keith thought we had it right, we took a cassette to this giant L.A. disco to debut it and get people's reaction. They went mad, dancing to the song with wild abandon.

Hearing the tracks, the record label thought we needed one more song, so Keith and I came up with "Love Calling." Keith laid down a heavy tom-tom beat that we tracked to Steve Stevens's bass as well as guitar. We added some faux African backing vocals, wood blocks, and heavy percussion, finishing it with a sax solo. It was cool experimenting with different instruments, since, up until this point in my musical career, I had never tried anything other than the usual guitar/bass/drums/keyboards setup. We also did a dubbed-up dance remix, which was a lot of fun.

We had been trying to come up with something fresh by searching for a sound that was a mélange of all the best rock/blues/folk/punk/funk ideas rolled into one. We tried to come up with something fresh. We wanted to access all of music's various styles at the same time, mixing them up to create a unique new brand, Billy Idol Music. We hadn't perfected it yet, but with the sound and feel of this peculiar little record that would go on to sell more than a million copies, we were on our way.

JUST BEFORE LEAVING L.A., I RAN across a book about a comic super-heroine named Octobriana, believed to have been created in Russia in the late '60s by a group of dissidents to protest the Soviet authorities' hard-line stance and the lack of freedom under the regime. The heroine of this graphic novel was a female James Bond–type freedom fighter/spy who embodied the ideals of the October Revolution, betrayed by the Soviet government.

Octobriana was like a Russian cartoon Statue of Liberty who came to life to battle the forces of Stalinism with a red star on her forehead. She was kind of like a Mongolian version of Wonder Woman with huge tits and a skimpy outfit.

I thought the character would look great as a tattoo but I was lacking the courage, so I downed a load of booze and a quaalude and went to Sunset Strip Tattoo and showed the artist there, Kevin Brady, the picture. He traced it onto some see-through paper, made an outline on my left arm, and began to stick needles in me. I fell asleep occasionally while he worked, but I woke up every now and then to say, "Not too Mongolian," before returning to my snooze. When he began to write his tag in Chinese figures, Kevin really dug in, and that was the one bit of the tattoo where I felt some pain. When he was finished, I was pleased. I thought the tattoo came out really well. Of course, news of my ink scared everybody back in New York, but I liked Kevin's work, and still do to this day.

Not too many people in New Wave rock bands had tattoos back then. This was 1982, before Guns N' Roses and the later-'80s bands, who really got tatted up. I don't know what possessed me, but I liked it and thought it went with my look. In fact, my Octobriana would become quite famous later that summer.

CHAPTER TWENTY-TWO

I WANT MY MTV:
VIDEO THRILLS THE RADIO STAR

Midtown Manhattan

IN THE SPRING OF 1982, MTV had been on-air for over half a year, but it had yet to make an impact because many cable systems weren't yet carrying it, even in New York, where it was born.

Bill Aucoin had told me about this new network, and we decided to make a video for the first single from my debut LP, "Hot in the City." It was very crude, and I don't believe we ever ended up submitting it. It had me walking on some *Tron*-like computer grid.

The single came out and did quite well, getting to number 23 on the *Billboard* Hot 100. Chrysalis didn't put my picture on the sleeve, as punk had been shunned by most radio stations and was not selling. This way, Chrysalis thought we might get a fair shake from radio, and they happened to be right. I also did a callout of a hundred American cities, so that each market could personalize the song in the space on the record where I shout, "New York."

With the chart activity, I did another *Solid Gold* performance, this time with my new band. In addition to Steve Stevens, there was Gregg Gerson on drums, Phil Feit on bass, and Judi Dozier on keyboards. Having a woman on keyboards was part of our fresh edge, a combination of sexes at the dawn of this new era in music. Beginning in April, and through the summer, we played shows across the Northeast to introduce the new music and band members.

On the night of August 4, we played two separate gigs in New York, first at the Ritz and then later at the Peppermint Lounge. The Ritz was a prestigious venue for us, one of the Manhattan rock clubs where you had to go down well in order to proceed on to bigger and better bookings. I don't know how many bands would've dared to play two venues in a single night, but it was fun, and the reaction was encouraging.

We then flew to the West Coast, beginning in Palo Alto at the Keystone on August 9, Bill Graham's Stone in San Francisco on the 10th, and then to L.A. for two consecutive nights at the Whisky and the Roxy the following night. I was a bit dope-sick during this leg and had some wine before the Roxy gig to feel better, but it didn't help! The *L.A. Times'* Robert Hilburn reviewed the show: the caption under the photo of me read simply, HUBRIS. Bob was just a little more than a dozen years early in his prediction of what would bring about my fall, but I was already walking a fine line between success and disaster.

After that, the band and I headed to Europe, where we first played London, and then traveled to Germany for a gig followed by a TV show appearance, for which we spent the day in a freezing castle for an old-school video shoot for "Hot in the City." The shoot was so long and arduous that I understood from that point on the value of having a preproduced video when promoting a record.

We returned to the UK to shoot a video for "White Wedding" for MTV, which was now beginning to become more meaningful in the States. We reached out to director Russell Mulcahy for a concept, but after a few promising preliminary discussions, where he suggested blowing up a kitchen, we decided to look elsewhere. So, we turned to David Mallet. I knew David from the live Generation X Marquee shoot he'd filmed in 1977. He had directed the *Kenny Everett Video Show*, a favorite of mine, and I had previously met him when Perri did a Def Leppard video with him. Knowing how great Perri was, he hired her to suggest choreography ideas for the shoot.

David and I put our heads together and came up with a concept. It

was a very simple but effective idea involving churches, a gothic wedding, and a motorbike smashing through the face of Jesus. The set was
a mocked-up graveyard with loads of crosses. I suspect the video had
something to do with a fantasy about the heroin I was doing in private,
but the song itself was really about not being tied down by society's
conventions.

At the time, I had begun to wear many rosaries and other items
around my neck to create a self-made image that I had culled from my
walks among the Catholic shops while I was in New York the previous
year. I had a leather vest made in bright red that could be turned inside
out for an interchangeable black look, to which I affixed a sheriff's
badge. I wore black jeans with a black rubberized pattern along with
some long Vivienne Westwood socks that came above my boots and
went over the lower part of my leg beneath the knee. I wore nothing
underneath the vest, exposing my chest, covered in crosses, rosaries,
and ornaments.

We bleached my hair the night before the shoot, and then I hooked
up with some of my UK mates, whom I had not seen for a year and a
half. Somehow, despite the late night/early morning partying, I still
managed to turn up early to shoot the gravedigger scene outside a
deserted church, arriving by motorcycle. Then we shot the part where
I unwrapped myself from the shroud I might have been buried in as
though I was coming back to life while singing the first verse. It was
Idol resurrected—undead, but still rocking.

David then began securing the mock coffin lid by knocking in the
nails in time to Keith Forsey's tom-tom beat. We had Mark May play a
male nurse, and Perri played the bride. Mark mopped Perri's brow as
she lay on a stretcher. I bloodied her finger by affixing a barbed-wire
wedding ring, and her kitchen exploded as she pirouetted like a prima
ballerina. In this video world, domestic bliss was not guaranteed. Perri
also recruited her friends Dominique and Alison from Hot Gossip/Spi-
nooch to choreograph dance moves that involved slapping their butts at
the front of an altar in time to the claps on the record. We had a stunt
rider playing me to crash through a huge stained-glass window with
Jesus' face on it, entering the church to exact some kind of revenge. It

was anarchy, and a spit in the face of convention. We shot the entire video in one very long day.

The video premiered on MTV, minus the barbed-wire ring and blood—which they had determined was not suitable for viewing—and it became an instant hit. At the time, MTV didn't have that many videos to program and was in need of content twenty-four hours a day. So "White Wedding" was running at least once an hour, which was amazing exposure, considering their viewership was growing exponentially every day, as more and more people hooked up to cable. There I was, in America's living rooms, and whatever residual radio airplay problems we had vanished as soon as the kids at home saw the video and began to call their local stations to request the song. As such, radio programmers overcame their fear that advertisers would be turned off by my punk-rock image. In fact, it was the beginning of radio opening up their playlists to many new artists as MTV began to gain influence. A new generation of listeners was emerging, hungry for new music.

At this point, the MTV exposure led us to embark on our first club tour of the U.S. and Canada. The band and the roadies were on a single tour bus, so it was very crowded. I used to wait until everyone was asleep to lie down on one of the couches, as I didn't care for the coffin-like bunks. Ace Penna, from my Sheridan Square days, was our road manager, and it was good to have a mate in that post. We rolled from one town to another, the bus becoming one with the road, the mind-numbing mileage stretching on and on, only to be relieved by the show, some drinks, and a bit of a hang with the fans before the crew loaded up and we were off again.

It was cool to be able to meet these fans and hear what they thought of the new music. I was still one with them. At this point, there was an intimate, human element to the tour, one that fame and notoriety would later prevent. These fans enjoyed the new scene. They had either been too young for punk or had never had the opportunity to experience it, since the music never really conquered America. Most of them had never seen any of the main characters in the flesh. During the show I would watch the audience near the stage as their eyes shone in the dark, the light show playing on their faces, the slashing whites and sonic blues blasting through with the onward pulse and throb of the music.

The band and the crew were rising to the occasion and taking their responsibilities seriously, but there were also lighter moments. One night on the bus, Steve Stevens was sitting at a table while in front of him the lighting tech and his assistant discussed the show. Steve mentioned that he wasn't sure he liked the green light they used on him during "Shooting Stars." The two technicians looked puzzled. "We don't have any green gels," they insisted. "But there's a green light on me during the show," said Steve. "Oh," nodded the lighting guy. "You mean chartreuse!"

RIDING THE MOMENTUM OF THE SINGLE and album later that fall, we traversed some of the U.S. and Canadian cities I had read about but never actually seen in person.

In the shadow of the Capitol dome in Washington, D.C., we stayed at a flea-bitten hotel, where the rooms smelled like golden showers and prostitutes plied their trade openly outside the entrance.

With its links to Britain, Canada already knew about me, and the single and album received immediate play. The fans there were excited to see an English punk. I played a town called Kamloops. The main street boasted a corral and railhead at one end, with a blanket-coated Indian tribesman who gave me a T-shirt that read FIRST KAMLOOPS AND THEN THE WORLD! They went nuts in Vancouver and Edmonton, where there were large punk-rock followings. In Calgary, a kid was dancing so crazily, he fell from the theater balcony and ended up bent backward on the PA stack. That must've hurt, though it was hard to tell whether he felt any pain. I spoke to the kid later at the hotel (where he miraculously showed up after the gig) and told him he should go to a hospital, but he refused. He wasn't leaving, nor were the other two hundred fans who seemed to have come to the hotel with him. They had enjoyed the show's high energy, and it was great they were so enthusiastic. It made me believe what I did mattered to people.

Before leaving Canada, thinking that they still put codeine in cough syrup, one of the roadies and I drank a whole bottle each before realizing there was nothing we wanted in it. I ended up spending the following forty-eight hours from Winnipeg to Trenton, New Jersey, out of my mind, and not in a good way. It was like a bum acid trip. The lyrics describing this experience—"I'm on a bus on a psychedelic trip / Reading murder books and trying to stay hip"—ended up in "Eyes Without a Face." To pass the time and ignore the effects of the cough syrup, I watched *The Texas Chainsaw Massacre* over and over, which gave me an idea for a future music video director.

The fact is, I had started chipping the H regularly again, so going on tour proved to be a bit of a nightmare, as I was often dope-sick on the road. Every now and then, Perri somehow managed to send me some methadone she'd gotten back home to the hotels we stayed in along the way. It helped to temporarily stave off the heebie-jeebies, but not for long.

With my drug habit, I was gradually slipping into a way of life that one day would take more than it would give. I was a functioning drug addict, capable of playing the gigs, but I was losing sight of all that was important. My dreams now came in the form of an addiction that insisted, "Abandon all hope ye who enter here." I wasn't addicted to any one drug, but to a constant cocktail. I functioned stoned or dope-sick; somehow my heart drove me on, but how far could sheer willpower take me?

I kept trying to clean up, which I suppose is commendable. Downtime meant a chance to pick up the habit again, and in trying to be clean, I turned to alcohol to salve my hunger temporarily. I knew the pitfalls of what I was doing—by then, Perri and I had long been estranged from normal society. This world seemed quite welcoming and alluring. Its womblike atmosphere promoted an unrealistic air of well-being that permeated everything.

I was a kid, like any kid, trying to see if there was some rationale in life I could hold on to and somehow get a sense of myself to buoy me up. I had convinced myself that this could only be attained by reaching into the dark and making sense of the movements in that indistinct place where light fades, blackness rules, and figures play in the mind.

From that imagination came fierce wild animals, searing deserts, a young prince and his lady caught up in a deadly web they've woven around themselves.

My princess waited for me in a tiny garret in New York while I stormed the barricades, a dope-sick punk-rock prince devoted to a kind of sensibility I thought was missing from this world, lusting for forbidden adventures and misadventures, needing to stare the world in the face before being finally undone and swept into the void.

As *Flash Gordon*'s Ming the Merciless put it, "Pathetic Earthlings. Hurling your bodies out into the void, without the slightest inkling of who or what is out here."

CHAPTER TWENTY-THREE

REBEL YELL WITH A CAUSE

New York City

THE END OF THAT CLUB TOUR coincided with the close of 1982. The picture of life for me had altered considerably in the few years since I'd moved to the U.S. I was no longer an unknown quantity or some left-over from the punk era but a bona fide '80s rock star with an EP, a hit album, and several big MTV videos under my belt. I was also a junkie and an alcoholic, but at that time none of that fazed me, as the forward momentum of my new life swallowed up any fears or cause for alarm. In fact, the last thing I thought about was my drug problem.

We were back in New York to begin writing songs for a new album. With the advances I'd received for the first solo album, I had enough money to feed whatever desires I had, so I no longer had to worry about my dope sickness—we started taking dope every day, as we could now afford to buy our own. With that, I returned to living on it, maintaining when I had to with a small amount to stop from feeling bad, functioning in the daytime, taking a little more at night just to get high. Sheridan Square off Seventh Avenue offered easy access to sub-way stations, but now I was able to afford cabs, which made traveling around the city that much easier.

First off, we decided to make a video of "Dancing with Myself," which was still being played like mad in the clubs and had now started to pick up radio airplay as well. We got in touch with a chap named Jeff Abelson, who told us he could get Coca-Cola to help with the financing. A number of ideas were considered, including designing a set as a gigantic pinball table, which would allow Coke to advertise their product and give us access to a bigger budget. In the end, these plans fell through, but so do many early video treatments, as you tend to brainstorm a million scenarios before coming up with the concept that will eventually appear on-screen.

We approached *Chainsaw Massacre* and *Poltergeist* director Tobe Hooper, who agreed to do it, much to my surprise. It may have been the first time a feature director helmed a video for MTV. We met with Tobe in L.A. and came up with a sketch of break-dancing zombies, a mad sledgehammer-swinging killer dad, karate-kicking kids, and a woman tied up, which was supposed to be my Octobriana tattoo in bondage.

I would be the protagonist, poised atop a futuristic tower being climbed by zombies attempting to pull me down. I would then destroy them by grabbing two electrodes, which charge my body. It was a simple idea, but there were censorship constraints being put on us by MTV, so the final result had to comply with their code or they wouldn't play it. We had to hold back on some of the horror elements, and at times would only vaguely suggest the corruption in the world that had led to a mad sledgehammer-swinging dad killing a mother as the kids kung fu–kicked their way into the future.

Tobe was cool, bringing his production team to the table and giving us access to his wardrobe and makeup artists. In keeping with the futuristic tone, they constructed a skeletal top that exposed my body but was unlike anything I had ever worn in my stage show. To cast our zombies, Perri and I headed down to Radio, a club beneath an archway where break-dancers met to show off their skills. We chose a few we thought were exceptional to appear as zombies in the video.

Once again, we bleached my hair the night before the shoot. I nodded out while waiting for the bleach to take and woke up an hour or so later with most of my hair fried, leaving a tuft at the front stuck up just enough to prevent anyone from seeing just how short it really was.

Tobe used a lot of refracted lights, the reflections concealing my bald scalp.

The shoot went pretty smoothly. The break-dancers jerked in and out, contorting their bodies in their signature moves as they climbed to the top of the tower. Tobe's special-effects people used a painted-glass shot to show the view looking down from my perspective, then combined the footage with shots of the break-dancers tumbling from a trampoline to get the effect of them falling into the vast depths when I zapped them from the tower. Another piece of glass was painted to show a huge billboard of my tattoo above me at the top of the tower in the ending shot. Octobriana, my tattooed love goddess, who appeared to be tied up during the video, was now free, the image showing her standing in as a female symbol of liberty for this dark world. Thank God Coca-Cola said no to the pinball idea, as I think this version was more in keeping with the dark style we first portrayed in "White Wedding." It was a futuristic vamp, a take on a larger-than-life comic-book world.

The "Dancing with Myself" video did really well on MTV and kept my album alive while we started to write songs for the next one. Having a well-known movie director work on it gave it a pedigree and backstory very few videos had at the time.

After the video shoot we began meeting at a rehearsal studio below Fourteenth Street, working on ideas and songs for the new album. Walking across Sixth Avenue, I started to hear a tune in my head, like a series of notes running up the scale. I had always been interested in how classical composers created some of their best themes by moving directly up the musical scale, with one or two minor variations or strategic pauses before cascading back down the scale.

I've always had a fascination with the titles of horror films. I had been reading a book about the genre's history, with riveting concepts and titles such as *The Cabinet of Dr. Caligari*. I was particularly intrigued by the '60s French nouvelle vague forerunner *Les Yeux sans visage* (*Eyes Without a Face*), about a brilliant plastic surgeon who vows to restore the face of his daughter, who has been horribly disfigured in a car accident. This vow leads him to murder, as he sets out collecting the facial features of his victims, which he then grafts onto his daughter's hideous countenance, attempting to restore her beauty. Her staring eyes remain the only thing visible.

When I got to the studio, I told Steve Stevens about the tune I had in my head, though I didn't have any chords. He showed me a revolving four-chord pattern he'd been working on that fit really well over the top of the tune. I started to use "Eyes Without a Face" as a possible title/lyric/chorus for the song. I began to write words that, in some disguised form, spoke about my life in New York and a relationship gone wrong, on the edge of disintegrating into madness. Perhaps I was reflecting on my own touring infidelities. In a way, those can leave you feeling soulless, especially if you're already in a relationship that you value but are degrading by looking elsewhere for additional sexual kicks.

The early '80s were a time of sexual freedom, as AIDS had yet to fully impact the heterosexual world. In the '50s, syphilis had been cured, and penicillin had wiped out gonorrhea. Only herpes remained as an STD scourge, so we were left in a fool's paradise, believing that sex had no permanent consequences. The age of free love was in its last stages, and science was about to make us aware of the perils of this kind of behavior.

Steve and I were now working closely together as a writing and creative team, continuing what we had started on our first album. Steve owned a small four-track recording machine, which allowed us to make demos of music soundscape ideas that we used to record melodies and lyrics that I came up with.

Keith Forsey flew to New York to check on our progress. One of the songs he thought had potential, though still as yet unrealized, was a song Steve and I had begun working on called "Flesh for Fantasy." It was initially an upbeat rock 'n' roll song, a speedy, punk-rock number with a title I had thought of after seeing an old "portmanteau" film, *Flesh and Fantasy*, starring Edward G. Robinson and Barbara Stanwyck. I wasn't yet convinced of its worth, as I didn't feel it had a solid foundation. While the title spoke of something sexy, it proved an effort to put some soul into it. We soon devised a different, slower, syncopated groove in the verse and tried joining it with the punk-rock chorus and a new soulful beginning. It still wasn't right, but at that point we were working on a number of different songs, so we put it aside to continue working on the others. Keith felt we had made sufficient progress with several songs, and as the winter was turning to spring, we began to talk about starting to record. Both Steve and I wanted to record the album in New York this time, so we began making arrangements to book time in the legendary Electric Lady Studios, a studio built by Jimi Hendrix in the heart of the Village on Eighth Street and Sixth Avenue, less than two blocks from my apartment. We still needed a bit more time to work up material, so Keith went back to L.A. while we continued searching for new ideas.

Perri and I began hanging out with Rolling Stones guitarist Ronnie Wood and his wife, Jo, in their Upper West Side brownstone. It was fun shooting the shit with Ronnie; I enjoyed the English camaraderie and his comfortable surroundings, unlike our tiny unfurnished Sheridan Square apartment. Jo was lovely, and it was cool for Perri and me to have an English couple with whom to socialize.

One day, Ronnie invited us to a birthday party at the brownstone. I forget whether it was for him or one of the other Stones, but I soon found myself standing with and talking to Mick Jagger, Keith Richards, and Wood, noticing each had a bottle of booze in his hands. As the bottle moved toward their lips, I followed its path and saw it had a Confederate cavalry officer dressed in gray riding a horse on the label. Above this figure was the name REBEL YELL. I had been interested in the American Civil War ever since I'd visited Gettysburg when I was five.

Gazing at the three guzzling Stones, I asked them if they had the bottle custom-made. "It's a Southern mash bourbon," they answered. "And it's called 'Rebel Yell'?" I asked. "Do you think you'd ever use that as a song title?" I tried to convince them it wasn't quite as iconic for them as "Jumping Jack Flash" or "Gimme Shelter," and they shook their heads and said they wouldn't use it. "Great," I said. "Because I might just use that title for a song, and maybe even call my next album that." I'm sure they couldn't have cared in the slightest, but up until that point, I'd had no idea what I wanted to name the album we were about to record. Here, right in front of me, in the public domain at the very mouths of the Stones, I had my answer. Thanks, lads. Now all I had to do was write the song.

A day or so later, I sat down, cradling my trusty Epiphone guitar, and began pumping eighth notes in the chord of B. I decided to make "Rebel Yell" a cry of love instead of the battlefield, as I had no intention of singing about the Civil War. After all, ladies are the most powerful creatures in this world, and this would be an anthem to love between a man and a woman. I thought about Perri and started to sing:

"Last night a little dancer came dancing to my door / Last night the little angel came pumping on my floor / She said, 'C'mon baby you've got a license for love / And if it expires pray help from above' / In the midnight hour she cries more more more / With a rebel yell, she cries more more more more more more!' "

I went to rehearsal, and we came up with a verse-chorus-verse-chorus setup. Steve then produced a middle sixteen bars to go before his solo. In looking for an introduction, I suggested using this new middle piece. Once we fitted it all together, we had the bare bones of the song to show Keith Forsey when he returned to New York.

At the time, the Stones were recording "Undercover of the Night," from, I believe, a Mick Jagger song idea. I was invited to the Hit Factory in New York to watch as Mick laid down a couple of vocal tracks, with Keith chiming in occasionally. Jagger did all his classic stage moves, and it was a blast seeing him in action in the studio. The song had a dance-rock beat, and I observed as they tried to tighten up the groove to make it more club oriented. At the time in most dance clubs, the DJs kept careful track of the beats per minute, or BPM, of a song so that they could seamlessly mix different tracks together without the intensity of the beat ever letting up, interrupting the flow of the dancers. I could tell the number sped up or slowed down slightly as it went into the different sections, which was cool, except it probably wouldn't flow in a club.

Knowing the tricks we had used to enable a song to be machined into a groove, I caught a glimpse of the band lined up behind the control desk. "Have you ever tried locking the drums up and triggering a pulse to drive the rhythm of the music and get that machinelike groove?" I asked. I wish I had a camera to catch the look of disgust that came over their faces one at a time as they peered up from the control desk, a look they might have given upon sniffing a particularly foul odor. I laughed and said, "Just an idea from the people at Idol," and realized I'd better shut up, as they knew what they wanted.

CHAPTER TWENTY-FOUR

A CHANGE IN PACE OF FANTASY AND TASTE

Electric Lady Studios, Greenwich Village, New York City

THE HOT, PULSING HUMIDITY OF NEW York bore down, and the droplets of water falling on one's head from the millions of air conditioners felt like the beginning of a rainfall that never came. Nothing could stop the relentless flow of hot air that whirled about the city streets as I made my way to Electric Lady Studios and into the dark and cool of the chilled rooms that sent a shiver through my body as I adjusted to the lower temperature. I moved along a snaking corridor that fed into the studio, where the lads had set up the drums and backline equipment, ready for us to start laying down some of the tracks. The carpeted, soundproof floors and ceilings betrayed no echo of my footfalls as I passed along the curved passageway and pushed myself into the bright glare of the control room.

Founded by Jimi Hendrix in 1970, Electric Lady was an oddball for its time. Instead of following the usual studio model—a big, impersonal box—it was a psychedelic den, with curved walls, groovy multi-hued lights, and sci-fi erotica murals to aid the creative flow. Hendrix had died barely three weeks after its opening party, but the list of greats who then recorded albums there included Led Zeppelin, Bob Dylan, and John Lennon. Would what we were about to lay down have the same kind of resonance? We had yet to find out. The purple carpeting and psychedelic wall murals that echoed the '60s seemed a little dated in 1983, but at the same time, we wanted to record there, not just drink in the ambience. Somehow, we would have to leave our impression in these hallowed halls, just as so many others had over the years.

Keith arrived from L.A. and we began to work up the songs to ready them for recording. We began by cutting "(Do Not) Stand in the Shadows," with a drummer who had been working with us, but after a while, it was like pulling teeth to get what we wanted. After that, the drums lay silent, and we tracked everything to Keith's patterns using a Linn drum machine that had decent rock sounds. We used both the Linn and a Roland 808 that had a much softer sound and was a favorite of a great many R&B acts. Keith's drum patterns were very distinctive and usually ended up as the hook in the song. Keith always thought *song* first when he came up with his parts. Other drummers were too busy worrying about what their friends would say about their performance to give us the relentless pace we were looking for. A drum machine had no ego and no friends to impress, and Keith could work it like a master. We were not playing just one style of music but a mixture of soul, rock, R&B, and punk, so a drummer needed to be versed in all of these styles, making it expedient to use the drum machine. Although the drum machine was soulless, Keith had worked with it long enough to know how to infuse it with the passion we needed to lay down the new tracks.

When it came time to do "Flesh for Fantasy," we recorded a version that still had a punk chorus, but we dropped that pretty fast and went back to the drawing board, deciding in favor of the final arrangement you hear on the record. Thank God for that, because it was now a silky smooth soul song with a dynamic chorus that let the title act as a cry of sexual need rather than a punky put-down. I sang the song while clutching Leopold von Sacher-Masoch's novella *Venus in Furs*, the very one that gave the Velvet Underground song its name.

"There's a change in pace of fantasy and taste / Do you like good music / Do you like to dance." I wrote the lyric as if it were a sexual advert someone had placed in a newspaper or magazine. "Hanging out for a body shop at night / Ain't it strange what we do to feel alright."

It is strange what mental and chemical processes our minds and bodies go through that send us searching deep into the night for sexual satisfaction. Some people took my advert literally. Mainly, it's a sexy song that spoke to the audiences of the time, who were in the process of discovering their own sexualities.

When it came time to record "Rebel Yell," we had no idea how to end it, so we just left a massive groove section to play out at the end. After doing most of the other tracking, the song was musically complete. Keith placed me in the middle of the studio with a handheld mic and let me vamp away over the drop-down ending. I had no idea what I was going to say or what tune I was going to invent. But believe it or not, on the first pass, the words "I walked the world for you, babe / A thousand miles for you / Who'll dry your tears of pain, babe / A million times for you" just came out. Basically, I just riffed and jammed the whole ending on the recording. I later perfected the performance with a better microphone, my standard Neumann 48.

We proceeded to lay down "Daytime Drama," "Blue Highway," and "The Dead Next Door" in short order, as we already had decent demos with the words and arrangements pretty much all there.

I SPEND SO MUCH TIME / BELIEVING ALL THE LIES / TO KEEP THE DREAM ALIVE /
NOW IT MAKES ME SAD / IT MAKES ME MAD AT TRUTH / FOR LOVING WHAT WAS YOU /
EYES WITHOUT A FACE / GOT NO HUMAN GRACE / EYES WITHOUT A FACE.

I used to tell people "Eyes Without a Face" was a murder song. I wonder if I was aware that it was my hijinks and gradual infidelity that were killing Perri's and my love story. Certainly I was beginning to drift into a strange world where you usually don't touch the ground and the only way to find human comfort is with a fresh someone for the night in a strange town on a strange continent. It's possible I was predicting our eventual dissolution, even though our love hadn't begun to fade. But the ten-month-long Rebel Yell tour was soon to begin, and that, coupled with the drug consumption and nonstop sex, would be enough to erode anybody's relationship.

NOW I CLOSE MY EYES / AND I WONDER WHY / I DON'T DESPISE /
NOW ALL I CAN DO / IS LOVE WHAT WAS ONCE / SO ALIVE AND NEW /
BUT IT'S GONE FROM YOUR EYES / I'D BETTER REALIZE.

The recording of "Eyes Without a Face" went well. Steve came up with a blistering guitar riff for the middle of the song that added a whole other dimension, rendering it more than just a ballad. I improvised a rapping part to go over the top. Rap was everywhere in New York at the time, in all the discos and clubs, so it made sense after my croon to start talking streetwise over Steve's supersonic barrage of sound. I thought to myself, *This album is getting really exciting.* I wanted a deep bass groove like those Sly and Robbie reggae records I loved, but it was difficult to get that. We tried quite a few bass players before we found a guy who played for the Broadway musical *Dreamgirls*, a Cuban bass player named Sal Cuevas, who really got what I was looking for. That must have been one of the heaviest bass sounds on any '80s record. We had a terrible time trying to convince the person cutting the vinyl record to make the bass loud enough, because the deep grooves that accommodate bass notes on a record—if too loud—can flip the needle off the record entirely.

We still didn't have the full complement of songs for the album, so I came up with "Catch My Fall" as an idea. It was a simple croon that mostly just described how I struggled with life's successes and failures, much like anyone else in the world, but it made a nice addition to the album. We threw on a Mars Williams sax solo as a change of pace from the guitar solos on every other track.

One of the last songs we came up with was "Crank Call," which I was still singing the night before we delivered the album in November. We partied a great deal during the making of the album, but only after the day's work was complete. I was taking just enough heroin to maintain in the studio; then, later at night, when I got home, I would do a bigger line to get high. A Russian guy named Ivan used to turn up at the studio with his foxy girlfriend and tons of blow, but I wasn't so into that, even though it was nice to snort a couple of lines and have a cocktail after finishing up the session. Coke was handy if you did a quaalude and wanted to stay awake to party, but it wasn't my drug of choice at the time.

I was busy getting the album cover ready with a couple of photo shoots. One had me standing on a pile of Rebel Yell bottles. Afterward, the photographers' lovely female assistant and I started to drink from them. About halfway through, we both got the worst hangover of all time. When I got home, it took two lines of heroin to rid me of the feeling. How the fuck did the Stones guzzle that stuff? They must have cast-iron livers! Jesus! I was basically a vodka and tequila man. When you're on heroin, you don't drink or want much of anything else. It's only when you stop doing smack that you start boozing or taking other drugs to try to get over the withdrawal.

At the eleventh hour of finishing the album, we knew we needed a real drummer. As good as the Linn was, it still sounded a bit too unreal at times, especially for the uptempo songs. All the parts were there; they just had to be copied and played by someone. That someone ended up being Thommy Price, who had been playing for Joan Jett and Patty Smyth. He really copped the feeling of the songs, and it was incredible fun watching him blast through "Rebel Yell," giving it the thunder you can still hear on it today. He tracked most of the album and then joined the band for the upcoming tour.

We almost missed our release date when the guy designing the album cover started to bullshit me about problems with the shot I had chosen, telling me a blemish in the background on the mock-up would look all right once it was blown up. I knew if it was enlarged, the blemish would only look worse, so I refused to let the album release without the alterations that I felt were important. The record label was threatening to put it out as it was because there was no time before the release date to fix it. I went to the studio where we were now doing the final mixes, and when nobody was around, I took the master tapes and held the album hostage until my wishes regarding the cover were addressed. I left the masters with my heroin dealer for safekeeping to really give them the shits. That got them listening, especially when I said I would bootleg the entire album first rather than let them put out the cover as it was. In the end, I got my way. Sometimes you've just got to go to the wall or people, if you let them, will walk all over you.

CHAPTER TWENTY-FIVE

EVERYBODY MUST GET ROLLING STONED

New York, Tristate Area

WE STARTED TOURING AS SOON AS the album was finished, play-ing mainly clubs. *Rebel Yell* arrived in stores in November 1983, just in time for the holiday season. We supported A Flock of Seagulls at Rutgers University one night—I don't think they expected us to be as good as we were, since most people from England had pretty much dis-missed us. They didn't know what I was up to in the U.S., or that I had an American following.

I was still relatively new to the States, but the audience felt they were getting a real show with authentic punk attitude. What I was doing now suited the young ladies in the audience, but the guys dug it too, because there were so many girls at my gigs. And, in my own way, I was still a rebel. We were ending our set with "Rebel Yell," then com-ing back with "Mony Mony." We were a tough act to follow! It was great playing "Blue Highway" and "Flesh for Fantasy," too. The new album was a lot more fun to perform live, and more solid in its intent. We also did "Hot in the City," "White Wedding," Generation X's "Un-touchables," and "Dancing with Myself."

A Flock of Seagulls didn't really have many recognizable songs other than "I Ran," so we pretty much blew them off the stage, leav-ing the audience shagged out and exhausted by the time they came on.

We were also using many of the same ideas as them: the low, rumbling bass, the spaced-out guitar effects. Steve Stevens simply wiped the floor with most guitarists he came up against, and Thommy Price rocked the house on drums, with the Canadian Steve Webster, who had also played on the album, most notably on "Flesh for Fantasy," on bass. We also had Judi Dozier on keyboards, which was cool because the girls loved seeing a chick playing with us wild guys.

It was a great gig, with the early-'80s fans digging on the new decade and loving it. They weren't jaded like most rock critics. This wasn't the boring pedestrian rock of yesteryear. No, this was fired-up rock to grab you by the loins and drag you into a decade that had hope and excess running side by side, where the corruption of the '70s was forgotten in a brand-new world.

We also played a nationally televised live show for MTV on New Year's Eve '83 with the Stray Cats and, via satellite from Wembley, England, the Police. We performed several of the new songs, giving them an incredible launch, letting viewers see how exciting an Idol show could be. It proved we were much more than just a video band and really fueled interest, with the attendance at our club dates swelling.

But during this whole period, I was still a junkie, trying to kick it and straighten out enough so I could go on tour and promote my album. I was struggling, but not admitting it to myself. The sum of my efforts to clean myself up would amount to replacing the heroin with booze and, later, cocaine, which today I realize was a disaster for me. Still, I was young, and didn't sit there and mull over the possible negative effects of my actions. I had too much to think about with this new venture to consider a possible downside to my addictions. The party was too good to leave, so while I continued down the crooked path, those around me were left to deal with the different facets of my personality that started turning up when I had a bad reaction to doing too much liquor and blow in addition to smack.

I would go into a rage if somebody set me off. I only see this now in retrospect. At the time, I thought the tantrums were funny, once they were over, as they wouldn't last long. But my hair-trigger temper would become a problem because I wasn't in control. I was completely unpredictable with what I would say or do, and whatever it was, I couldn't remember afterward. One of my video producers, T'Boo Dalton, would later give the ugliest of my many drug-fueled personalities a name: "Zool."

"Rebel Yell," the first single from the album, was about to be released and we didn't have a video, so we decided to make a live performance video to showcase the new band and album. We chose to hire the American director Jeff Stein, who shot the Who documentary *The Kids Are Alright.* I loved the documentary and liked that Jeff was a film director with experience but was used to shooting rock 'n' roll bands. When we got together to plan the video, it was at the end of the first three weeks of shows, and I don't think I had slept much due to the dope sickness. It was taking a while to set up and I had fallen asleep in a chair for a bit when Jeff innocently woke me to ask about something, and I flew off the handle and in a flash had him up against a wall.

When you are strung out, you have a tremendous amount of pent-up, nasty energy, and if it gets channeled via the wrong emotions, the results can be noxious. A person can become dangerous even if he is not usually violent. On this particular occasion, even though I am not a violent person by nature, being awakened so unceremoniously by Jeff pissed me off, and I lost it. I realized quite soon that I had overreacted and that Jeff had no ill intentions. I quickly calmed down, apologized, and proposed I go home and sleep, then come back the following day refreshed, ready to work.

It was the holiday season, so all the equipment houses were closed and we had nowhere to shoot the video. Somehow, Jeff and his crew managed to secure the Capitol Theatre in Passaic, New Jersey. They bused kids out of New York City to the theater. Of course, they loaded the buses with wine and beer, which nowadays you could not do. At the theater, everyone was very merry. Jeff put the hot-looking girls with the big tits up front. We had a mosh pit—Jeff's cameraman had the footprint of a Doc Martens boot in his cheek for a week.

Even though the video was a triumph, it was a hair-raising experience. About an hour before the "Rebel Yell" world premiere, MTV called, demanding removal of a shot of a kid in the front row holding a Budweiser can. So Jeff got the master tape and had to find a shot to slug in, just one more shot of hot-looking girls with big tits. They ran it over to MTV ten minutes before the world premiere. If they hadn't, there would have been nearly five minutes of black. That's what it was like in those days.

Jeff Stein is a great guy who didn't take my blow-up personally, and instead produced an incredible video with one day's notice. . . . But Zool had struck and would strike again.

THE COVER OF *ROLLING STONE* MAGAZINE, especially in those days, was the ultimate recognition of credibility for an artist and his music. So, when informed by my publicists, Howard Bloom and Ellen Golden, that they wanted to do an interview with me for a possible cover, I was excited. However, that enthusiasm became tempered with increasing paranoia, especially when I learned the magazine had a reputation of being antagonistic toward MTV and those artists—like me—who were heavily promoted on the network. This was of particular concern for my press reps. When I heard that the article about me would be called "A Date with Billy Idol," it sounded like something out of a teenybopper magazine and only added to my fears about how I would be portrayed.

Upon arriving at the cover shoot, which took place prior to the interview, E. J. Camp, the photographer, didn't seem satisfied until I was bare-chested, wearing a loincloth fashioned from a T-shirt, with bleached blond bog-brush hair, dangling chains, glow-in-the-dark rosaries, and metallic crosses around my neck. The getup made me uncomfortable, as I remembered the terrible reaction John Travolta had gotten by shedding his shirt for the cover to promote *Staying Alive*, the *Saturday Night Fever* sequel he'd made with Sylvester Stallone. I naively asked E. J. to promise me she wouldn't use the pictures if I didn't like them, not realizing publisher Jann Wenner was the final arbitrator of all such decisions.

All my misgivings were at the forefront of my mind when I came to do the interview with E. Jean Carroll, the journalist. She was a nice enough lady, but unfortunately, we (in truth, mostly I, in my dope-sick state) consumed several bottles of red wine with our dinner at Emilio's in Greenwich Village. By the end of the interview, when Ellen Golden showed up at the table, my insecurities rushed to the surface, and I found myself leaning into the tape recorder raging on about how much I hated *Rolling Stone* and didn't want to be on the cover. If we had done the interview earlier in the day, and I hadn't been so drunk, I would never have said anything like that. But once it started, the vitriol came pouring out.

By the time the check came, I was already pretty wasted. "I'll let you pay," I slurred, "but it better be a *good* article, you cunt. Otherwise, stick it up your ass. Anyway, *Rolling Stone* sucks. . . . If they were clever, they would have bought their own TV channel and put me on it. I know *they're* rich enough." Meanwhile, Carroll's tape recorder was silently whirring, taking it all in.

I couldn't stop myself, and of course my rant made it into the final article. "Don't fuck with me, motherfuckers!" I rambled. " 'Cause I'm going to be rich enough soon. I'll be at your economic level, and then fuck *you*, *Rolling Stone*.

"I want to be on the *back* of that motherfucker! Don't put me on the front! I think it *sucks* being on the front of *Rolling Stone!*"

Speaking into the recorder mic, I continued to drunkenly ramble, "I love you all, you motherfuckers. But you should have fucking had a bit more respect when I came up in 1977, '78, to see you in your Fifth Avenue offices! But I don't care. Maybe now you understand that I *am* worth being on the front cover of your magazine—for the right reasons, motherfuckers! Don't fucking put me on if you don't like me or my music! Fucking *don't* put me on it!"

Carroll responded that her story on me was probably going to be a cover.

I told her I didn't like the picture they used of me in the year-end issue. "I thought it sucked," I said. "And they better not fuck with me again."

The irony of my knee-jerk reflex "punk vs. establishment" bashing of the magazine was that I actually loved many things about *Rolling Stone*. In its coverage of John Lennon and Yoko Ono, the publication was one of the few media outlets that actually stuck up for the ex-Beatle in his immigration fight against the U.S. government. I admired their books on Dylan, and of course I was a huge fan of Hunter S. Thompson's gonzo-style journalism. Unfortunately, I shot myself in the foot, and what came out was this drunken, dope-sick rant that I couldn't justify even if they betrayed my request not to use the photos I shot with E. J. Camp. Admittedly, when the magazine came out, my audience was thrilled to see me nearly naked on the cover, with my buttocks on the pages inside, even if the "end" didn't justify the means. With the benefit of hindsight, my mindless venting would've been better off consigned to a garbage can. I should've been just happy to talk about how well the *Rebel Yell* album had come out. Unfortunately, I don't believe we talked about music at all in the interview, which was mainly my fault, and a missed opportunity for me to have picked up artistic credibility from the critical community.

I should have known better, but I was under stress, addicted, drunk, and slightly hopped up on coke. And this was the result. Even though it made me look like I didn't give a shit about anything at all, I really cared about the music I was making with Keith and Steve. It's just a shame none of that got in the interview. I have no one to blame but myself.

Those ragged interviews only confirmed that I was just a ticking time bomb hastening my own fall from grace. And it wouldn't be the last time I put my foot in my mouth. Dickens's oft-quoted line "It was the best of times, it was the worst of times" could well have been written about me. That infamous *Rolling Stone* cover might have boosted my short-term career prospects, but it harmed my chance at earning a measure of long-term credibility for my music, all thanks to me.

In part due to the notoriety, the "Rebel Yell" video was a huge success on MTV and the record was a hit on rock radio, where it would often get played after Van Halen's "You Really Got Me." I suppose that was one way radio could rationalize it for their playlists, playing it back to back with the song nearest to punk, a cover of an old Kinks tune. Radio programmers tended to play it safe by opting for an image and a sound that was pretty consistent and within a formula. It was the job of the record company promotion staff to persuade them that they had everything to gain and nothing to lose by playing a song by an artist that might stretch the limits of their format without alienating their audience. It might even expand their audience, or allow them to beat their competitors to the punch by discovering a hit before other stations did.

MTV wasn't constrained by those rules. They were the only game in town when it came to playing videos, and at the time, their audience was growing by the millions every month. If they liked the music and the video, they played it. And so it was for me with "Rebel Yell." MTV led the way, and radio, spurred on by an enthusiastic promotion department at Chrysalis, quickly followed.

All I cared about was getting people to know about the album, and it seemed that all my dreams and hopes for success were coming to fruition. The video images of "Rebel Yell" were jumping out of TVs in millions of living rooms across America, and the signal from radio station towers zoomed and thundered the song through the speakers of a million boom boxes—the listening device of the day. Also not to be forgotten was the song silently filling the ears of joggers on their morning runs and workers on their way to and from the office, wearing the newly invented Sony Walkman.

It was so great to see the joy our music was giving our fans on the road and to hear from many of those we met that the music meant so much to them. As the record took off, we graduated from clubs to small theaters. Everywhere we played we could feel the excitement in the air from the punters who just wanted to have some fun on their night out. It sure was an exhilarating time to be alive. I was living the dream, and that was a great feeling. But despite all this success, or perhaps because of it, I had done nothing to solve my own addiction to the lifestyle that was continuing to take its toll on me. Could I dispel the nightmare I was inevitably conjuring? Could I live beyond the hubris that rock journalist Robert Hilburn had predicted would eventually doom me? We would soon find out.

CHAPTER TWENTY-SIX

THE ROAR OF THE LION
AND A NONSTOP GLOBAL ORGY

All across the USA

I WALKED INTO THE GARDEN OF time and saw the Lioness standing beside a tree. I had no fear but couldn't wait until I was entangled, ready to be torn apart. I could see the powerful sinews of her long, sleek muscles and caressed her powerful fangs, begging her to sink them into me, but when she did, with a low growl, I was set loose, and a paradise of passion carried my senses, sending them silently into a wilderness lost in sunshine and shadow. I burst forth from her jaws deep inside the forgotten land, dying a thousand times before the Lioness let go of her love, for her love was death and I was so near the edge.

The Lioness said not a word, her huge tongue licking me as waves of orgasm hunted my soul and would not, could not, let go. I was a prisoner, caught in the Lioness's smile. Gone was time; gone was ambition. Dance with me, for I have lost the Lioness's embrace. Die with me, the thousand deaths that flesh can die. But I was reborn, and the cycle remains unbroken. Writhing naked bodies dance among the white-hot burning flames as the Lioness purrs, for she holds sway here, and I am but a slave to my mistress.

If you want to know what I'm talking about, enter a world where white is black and black is white, for that's where the Lioness lives, feeding on human souls. Take heroin, add cocaine, pot, alcohol, and ecstasy, then get together with like-minded people and orgy as in Roman times. The sexual act and the drugs go hand-in-hand. Pleasure seekers of the world, unite, for we set sail and we are not coming back the same. The wedding feast is here, and I must tell of the forbidden journey where sanity is best lost. Abandon all reserve, for we orgy in the '80s, as that is all we have.

Many people were using the moment to discover their sexualities and private fantasies, and what better way to do so than to join in with rock 'n' roll, where there were no rules, the party was 24/7, and we could stretch, suspend, and fold time like it was elastic.

The Rebel Yell tour certainly took on dimensions in the sex-and-drug department that felt like the descriptions above. My manager, Bill Aucoin, did nothing to stop it, preferring to egg on our wild behavior, condoning it as he practiced his own edgy sexuality that most managers of the time knew nothing about. Bill's jaw would grind back and forth some days, the result of the previous night's cocaine binge. When he'd visit us at one of the promotional in-stores we'd do around the country, we would stand in a line behind the counter and place our fingers above our top lips to replicate his mustache, moving our jaws back and forth, imitating that sawing motion as a kind of salute.

All along the way, there were usually scenes of crazy fans hurling themselves at our car, sprawling on the hood or lying down in front to prevent us from moving. They screamed, they moaned, they grabbed us or one another, crying, "Oh my God," jumping up and down, pressing forward and overwhelming security, their red faces wet with tears, their screaming mouths begging for release. They ripped off what few clothes I had on and held their trophies aloft, then fought each other to keep the prize. It felt like Beatlemania all over again, except this time darker and more troubling.

The gigs had the same wild abandon as our audience found its voice, which usually entailed a scream. Edvard Munch's famous painting was on almost every face; a strange twisted skull with hands on either side, groping for God knows what. We moved around the U.S., virtual prisoners on our bus or in hotel rooms as the record boomed away on a thousand, nay, a million speakers. Many found their way to our rooms, and we obliged our lusts and theirs, the same young lust that knows no boundaries, with no end and no beginning, as it is insatiable. The few hours we traveled or played the shows gave us just the respite we needed to do it all over again the next day.

The "Rebel Yell" video and radio airplay had done their work well, but now it was time for a follow-up. When we'd finished recording the album, Aucoin had played it for a top New York DJ, who thought "Eyes Without a Face" was the obvious successor. During a two-day break from the shows, we met up with David Mallet in L.A. and concocted the blueprint for a new video. I recalled my affinity for the German Expressionist silent horror film *The Cabinet of Dr. Caligari*, and the strange, twisted nightmare sets suggested the psychotic world of the somnambulist killer.

Using that influence to create the concept, we shot a video a few weeks later in L.A., beginning with a shot of my disembodied head, coming in close on my eyes, filmed through flames to distort the picture. Then I descended a twisted staircase to enter a pit surrounded by fire. Silent, hooded monks dressed in black loomed on a raised circular plinth behind and around me. The video ended outside with Perri and me being blasted by a pressure hose you couldn't see. Finally, there was a shot of me standing with my fists in the air in triumph, kind of like Charlie Watts on the cover of the Rolling Stones album *Get Yer Ya-Ya's Out!*

During the two-day shoot, I listened to Creedence Clearwater Revival's "Green River" and "Keep on Chooglin' " over and over, which proved handy when Dennis Hunt, the *L.A. Times* critic, came to interview me during a break from filming and was disarmed, impressed to see my trailer rocking back and forth as I danced around to classic rock 'n' roll.

Wrote Hunt: "Idol, 28, is arrogant, abrasive and often snarlingly sarcastic. But he's still very likable. His intelligence and, believe it or not, sensitivity temper those other qualities, but his most distinguishing characteristic is his smoldering intensity. When talking about something he feels strongly about, he gets so wound up that he seems ready to explode."

I had held it together during the interview and was thrilled with the results.

IN THOSE DAYS, I WORE HARD contact lenses to correct my shortsight-edness. As the video for "Eyes Without a Face" was shot over a mara-thon forty-eight-hour span, by the time I'd flown to the next gig in Tucson, Arizona, I'd been wearing them for thirty-six hours. I hadn't slept that much—if at all. While waiting for the sound check, I went outside, lay down, and passed out on the cool grass verge outside the college venue. I was dressed in a Vivienne Westwood outfit with a Dickensian touch, and with my crumpled top hat, I must've looked like the Artful Dodger, which was the desired effect. However, after my eyes closed and I entered dreamland, I was blissfully unaware that I hadn't removed my contacts, until without warning I was awakened rather rudely by a sheriff pointing his gun directly at me.

"We don't allow no bums to sleep on the grass," he growled.

I heard his voice distant and hollow in my head. I opened my eyes but could only make out the outline of his weapon, while tears came pouring from my eyes. Something was wrong! I realized I had fallen asleep without taking the contacts out. You can scrape the cornea of your eye, exposing your nerve endings, making you ultrasensitive to the light. The pain was intense and my eyes were gushing. All the while, the cop kept saying something about bums not being allowed on the lawn.

"I'm with the band playing tonight," I offered.

"Well, let's take a look, buddy, but you better not be wasting my time," he said pointing out the way with the gun barrel.

We went into the building and found my road manager, George. "He's with us, all right," he told the officer with a glint in his eye, be-traying a worried expression.

"I don't believe you," the cop insisted. "Get everybody working here to line up on this stage and identify who this is."

I went to remove the lenses from my eyes that were literally stream-ing tears. "You! Don't move," he ordered, gun still drawn.

So the crew lined up in front of me, my eyes still dripping, as the cop asks, "Who is this bum?"

"The boss!" they answered in unison to the police officer's sur-prise, to which I added, "Right! Now, I'm taking these things out of my eyes because I think I'm going to need to go to a hospital. They're killing me."

So they rushed me to a hospital, where drops were put in to relieve the pain. Unfortunately, we had to postpone that night's gig. My eyes remained bandaged for two days, and only after that had my corneas healed enough for me to recommence playing.

When the "Eyes Without a Face" video debuted in June of 1984, it went to number one on MTV for six weeks. Add to that the over-the-top radio play for this twisted ballad, which was always paired with the Cars' "Drive" on the NY drive-time station, and we climbed into the Top Ten singles chart at *Billboard*. At one point that spring, we were at number 4 on the album chart and number 6 on the singles tally. After that, we began to play arenas. For ten months, we crisscrossed the States and Canada several times. Somewhere in the darkness, the Lioness roared her approval. I had become a massive star in the States, with a punk pedigree to boot. Everything was falling into place.

We rolled through the American heartland on a bus to nowhere, stealing through the night, caught up in a dream, inhaling it in and then blowing it out. City after city, town after town, and then continent after continent, on a never-ending ride at a worldwide rock 'n' roll fun fair, dazzled by the lights, buried in the sound, and caught in a crossfire hurricane. For all that, it was the songs that would sustain and soothe you, the magic moments written on the heart and soul. Every show was packed with frenzied fans, creating a charged atmosphere that is difficult to describe. Keith Forsey showed up at the Pine Knob show outside Detroit on June 2, and was knocked out by the scenes of mayhem in the crowd. He loved hearing the songs from our new album, expertly played by a well-oiled, road-tested band.

Steve Stevens was ablaze on this tour, firing bolts of lightning from his guitar rig like a musical god. Even my fans were really only just starting to realize what a great and subtle guitar player he is. My drummer, Thommy Price, thundered like a man possessed on "Rebel Yell."

All the band members had a great sense of humor. Steve was a marvelous mimic who imitated many colorful characters along the way, including our bus driver, Earl, whose CB handle was "Lonesome Hobo."

Steve would get on the CB radio when Earl wasn't driving and call the other truckers making believe he was Earl, with a high-pitched southern accent, calling himself "the Lonesome Homo," which would have the homophobic truckers crying out in disgust. It sounds silly now, but on a long day's journey into night, humor got you through to the next tour stop with at least part of your sanity intact.

CHAPTER TWENTY-SEVEN

JUST A PERFECT DAY

London

In July 1984, I traveled back to England in triumph as a solo sensation, unlike the has-been who had left three years before for a new chance. Perri was with me as we touched down at Heathrow in London. We were in the UK for an appearance on *Top of the Pops*, performing "Eyes Without a Face" together with Steve Stevens, with Perri dancing and hitting the background vocals behind me. The song was my breakthrough solo hit in the UK. To celebrate, some of Perri's dancer friends met us at the airport. We went to a flat and a friend got out what he said was "very strong Persian brown heroin." All of us did a line and everyone nodded out except our host and me, so we did another line. I remember five more lines before I touched the face of God.

All went black, and then began wild dreams of a pleasure palace. As king, I had set it up with warm surrounds, waterfalls, greenery, and sexual delicacies, inside a dome peopled with lovers whose naked, open lovemaking was de rigueur. There, I smoked my pipe, anointed with the best oils, surveying the scene: a Chinese opium dream. A pure sleep of the gods overcame me. But soon the water sounds increased and streamed down onto my warm, naked body. A flood of water caressed by sin. Sin screamed at the water, "I don't want this to end! Who dares destroy the king's reverie?"

I was coming to, in a bath, in cold water. *Why won't they let me sleep?* I wondered. All around me people were screaming, hitting me, ripping me from my dreams, from the abyss of the overdose I'd taken. Somebody came into the room, opened a blind, and saw that my lips had gone blue. I was dying. As they tried to save me I kept thinking, *Let me sleep, let me dream. I don't want to awake—I'm an emperor!* But they took me to the roof and walked me around and around for hours to stop me from falling into death.

As I CONTINUED MY DANCE ON the edge, Idolmania was sweeping the world. After the UK, it was on to Europe, Australia, Japan, and New Zealand. The album and singles took off seemingly everywhere, thanks to MTV's expanding international penetration. We received gold and platinum albums from many territories as the record became a global smash. Onward and onward in a blur we continued, the capitals of the world flying by—Sydney, London, Paris, Oslo, Frankfurt, Rome, Toronto, Washington, Dublin, Zurich, Tokyo. It was as if we were Time Lords from a *Dr. Who* TV pilot, mounting our time machine, the TARDIS, to enter a rock 'n' roll dimension. I was on a roll. Any resistance we'd felt in 1982 fell away as more people started to dig what I was doing.

While in England I made a visit to my parents in Bromley, partly for my father's sixtieth birthday, and also I hadn't been home for ages. I wanted to give my platinum *Rebel Yell* disc to my dad as a present, as a way of saying, *I fucking told you so*. As I told Neil Tennant for *Smash Hits*, "There you are, Dad. A million Americans have bought my record. Five hundred thousand Canadians have bought my record. So many hundreds of thousands of people in Australia have bought my record. And you told me I was a fool. My dad, he might be sixty years old, but my choice in life is to tell him: I was right. I've done something more than you can ever do. Which is that I did what I wanted. And I did it with the weapons of rock and roll."

I can see now I still had a really big chip on my shoulder about my dad's view of my chosen profession and how I would never be successful or happy doing it. Today I can appreciate a bit more about where my parents' generation was coming from, how all they had been through—the Depression, World War II, and post-war reconstruction—would limit one's belief that they could step outside of their accepted lot in life. Now I understand, we could dream big only because of what they went through.

I dreamt audaciously big. I also went to visit Chrysalis's London headquarters. Failing to see any sign of *Rebel Yell* on the wall upon entering the building, I proceeded to smash the office up as a sign of my disdain, leaving graffiti spray painted all over the walls. I'm sure the staff was appalled. I also trashed the record company apartment where I was staying. I felt they had sent me on this journey and, as far as I could see, I had returned with the goods they wanted, but there was no sign of respect for what I had accomplished, the goal I had set out to achieve.

I was the fool—jet lag and being hungover led to my manic and de-structive behavior—but we were working our balls off with very little downtime, and I felt that it was crucial that everyone involved with selling the album got off their collective backsides and really worked it with a purpose or got out of the way.

Chrysalis boss Terry Ellis could see we needed a break, so he in-vited us to stay for a few days at his home on Tortola, one of the Virgin Islands, before we returned to the U.S. to continue the tour. This is where I first heard the remix of the next proposed single, "Flesh for Fantasy," done by Gary Langan, who was one of the founders of Art of Noise, a band that seemed ahead of its time, with wild editing and off-the-wall sounds, which I liked. I had suggested him for the remix, but I was concerned because it would be the first remix done without me being present. I needn't have worried, as it came out great, featuring Steve's explosive guitar riff as a repeated flag entrance with a measured gap between each power chord. We started to use this remix as an intro in our stage show, and still do to this day. "Flesh" always seemed to be paired with Yes's "Owner of a Lonely Heart" on U.S. radio rotations. Coincidentally, Gary also mixed that track.

The record company wanted a video for "Flesh for Fantasy," and we sandwiched it into a three-day break between shows on the Silver-cup Studio soundstage in Astoria, Queens, across the bridge from Manhattan. Perri had organized a dance troupe of her own, working out of a place called the Cat Club a few blocks east of Sheridan Square. It was a cool hang, giving us a place to go that was ours. It was tiny, with a small stage where a group could play or Perri's dancers could showcase their routines.

The girls were already familiar with her choreography, so we decided to use them in the "Flesh" video to, no pun intended, flesh out some of the scenes, which were really just composed of me taking a glorified walk through some sets, which included a triangular-shaped tunnel and a futuristic cityscape.

We used a different director this time, an American named Howard Deutch, a John Hughes protégé who worked on the *Apocalypse Now* trailer and went on to direct such films as *Pretty in Pink*, *The Great Outdoors*, *The Replacements*, and *My Best Friend's Girl*. The budget was relatively small, and Howard took a bit of convincing to take on a rock video of the style we were going for. This was the second time we used the husband-wife team of John Diaz and T'Boo Dalton as producers, as they had worked on the "Eyes" video. Perri and I became extremely close with John and T'Boo. John likes to say the "Flesh" video was the most difficult video he ever produced. Jeff Stein didn't direct this one—Howie Deutch did—but Jeff is the reason it was so difficult to execute. Howie's entire crew was working for Jeff on another video that went over deadline. He had to push our shoot back and charter a LearJet to fly the crew back. On the day he was supposed to light the set, the director of photography, Tony Mitchell, arrived at 4 p.m., totally wasted because he hadn't slept in five days. Our first day ended up going thirty-six hours. The second day went about twenty-four hours. The final setup was a long dolly shot, and Tony told an incredulous John, "You gotta take over this shot. I'm blind." He couldn't see anymore. The pace of the last six days wrecked his vision.

One advantage to having a sizable female audience is if you are playing songs that are groove-oriented, it gets them in the pit of their stomachs and eventually gravitates to their loins. Then you are speaking a special language that most men will never get. My experience is that women can access their erogenous zones more easily when the music speaks this sensual tongue and they become relaxed. And needless to say, this was happening on the road on a nightly basis.

The quantity and quality of good-looking and sexy girls at the gigs was phenomenal. It made it nearly impossible to be faithful to anyone. It would be a lie to say anything else. Wherever we went, a whole different slew of women were available. If you weren't a sex addict at the start of the tour, you soon would be. Shit, the mind boggles at the thought of it. Hotel after hotel, gig after gig, a million scantily clad chicks all hopped up on excitement. Many of them had drugs, a great combination. It was nonstop sex, drugs, and rock 'n' roll music. You got a license to live fast and leave an incredible-looking corpse. After moonshine washed down with Mountain Dew, anything was possible.

In Rochester, New York, I was accused of "sexual deviancy," so I attended the pretrial hearing in a Vivienne Westwood tartan plaid suit that featured penis-and-balls buttons that blended in so well you would have had to really look hard to see them. No one noticed, and I denied being a "sexual deviant," but indeed that was exactly what they had on their hands. In this case, I was trying to get a girl out of my hotel room by saying she could only stay if she made it with the other girl I'd let in, who just happened to be younger and better-looking. When she wouldn't, and why not I don't know, I told her to leave and ended up throwing her out of the room, which was a mistake. I should have called the road manager. Later I would have a security guard, but back then I was on my own. The girl's case was thrown out, but the fact is, I should have known better.

Somewhere during this nonstop ten-month whirlwind, we paid a weeklong visit to Japan to do press, radio, and TV promotion. The Japanese record company worked our balls off from 9 a.m. until 11 p.m. every night during the week, with time off only to sleep. Suffering from jet lag and needing to have some fun in between the nonstop round of interviews, Steve and I, after the day's last interview, would go straight to a place called Lexington Queen, which was populated with Japanese, American, and European models. We did not return to our hotel rooms until four in the morning.

Every morning we'd arrive a few minutes late, and the Japanese company reps would throw a fit, as they worked on a very strict timetable with no room for deviations, whatever the reason. One day I was dressed in a traditional samurai outfit for a photo shoot, but apart from that, I had no contact with any Japanese culture except for having sex with a couple of local models in the hours when we should have been sleeping. On our last day, we got back to the hotel at our usual early dawn hour after a dinner with people from the Japanese label who had finally let their hair down and gotten pretty sloshed. We decided to pack and get our stuff down to the lobby, so we would, for once, be on time and waiting for them. They turned out to be a few minutes late, and we really gave them hell, prompting them to apologize profusely, bowing over and over until we burst out laughing. It took a while for them to understand that we were joking and didn't care that they were a few minutes late, but it fed our sense of humor to see them so mortified at fucking up their own schedule. After one more TV show on the way to the airport—they worked you until the last possible instant—it was sayonara, Japan.

A few months before the never-ending tour finally concluded, we released a fourth single, "Catch My Fall," with a video directed by David Mallet from a concept we came up with together. We shot the clip in London with a remix of the track that Steve and I produced, the *Rebel Yell* album continued rolling with more exposure on MTV and regular play in the dance clubs.

One night, I happened to meet one of Prince's lovely protégés, Vanity, a beautiful singer whose real name was Denise Katrina Matthews. I went to a screening of *The Last Dragon*, a martial arts movie she starred in, and that began a clandestine but short-lived affair. Her beauty was so undeniable, it was hard not to fall for her, which I did, forgetting for a moment about my relationship with Perri. Vanity's beauty could force you to stretch the truth to live in a dream world where all was possible. She attended a number of shows on the tour, and I was very excited about her, but I truly cared about Perri. Time, distance, and constant temptations meant that in the end, I was playing

a double game. Perhaps that was what I meant about being a double
agent in "Eyes Without a Face."

THE PLAN FOR THE FUTURE UNFOLDS slowly, delicately, like a shot
taken by a time-lapse camera of the gradual opening of a flower, each
petal blooming to reveal its brilliance like a Technicolor yawn. The
Lioness lazily licked her paws clean, enjoying her downtime as she
slowly gazed far off into the distance across a wide savannah.

It was the '80s, the midst of the Reagan go-go era, and plenty of
people were living as if there was no tomorrow. Nothing succeeded
like excess, so staying on a party edge was the norm. A haze of rock 'n'
roll splendor and increasingly hard drugs had blown the '70s away.

I carried a copy of the Jim Morrison biography *No One Here Gets
Out Alive* in my back pocket, in my search for a permanent derange-
ment of the senses. I had added cocaine into the equation in a major
way. I had snorted coke intermittently before, but it was way too expensive at the time and I didn't really need a speedy high. But over
the course of the Rebel Yell tour, I gradually started to use it more and
more frequently. I was now earning some real bread, and I used coke
to keep up with the pace of the tour, but also to stave off the body-
wracking heroin withdrawal. And, of course, to just plain party.

Also by now, it was impossible to ignore the fact that women, in
particular, would find me to be the subject of their attention wherever
I went. Flying on a silver bird high in the sky, we were continuing the
party in the first-class lounge, downing free booze and doing some
blow in the toilet.

At 30,000 feet in the air, as I entered the lavatory, a sexy bird of a
different kind took my arm and entered with me. I looked into her
excited eyes and could see the score. I laid out two lines of blow on the
top of the porcelain loo. The cool white gleam excited us and the pure
flakes called out to us as I took a prerolled bill out of my pocket. "Ladies first." She bent over to inhale the line, and her tight curvy bottom
was exposed by her action. I rubbed up her long leg and then slowly
placed my finger against her hole and worked her panties aside to rub

her wet pussy. As I slowly penetrated her with my finger, she gasped when the force of the line buckled her senses. "While you're down there, do the other one," I said, and unzipped my fly. My hardening cock pushed its way out and I covered it in saliva, slowly working it inside her now-drenched vagina. The effect of the second line smashed into her senses as my dick reached deep into her cavity. Slowly, I thrust my hips and we started to move in a grinding rhythm, matching thrust for thrust. She moaned out loud and I responded with a low, animalistic grunt, letting loose a throaty growl as the sweat dropped from my forehead onto her naked back. Then our mouths opened and the noise we made was a wild "*ahhhhhhh*" as we both reached a simultaneous climax. I kissed her; she straightened herself up and slipped out of the door, back into the plane. I did a line and then, after waiting a second, I followed her.

I was having a great time. My career was riding an amazing wave of success and I was plowing through it seemingly unscathed despite my best efforts to destroy myself. Today I can see I was on a tightrope hovering between life and death, but at the time I didn't care. I ignored the dangers. As I looked to move on to the next event in my music career, I would go down any road to find the muse. The perfect thing would have been to immediately follow up *Rebel Yell*, but Bill Aucoin had some other ideas that would take us into another world completely.

CHAPTER TWENTY-EIGHT

KING DEATH: AN ABORTED FILM PROJECT SIGNALS THE END OF AN IDOL MAKER

Hollywood

I WAS ONCE AGAIN RIDING A giant bird, headed to L.A. with Bill Aucoin and producer John Diaz. Earlier that year, at the "Flesh for Fantasy" video shoot, John had introduced me to the Hollywood producer Joel Silver. Joel was a very in-demand producer who had recently produced *48 Hours* and was fresh off the futuristic rock 'n' roll fable *Streets of Fire*, with Willem Dafoe and Diane Lane. Joel had expressed excitement at the possibility of working with me on a new film, and we were off to L.A. to meet him and a series of Hollywood studio moguls to sell them on a concept—one that I had yet to come up with.

While enjoying the first-class privileges of free food and booze, bullshitting various ideas back and forth, I suddenly remembered a novel I'd read, *King Death*, by Nik Cohn, someone who had some current cachet in Hollywood for writing the short story that served as the basis for *Saturday Night Fever*. The story involved an assassin whose handler/manager would send him out on various assignments, which I thought might be some kind of allegory about Elvis and Colonel Tom Parker. Rod Steiger, whom I'd always liked, struck me as perfect to play this older father figure. I wasn't sure how music would fit into it, but perhaps the central character could be a rock singer who doubled as a professional hit man.

Eddie, the book's title character, is asked, "How does it feel to kill?" He answers, "But it isn't killing. Death is a science, almost a vocation. I'd like to think I'm a performer." Indeed, Eddie's mystical power allows his targets to avoid the fear of death. They are, instead, transported to another realm after getting shot. "Death is a completion," Eddie says, finding fulfillment, satisfaction, and pride in each assignment he carries out. When a top TV entrepreneur named Carew chances to see Eddie in action, he takes him in as his protégé, and together they plan to bring his gift to America. After overcoming several obstacles, they literally ride to glory on the Deliverance Special, a train carrying King Death and his entourage across the U.S., until Eddie undergoes a disturbing change. "Part nightmare, part modern-day fairy tale, *King Death* is a shocking tale in which perversity, violence, and the contradictory morality and immorality of American culture are explored with striking power." So reads the quote on the book's inside jacket.

As we crossed the country at 30,000 feet, I talked myself into believing, with some plot twists, that this could be more than just another rock star vehicle, like Prince's *Purple Rain* or Madonna's *Desperately Seeking Susan*.

Aside from his managerial talents, Bill Aucoin had been a TV producer, and the story had a vague parallel to my own rock 'n' roll career, with Bill sending me out on various assignments in my chosen vocation. Over the next few days, we proceeded to float our over-the-top idea to the Hollywood studio heads we met.

In Los Angeles, we met with Silver, and when I told him my idea, it shocked me that he immediately liked it. Shit, it was just a daft idea that I'd concocted on the plane ride over. The next day, I was feeling pretty rough from the excesses of the night before, but somehow I managed to straighten up. Joel picked Bill, John, and me up at the Bel Age in a stretch limo and we began to visit the major studios—names I knew from the credits of every movie I had ever seen. I pitched the idea to all of them pretty much as I had done with Joel. At each meeting, I spoke for thirty minutes or so, mostly flying by the seat of my pants, improvising wildly whenever I was asked about the plot or characters. Our first meeting was at 20th Century Fox and it went extremely well. Upon arriving at Universal for our next meeting, there was already a message waiting for Joel that Fox was prepared to offer a development deal. But the Universal pitch was completely over the top. The executives vowed not to let us leave their offices until we signed a guarantee with them, but we had another scheduled meeting, so we left, with Joel promising to call as soon as we reached our next appointment. John and I ended up taking the meeting while Joel spent almost the entire time negotiating a deal with Universal on a phone in another room.

The offer included a guaranteed budget of $10 million for the film and another $1 million for the sound track album. I was pretty amazed when Joel came in and whispered that we now had a deal with Universal, but I kept it together and continued delivering my spiel to the Hollywood suits gathered in front of us. We never even bothered to make it to our last appointment. I couldn't believe how well this was going. It was nuts. I was just glad that somehow I had made it through the meetings, and relieved they had been such a success.

Back at the Bel Age, Bill had taken a big suite, where he proceeded to party for several days, out of his mind smoking a water pipe filled with crack cocaine amidst his coterie of young boys. The smell in the corridor outside his suite was so pungent that the hotel threatened to evict us all.

At first everything seemed to go smoothly with the film project, but before long, things began to unravel. Bill wanted more control and was willing to lose Joel Silver's involvement to get it. One day, Bill came to me and said Joel and John Diaz were out and that we would be making the movie independently. My immediate instinct was that this would be the death knell for *King Death*, because Joel Silver, not Bill, was the one who had the connections and the ability to actually get this movie made. Joel seemed to truly believe in the idea, which is so important when one is exploring the least-trodden path. I went along with my manager, but I could tell, once we began meeting with other possible producers, the idea just didn't make all that much sense to them under the circumstances. Joel was nice enough to sell the idea back to us, but the absence of his clout led to a dead end.

I spent six months in Hollywood that I could instead have spent writing the next album with Steve Stevens. By the time we did start collaborating on new material, I was a full-on cocaine and heroin addict. The drugs were ruling me. All the aimless time I'd spent after Joel stepped away from the project had left me with three months of dead time that I used to feed my drug addiction. I started smoking coke, which is its own form of King Death.

AFTER SIX MONTHS IN L.A. CHASING a dream that was never realized, I returned to New York a seriously debilitated and dependent person. Aucoin continued to smoke coke himself and didn't return to New York with me, leaving me without a manager. For a while, I managed myself, thinking that when Bill eventually came out of his drug stupor he would return to his Olympic Tower apartment and we would resume our work together. It was about a year before he actually returned, but he was never the man he was before, and I felt the need to move on. *King Death* was actually the end of our working relationship, which lasted from 1979 to 1986. What a shame. Drugs and ego dealt the deathblow, and that should have been a lesson to me.

Bill Aucoin was a fantastic personality who lived fiercely for the moment. But when that meant he was no longer doing the work with me, I was left to my own devices. Fortunately, Bill had populated his office with talented young ladies such as Kathie Dowling, his assistant; Stephanie Tudor, his production assistant; and Brigid Waters, his director of finance. Those three really held the fort for him and continued to be very loyal to his management schemes. That meant, in terms of day-to-day operations, I could still rely on their professional expertise, which was considerable. In fact, Brigid Waters still works very closely with me to this day.

In the meantime, I was continuing to work on the follow-up to *Rebel Yell*. After all, I had never needed a manager to tell me what to sing or write. But I would need much more than even Bill could ever give me to survive the hell the immediate future had in store.

CHAPTER TWENTY-NINE

TOP OF THE WORLD, MA

West Village, New York City

AFTER I RETURNED TO NEW YORK, Perri and I moved apartments. First to Jones Street, and then, due to fans hanging outside our front door, to Barrow Street near the West Side Highway, where our window overlooked the end of Christopher Street in the West Village. No one hung outside there because it was so far out of the way of everything. Barrow Street was the first place of my own that I had the money to decorate, so naturally, I bought a black couch, black carpet, and some red velvet drapes to go with the white walls and high ceilings. The black carpet proved to be a source of amusement, as I would sometimes drop a black T-shirt to the floor and it would remain "lost," sometimes for weeks, until I opened the curtains and discovered it camouflaged in the darkness.

Unfortunately, our life together in that Barrow Street apartment wouldn't last long. In the gray days of late winter 1986, Perri moved out, leaving me heartbroken, depressed, and alone. Our split was my own fault. My uncaring behavior drove her away. When I returned from the Rebel Yell tour, I carried on as if the tour had never ended, following my own desires, sexual and otherwise, when I should have been spending time with the love of my life.

Now, as I prepared to record my third solo album, eventually to be called *Whiplash Smile*, my songwriting was driven by the almost overwhelming loss of being separated from Perri. When I go back and listen to this album now, I can feel the aloneness in the very pores of the record. The eerie windswept echoes, the cold plate reverb, the brittle drum sounds, the lost voice echoing into oblivion.

My intent was to use my sadness over losing Perri to the album's advantage. I tried to evoke some of the great '50s spirits who took heartbreak and made it their own; legends like Elvis, Gene Vincent, and the late, great Johnnie Ray. My cover of Booker T. Jones and William Bell's Memphis classic "I Forgot to Be Your Lover," which was the album's first single, is all about saying how much I desperately needed someone.

I first heard "To Be a Lover" on a George Faith album of old soul songs given the reggae treatment by producer Lee "Scratch" Perry. Geoff Travis, who ran Rough Trade, an independent record store and groundbreaking label, turned me on to it back in 1977 in London. He knows his reggae, and years later I was still listening to my copy of it. The credits said that "To Be a Lover" was written by George Faith, although I later found out about the original, an early-'60s Stax Records recording by William Bell. While considering songs for my new album, I thought to myself, *What if you sped it up double-time and gave it an R&B/rockabilly feel rather than the slow reggae groove?* Keith got the idea right away. We went to work, realizing our gut feelings and creating something very special. With its electronic Juno bass and wild Richard Tee piano stylings, "To Be a Lover" was a definite statement that we were sticking with some of the R&B flavor we had previously used on "Hot in the City" and "Mony Mony." The track was exciting, upbeat, and serious to dance to. Steve Stevens played great on this track and really delivered on the remix, putting a killer flag riff at the beginning that wasn't on the single. He toughened up the remix, adding that extra ingredient that is a staple of Idol recordings.

After the "To Be a Lover" single came out, we played it at a party thrown by Dan Aykroyd's brother Peter. At the party, a long-haired chap came up to me to tell me how much he enjoyed what we'd done with the song. It was legendary Stax Records guitarist Steve Cropper, who had played on the original version. He was a hero to all of us, so his liking our version was a great boost.

"Sweet Sixteen" is a heartfelt lament with a story behind it. While making *Rebel Yell*, I read an article about the Coral Castle in Florida, built by a man from Latvia named Edward Leedskalnin. Ed was left standing at the altar by his bride-to-be, so he split Europe for America and, after contracting tuberculosis, made his way down to the warmer climes of Homestead, Florida. It was then he that began constructing an impressive monument made out of massive limestone slabs. A nine-ton slab standing on its side acts as a revolving gate that moves with just a touch of the finger. A giant moon is a functioning rocking chair, also carved from stone. The story goes that Ed supposedly levitated the blocks into place, since no one seemed to help him do it. A truck would arrive with a slab and he would ask the driver to walk away, and when the driver returned, the slab was on the ground with no one else around. This man, with only a fourth-grade education, worked alone at night by lantern light, and stood just five feet tall, weighing only a hundred pounds. He would take people on a tour of the Coral Castle for ten and twenty-five cents, and when someone asked him why he had built it, he would simply say, "It's for my Sweet Sixteen," referring to his lost bride-to-be who had so heartlessly left him. It was a coral memorial to her. "Sweet Sixteen" is mine for Perri.

Whiplash Smile had a lot of potential. It should have been a worthy successor to *Rebel Yell*, an album featuring a real band working, rehearsing, and recording songs collaboratively. But I insisted that I should be the only one writing the songs, and in true punk fashion I insisted on doing something completely different, making this album a synthesizer album. This might have worked if I'd been at the top of my game, but overall I slacked off. Left to my own devices, I fucked up and lost sight of what I could be. I threw away my guidebook of how to make a record. The result was an unfocused performance from yours truly, with a writing and recording process that resulted in alienating my partner Steve Stevens.

Ever since the *King Death* debacle and Bill Aucoin's unceremonious departure from my life, I had been descending into a state of virtual slavery to drugs. And with Perri gone also, the situation went from bad to worse. Usually, the manager acts as the voice of reason and keeps the artist cool, but in L.A., I saw Bill Aucoin run amok, and I did not hesitate to dive right in after him, ending up hopelessly wasted.

I replaced the emptiness I felt upon losing Perri with MORE. I built a massive monument to her with sex and drug addiction. I realized that I needed to stop taking heroin, but unfortunately, in order to deal with the withdrawal, I substituted cocaine instead. I had no intention of going through that hell. I preferred to stay in my own coke purgatory rather than having to face going cold turkey. After a while, my nose became so bloody that I reverted to smoking coke instead. From there, it was all downhill.

I would hole up in my apartment smoking and staying awake, at one point for three straight weeks. My concentration on making the album diminished. Everywhere I went I would carry around a small satchel with my pipe, some rocks to smoke, and a butane torch. Even when I made it to the studio, I shoved the satchel in the bathroom, hid it under the sink, and took hits as needed, not thinking the smell of coke would permeate the whole complex. Keith did his best to cover up the stench by spraying the bathroom with air freshener, but it was an exercise in futility. Nothing could prevent anyone in the building from knowing what was going on, particularly Mick Jagger and Dave Stewart, who were in another studio down the hall.

J. D. Dworkow was a great roadie and friend of mine who would come to my apartment to pick me up for my recording sessions. Sometimes I left him waiting more than three hours, as I couldn't get out without doing another hit of coke, smoking a joint, then freebasing. I would rationalize this behavior by telling myself that, since I was paying J.D., his time was my time. That's not usually the way I treat people, but I was so hooked, I could justify any action, no matter how heinous. I was fast losing my real personality under a ton of blow, but I couldn't see that. All I could think of was the next time I would be getting high and trying to avoid any comedown.

I had a drug dealer, Fred, who delivered, and if he couldn't make it for some reason, in my apartment building was a guy who also sold coke, so I never really lacked for a supply. I'd wake up, do a line, and then smoke a joint to start off the day. After that, I would cook up the coke as a way to relieve my bloody nose.

Eventually, paranoia set in, and I suffered delusions of being watched or filmed. I heard voices, as if people were in the apartment next to me, above me, or below me, and were plotting against me. Sometimes I could see ghostly figures of people just standing around in my apartment; a couple of schoolgirls in one corner; a businessman with a briefcase in another. They didn't interfere with my coke smoking, so I ignored them.

Finally, all the voices, spectral visions, and drug-fueled paranoia got so bad I called my good friend Bobby Belenchia to talk me down and convince me I was delusional, and that what I was thinking and seeing wasn't real. When he came to the door, he put his finger over his lips and walked me into a small guest bathroom, where he turned on the sink taps full blast and, as the noise echoed around the hollow, high-ceilinged room, began to talk to me as if anyone listening or recording us covertly wouldn't be able to hear us. His performance was masterful, just like in a spy movie. I burst out laughing and suggested I do a hit as we talk. Bobby agreed, probably thinking that I would be easier to reason with when I was comfortably in my stoned element. We walked along the wood floor in front of the bathroom doorway and down the three steps that led to the spot in the main living room where I had my pipe, torch, and rocks cut up and ready to smoke.

We talked while I smoked, as Bob did his best to explain that I was high as a kite and was going to have to accept that the coke was making me imagine everything. Just as he was explaining this, I saw what looked like the shadow of a large individual on the long, pale wood floor that led to the front door of my apartment. Bobby saw it, too, prompting us to crawl to the door and open it, only to be confronted by an actual, real-life large bloke standing up against the door with a beer in his hand. We both screamed at once in horror and I instantly slammed the door shut.

"Don't ever tell me I'm imagining this," I said, and Bob agreed. We both returned to the living room floor. There had been someone standing there, I wasn't imagining that. I later found out that the people in the apartment at the end of the hall were having a party and could smell the burning, acrid scent of freshly torched rocks. One of the drunken revelers had stood outside my door to see what was going on. For me, this was confirmation that I wasn't just imagining these things, which in my condition was convenient validation of my decision to carry on my self-destructive lifestyle with renewed vigor.

TRAIPSING AROUND NEW YORK WITH THAT satchel on my shoulder, I went from one bad scene to another. It's not the best idea to walk around the city high on that amount of blow because your mood shifts quickly. One day I found myself at a Rolling Stones recording session as out of my mind as I could be. Keith Richards and Ronnie Wood were there, and in the corner was the classic soul shouter Don Covay. I whipped into the bog to do a quick hit, hoping to level out, but that wasn't the effect, and soon after, I found myself having words with Keith. I went into a tirade about something or other, and I could see Ronnie smirking. Of course Keith knew I was pretty fucked up. He wrote in his autobiography, *Life*, that he doesn't like people under the influence of smoking blow and I don't blame him. I feel awful about my mood that day, since I was a guest at their recording session. I'm sad to this day that I let myself get that out of control. After pissing off one of my childhood heroes, I realized I was better off staying at home if I was going to be that high.

I was safer on my own in the dead of night, stoned out of my gourd with the red drapes shut, sitting nude on my black carpet, watching pornography 24/7, which somehow seemed to make sense on that much blow. At that moment, no one and nothing else mattered, only what I was thinking to myself.

Once the pipe split in pieces and I had to gaffer it up so it would work for a short time. Then I realized I was smoking tape instead of rocks. In the dead of night, I walked to the local twenty-four-hour store that sold pipes and butane. After making my purchase, the guy behind the counter looked at me quizzically and warned, "You're not doing too much of that stuff, are you?" "No," I told him, rushing back to my apartment in case anyone tried to stop me. I had become so recognizable from MTV that it wasn't just rock fans who knew me. In that state I didn't want anyone to see me, lest they interrupt my quick visit for supplies before my high dissipated, leaving me with a massive comedown on some side street.

SUDDENLY, I'M WIDE-AWAKE. A FORM OF consciousness returns and I find myself sitting on the floor in the same spot I fell asleep, head forward, hands curled around the pipe, still clutching the butane torch. With an instant click, I'm back in action, the blue-hot, white-hot flame dancing in midair as I place a rock on the inflammable glass at the top of the device. The center of the multitude of screens is carefully spaced apart that will slow the dissolving, melting coke as I chase it down through the sides of the pipe, carrying out a choreographed movement with my hand and butane torch. The torch is a white-hot symbol that would look perfect in the hands of the Statue of Liberty, which proudly stands in the Hudson just a few miles from my apartment window. I light the rock at the top of the stem, which begins to melt, the flame dancing around the stem in a motion I have repeated so many times it has now become ingrained; a measured, routine motion. I chase it down, follow it around, catch it, and burn it while the white smoke billows in the see-through glass, making its way into the bowl. I slowly inhale and the world becomes brighter, the mind expands, and gradually, I'm back in a state of grace.

Fourteen seconds, only fourteen. I hear in my mind the Chinese voice of Benny Gleek, the base guru, the one who uttered the immortal teaching on the correct amount of time to hold in a hit. Like a kung fu master, Benny had made a fortune in some business or other, and now spent his days and nights freebasing. Now, in his stead, I sit alone in my own reverie, enjoying the solitude where time is mine and I am beholden to no one but the white rocks that twinkle their message to "smoke me" in the low light of the white-hot flame. "Top of the world, Ma," I echo James Cagney in *White Heat* as I exhale.

Finally, after a couple more hits, I rise from my position and muse to myself that taking this shit is like diving from a board into empty space, guessing whether you'll land or not. What fucking time is it? Is it day or night? I've no idea. I stagger to the window to open the deep royal red velvet drapes, standing on the black carpet. I steady myself as my head spins for a second, and when it clears, I pull the curtains back to see that it is night and there are ten thousand men marching down Christopher Street to the West Side Highway. They walk in unison in a silent candlelit march to mourn the dead and spread the fight against AIDS, all of it right beneath my window. An entire way of life seems as if it is on the verge of extinction as a deadly disease strikes down members of the gay community. No one can anticipate how bad it might get. The world shakes. Who would be next? For the moment, WE MARCH AND SHOW OUR SOLIDARITY, according to the placards on display. After a while, the vigil continues and I shut the curtains, thinking about the living and the dead. I hear a voice inside my head—*I'm waiting*—and I forget the march, forget time, pathos, and empathy, and return to where I was sitting. I take another hit, as I know the pipe will have cooled.

I BEGAN TO ENJOY THE STRANGE solitude that came with shutting out the world. If I stepped outside my door, I would expose myself to coming down and being inexorably confronted with the pressures of an overpowering celebrity life that was turning into an out-of-control circus.

Before the success of *Rebel Yell*, I could move about pretty much as I pleased. Now I was a prisoner of that fame. The level of celebrity was unlike anything I'd ever experienced. And so I took some shortcuts to maintain for myself at least an illusion of choice while locking myself out, with the rest of the world clamoring to get in. With my drugs, I could still roam far and wide in my mind without having to worry about anyone disturbing my reverie. I was dancing with myself.

I should have been in a rehab facility, but I had convinced myself that I enjoyed being a drug addict and the weird, lonely world I created. It compounded my feelings of alienation from the world that welcomed the fantasy of me on their living-room TVs but wouldn't particularly care for the real me in my current state.

When I did venture out to some function, I would require bodyguards to accompany me. I could never be quite sure what was going to happen as I went in and out of places. The MTV audience was so large that I could be accosted at any moment, and scuffles and disturbances would break out if I hung around one spot too long.

Whether or not the bodyguards were protecting me or protecting the people from me is a hard one to figure out, but the old informality I had enjoyed when I first came to New York was a thing of the past. If I went to a club like Limelight, I would have to be ushered to the upstairs VIP section behind a red velvet rope that cut off access to where I was sitting. I would have to invite people to step over the rope just to occupy the same space as me. This sort of power may sound like fun, but I loved the freedom of being a punk rocker, and this stardom trip was a whole different ball game.

I ventured out one New Year's Eve, toasted from making the album and still reeling from the film that didn't happen. I went to a party at Limelight and found myself upstairs in the VIP section. A couple of English birds I knew came up, motioning that they wanted to join me. I had been having a bit of a fling with one of them, but nothing serious or regular. In truth, I had grown tired of her and had been hoping to meet someone else on that night, so I shook my head no. I could see she was hurt by my rebuff, and it made me feel vile. I soon realized I was burnt out and drug-sick, and not in any mood to hang, or perhaps I was embarrassed by the "daggers" I was now getting from both of them, so I slipped out the back way, went home, and decided to have a quiet night by myself. Who gave a damn if it was New Year's Eve anyway?

When I arrived at my apartment, I wasn't going to take or smoke anything, since I felt pretty knackered. But then I heard a knock on the door. I looked through the security lens and saw it was one of my bodyguards, who had only worked for me previously on a couple of occasions, outside in the corridor with the English girl I'd just left behind at the Limelight. "What did you bring her here for?" I said without opening the door, asking them both to please leave, as I didn't feel like having any company. Well, the girl didn't split—seems she had taken some ecstasy. I was getting increasingly annoyed that someone I had been paying to protect me would bring this girl to my home. I tried ignoring them, but the two just wouldn't leave. After an hour, I threatened to call the police, and while this succeeded in chasing away my bodyguard, he didn't take her with him. She started pounding on my door—she wouldn't let up. I called the police, but they didn't want to get involved. After much cajoling and explaining who I was, they finally showed up and restrained her so that I could open the door and talk to them. I tried to explain, and after a while the cops finally began to believe my story. I told them I didn't want her arrested, but she was obviously a bit nuts and was not about to leave voluntarily. All the while she was hysterically crying and moaning.

While figuring out what to do, one of the cops engaged me in conversation. "Is this a crazy night, or what?" I offered. "This is nothing," responded the officer. "We just came from a place where a nude couple stopped the elevator in between floors to have sex. Another resident rang for the elevator, and for some reason, the doors opened despite the elevator being stuck between floors. The resident wasn't paying attention, and when the doors opened, he plunged to his death. The girl he was with just managed not to follow him."

"Shit," I said. "This is nothing compared to that."

The girl still wouldn't leave, and it took three cops to haul her away, struggling to shove her into the elevator at the end of the corridor. I started to relax, but five minutes later, the buzzer went off in my apartment. It was the cops calling from the ground-floor intercom, and judging from the background noise, they were still trying to subdue her.

"Just tell her you love her!" the policeman shouted into the intercom.

"But I don't," I answered.

"That doesn't matter," he said. "Just do it!"

So I did, and that seemed to finally get her away from my apartment. So much for my desire for a quiet New Year's Eve alone.

CHAPTER THIRTY

RETURN TO SPLENDOUR

West Village, New York City

As the *Whiplash Smile* sessions progressed, I became even more volatile. Zool continued to rear his ugly head. One day, disagreeing with something Brendan Bourke had said, I threw an unopened Coca-Cola can at him, which just missed, violently exploding against the wall. My mood could shift rapidly and people never knew exactly which Billy Idol they were talking to. It was all taking a heavy toll on the creative process. Earlier on, when recording "To Be a Lover," I was having a rough day standing at the mic in the studio. We used to grind up coke with a Deering mill, using the large size that holds three grams. I had the top of the grinder off and was holding the bottom that was filled to the brim in my left hand, in the process of trying to record a take. Keith was trying to encourage me, but my mood was foul. I eventually threw a wobbler, kicking both the mic stand and the lyrics stand all over the studio, my arms waving as I shouted obscenities while maintaining a firm grip on the grinder.

"That's my boy," said Keith Forsey to the engineer behind the glass. "He didn't spill a drop of blow during that whole tantrum!"

I guess you can sense how unhinged all of this was getting. I was spending hours in my dark apartment with masturbatory fantasies bleeding into real life, a kid from Bromley in Kent alone and out of his mind in New York, gradually going more and more insane, out of control on a mind-numbing cocktail of drugs without anyone who had any power to make me see sense.

Everyone around me knew that I was in trouble, and they asked Keith Forsey to come to my Barrow Street apartment to try to reason with me and convince me that I needed help. Keith agonized over coming to see me, because he knew how volatile I could become at any moment.

When Keith arrived I let him into the apartment and into the living room, where instead of sitting down he stood right in front of me. I could see he was about to give me a massive heart-to-heart talk. I suppose I knew instinctively what he was going to say, so I spoke first, conceding that I needed to go to a hospital to sort myself out. He looked at me with astonishment and his mouth dropped open in disbelief at how reasonable I was being. "I can't believe you've said exactly what I was coming here to say to you. It took me hours to build up the courage to try to say what you just said to me, you asshole."

"Let's just do some hits today and I'll go tomorrow," I laughed. Keith went off to get Brendan, and in that time I split and managed to do a runner, leaving Keith's intervention attempt in shambles as well as everyone around me very concerned about my well-being.

At the same time, I still hadn't heard from Bill Aucoin. It's no wonder he couldn't bring himself to come back and manage me. He was in this same state of mind, but to the power of ten.

When Aucoin finally did return to New York after his L.A. bender, it was to carry on partying. I was having trouble accepting that Bill had stepped up his partying to such a degree that managing me was no longer possible. I guess I thought that we were true partners and that our relationship would continue. But now, without Bill and without Perri, I was left to my own devices, which meant basically doing what Bill was doing: surrendering to the void.

Bill's associates Brigid and Brendan might have given up on him, but thankfully they didn't abandon me when I needed them more than ever, after I experienced another psychotic event. This one frightened me. Because of the supposed demons I could see and hear, I locked myself into a closet and wouldn't emerge until Brigid and Brendan coaxed me out. That's when I finally agreed to be hospitalized and enter Beth Israel. For the moment, I'd had enough.

I lasted only ten days, and then I checked myself out, slipping past Brigid and Brendan in the lobby. I was back, off to new adventures. Why did I check out so soon? The monsters had receded, and I convinced myself there was nothing wrong with me. I'd just taken a little bit too much, that's all. At least that was my rationalization. I couldn't pin myself down. I was stuck in a revolving door, going from one drug to another.

Brendan and Brigid stepping in to help me was due in part to their kindly, sympathetic natures, but also due to the fact that my dad was breathing down their necks in the form of letters and phone calls from the UK. It was only a matter of time before word of my condition got back to my parents in England. My dad came to New York in an attempt to save me from myself.

He arrived carrying a big walking stick to symbolize the purpose of his mission. He didn't need the crutch, he was here with conviction, like Christ come to cleanse the temple! I was glad to see him, as I needed a break from my shenanigans. We were finalizing the album, the cover art, etc., so I didn't mind straightening out a bit. My dad's arrival was great because it was our first time alone in years. I was in the throes of serious addiction, so I made a big effort before he arrived to rewire my brain and turn myself into a slightly different person—at least for the time being. After going from extreme to extreme, how can you stop when you've made yourself believe that what you're doing is fine or even normal? But I had to come down to earth and get a hold of myself for his arrival.

He tried to reason with me and to become involved in my financial affairs. He had worked as an accountant and had built his own business, and so I knew he understood the language of financial matters.

I was lucky that Brigid, who had worked at Chrysalis before working for Bill's company, decided to continue working with me as my business manager. This allowed my business affairs to continue without interruption, and there was no lack of guidance there, since Brigid and my dad got on well. She is an excellent organizer and took on much of the tour management with first-rate business acumen.

I realize now that my dad's focus on my business matters when he came to see me as I struggled with my health in the throes of drug addiction was his way of relating to me and trying to connect with me. He was looking out for my overall welfare in the best way he could. I appreciated that I had a great soul on my side. His visit truly meant the world at that time: he may well have saved my life.

Dad was great, staying with me for three weeks, although I probably drove him just about nuts, listening to the collected solo works of Alan Vega all day and every night. At one point, my dad asked for a sandwich to eat while we were at the Hit Factory, and they ordered out from the Carnegie Deli, which sent over one of their huge chicken sandwiches. Dad made a smaller sandwich from the giant one they delivered and put the remains in my fridge, still dining on it weeks later. He even took some of it on the plane with him for a snack when he went back to England.

My parents had been worried about me for a long time. My mum had visited me earlier in the year, when we attended a wedding together. At the time, I was snorting coke and heroin, but not in front of her. So I was stoned and trying to maintain. A few days after the wedding, we went to see Les Paul play at his club Fat Tuesday's. That's where I got him to autograph the Les Paul Jr. guitar I used to play onstage. It's now so valuable I no longer play it for fear someone will steal it. On the way back from the club, I came very close to trying to get out of our car while it was moving, at about twenty miles an hour. There was other traffic around so I didn't attempt it, but the fact that I would even consider it makes me realize how little regard I had for myself and for others during that period. I could have easily been injured or killed myself—in front of my mother, no less.

The album and remixes were almost done and the cover art was starting to come together. I drew a planet with rings around it, placing the needle and arm of a record player as if the sound was in the groove of those rings. I also drew the RETURN TO SPLENDOUR circle with the yin and yang and the cross with PILGRIM written beneath it for the inside sleeve. Following my DIY punk ethos, I had designed most of it myself, however well or shitty it turned out. I was assured by the record company's art department that the vinyl disc would look gold, but wouldn't you know it, par for the course, it came out looking like diarrhea. Foiled again, another "oh bollocks" moment, but there wasn't enough time to play around or change it.

Whiplash Smile was ready to be shipped to stores. I was ragged but functioning as another tour loomed in the near future. I was determined to slow down.

I WAS EXCITED ABOUT THE PROSPECT of making videos to support the new album and having the band play live, but I needed a manager. Through my lawyer, Stu Silfen, I met and secured the services of Freddy DeMann, Madonna's manager, to replace Bill Aucoin, who remained missing in action. Signing with Freddy was seen, within the business, as a bit of a coup since it looked to the outside world that, despite managerial changes and the inevitable rumors and questions, everything was fine and the new album was about to come out. Freddy's first order of business was to arrange a tour for the spring and summer of '87.

Freddy was about forty at the time, shorter than me, graying at the temples, sometimes quiet, but sharp as a tack. His wide, searching eyes would see all and know all, but he didn't always let on that he knew what I was thinking. Diminutive in height, but a giant in business know-how, Freddy could pull off whatever he promised, and I had confidence in him being able to help sell *Whiplash Smile*. For a brief moment, I considered calling the album *Fatal Charm*, but Freddy said I had the right title and not to second-guess myself. I agreed, and it felt good to have a sounding board again.

The promotion for *Whiplash Smile* began in earnest in September. I did a video for the first single, "To Be a Lover," with David Mallet directing once again. The clip was set in a boxing ring, using the idea from Elvis Presley's comeback special, where he played on a square stage, as its rock 'n' roll reference point. We shot the video in England, and after we finished the shoot, my mum and dad whisked me off to a vacation in Majorca, a Mediterranean island off the coast of Spain. This took me away from my immediate surroundings of New York, where I was open to temptation and the possibilities of succumbing to that drug world.

Freddy had introduced me to a young Australian chap named Neil Bradbury to work with me on a daily basis and he, also, came out to Majorca. Neil and I had to acquaint ourselves with each other very quickly, because "To Be a Lover" had just been released, and there was plenty of promotional work to do. We were immediately in the fray, and time was of the essence. The luxury of getting to know each other had to be put on the back burner for the moment.

During the second week in Majorca, I had a young lady visitor named Anita. She was a singer in a band and was one of the backing vocalists in the "To Be a Lover" video. She was a gorgeous Indian/English girl who could outdrink me and we had become quite friendly. We enjoyed swimming, and the first night she was there, we both ended up walking fully clothed into the sea, me in my leather trousers. Each day, we would swim across the bay to another inlet with a large, prominent rock on which we would lie in the sun before swimming back. We generally relaxed and enjoyed each other's company. We sometimes visited the nude beaches and had fun in the sand and surf. The pressures of making the album and dealing with my change in management began to slowly fade away.

But work was not so far off. My British/European publicist, Sharon Chevin, soon arrived on the island and brought some journalists with her for interviews and pictures to promote the album's international release. Some cool photos were taken in the golden-hour sun that effectively masked the physical effects of the last few months. That kicked off the imminent album release in a relaxed and beautiful setting. Eating properly and swimming every day had brought me back to a decent state of health.

Throughout my stay, though, I was coughing up thick, dark phlegm from my lungs, which showed me just how much I had been abusing myself over the past few years. The long, hot sunshine days blurred into drunken nights and passionate squabbling with Anita, followed by makeup sex in the sand dunes of the nude beaches or in the sea in full view of the public. My lungs slowly expelled the black mush that had been accumulating, and my mind and body started to realize that by hook or by crook, I had kicked heroin and was now ridding myself of the nasty coke-smoking habit.

I enjoyed being with my parents in Majorca, but I was in rock 'n' roll mode and couldn't completely turn off the reality that my album was about to be released, with the underlying anxieties and concerns about how it would be received. I knew I had to stay on my toes when dealing with the very sharp English music journalists. With them around, I could not afford to switch off my mind entirely, which would have been nice. But the compressed nature of time in rock 'n' roll is such that things need to be done right at the moment of conception.

I went with my parents to a club for older people featuring guest musicians, and my mum asked me to sing a couple of songs. That meant being in front of an audience, and I had to be the Billy Idol that people expected. Though I was in Majorca as William Broad, even my parents at times still wanted me to manifest the onstage Billy Idol. This was jarring to me in the vacation setting. When I'm Billy Idol, I'm wired differently than William Broad. William Broad can quietly sit and read his history books, while Mr. Hyde shakes it onstage. It's a dichotomy in my personality. It's not that I'm putting on anything when I'm Billy Idol; I'm just reaching in and pulling out my extrovert self.

After that two-week break, I was in much better shape. I was off heroin and coke, but I was still drinking quite a bit. I had gone from the swings to the slide, but at least I had begun to try to get a hold of myself instead of being completely out of control and scaring all my friends and loved ones half to death.

By the time I returned to the States, *Whiplash Smile*, which I'd begun recording in June 1985, had been released; the LP on October 15, 1986, and the CD on December 10. This staggered release was how it was done in those early days of producing CDs, in part because record labels offered reduced royalties on CD sales, thievery under the guise of offsetting new production costs.

Within a week of my return, despite all good intentions following my stay in Majorca, I had become a belligerent drunk. In the past, I had OD'd on heroin and been hospitalized for going crazy on cocaine. Now liquor was my poison. I managed to function quite well, considering. I did do some blow, not quite the reformed lad I had hoped, but certainly a step in the right direction compared to my recent track record. The added bonus was that the booze fed my sex addiction. The orgiastic moments in between work were filled with casual sex, no strings attached, a young man's dream come true.

CHAPTER THIRTY-ONE

THE LUCK OF THE IRISH

Thirteenth Street, New York

I HAD TO LEAVE MY BARROW Street apartment because the lease was up, so on September 1, 1986, I moved into a place on Thirteenth Street between Fifth and Sixth Avenues. With a change of scene, I began making an effort to clean up, seeing a psychotherapist to talk about my addictions—although I probably didn't recognize them as such at the time. Today, I can see that I was completely caught up in a web of my own making, trying to find a way out.

The psychotherapist's name was Dr. Trigg, and we got together a couple of times a week. He would talk to me about not taking drugs, in particular crack, and I told him—a pack-a-day tobacco smoker—that he shouldn't smoke cigarettes. He was a nice man and tried his best to help me, and for a short time, he helped me keep my drug use in check.

After a few months in a fairly clear state, I realized just exactly how much I was missing Perri. Shortly before Christmas, we began talking to each other again. We both seemed to be in a better frame of mind and we were relieved that we still genuinely cared about each other, even after our long breakup of over nine months. Add to this the time I'd spent in L.A. working on *King Death*, and it seemed like we had been apart for longer. Brigid remembers coming to my apartment one December day and seeing champagne bottles everywhere. She found Perri and me there in bed together . . . reunited.

And so Perri moved back in with me, but things were still very rocky when it came to drugs. Though I had longed terribly for Perri while she was gone, I still had difficulty staying home and being faithful to her. I would sometimes stay in a midtown hotel to have various affairs on the side or just to get some space to myself. More than anything else, I wanted to carry on partying where I wasn't being watched by anyone who really cared about me.

All around me, people were dying. I met a waitress from the club Area, and she spent a couple of days and nights with me, and when I next heard about her the following week, she was dead of a heroin overdose. But reality didn't play a part in my thought process. I didn't or couldn't care about my own health or safety, as I inevitably gravitated toward people who operated under the same set of rules.

In late February 1987, I found myself on another coke-smoking binge, walking into a police anti-crack sting in Washington Square with another lady friend, Grace Hattersley. Everyone else in Manhattan had read in the newspaper that day that there would be a police operation in the park that night. The police only insisted on arresting one of us, and Grace kindly decided to take the fall for me. A true gift, since I could've been deported had it been me who was arrested. Nonetheless, it ended up on the front pages of all the New York papers.

Just prior to this incident, I had taken a meeting with my press agent, Howard Bloom, who was telling me we needed a major press event to help announce the tour, so when I saw him the day after the front-page exposure, I said to him, "Well, how's that for press coverage?" and he responded in an exasperated tone, "I didn't mean that kind of press."

The story didn't end there. Grace gave a press conference, mentioning that she was my girlfriend, which enraged Perri, who decided to call her own press conference to announce that she was my *real* girlfriend. The day after Grace's media chat, Perri appeared at hers, opening up her shirt to display a leopard-print bra to the photographers as she exclaimed to the assembled press: "I'm Billy Idol's girlfriend. I know something like this may split up some people, but we've been through a lot." That settled it.

When I headlined Madison Square Garden later that year, I opened the show with an insider's remark, "From Washington Square to Madison Square," and the audience roared with laughter.

THE VIDEOS FOR "To BE A Lover," "Sweet Sixteen," and "Don't Need a Gun" kept the MTV audience transfixed, and the Whiplash Smile tour was booked for summer and fall. The album would go platinum, but despite our overt success, this thing that Bill, Steve, and I had started, that had been rolling along quite nicely, was now coming apart at the seams. As far as anybody outside the inner circle was concerned, it remained in full motion. I certainly wasn't immune to ego and vanity at the time, and the drugs and alcohol were closing my mind to a lot of what was going on around me. I was living a fantasy that was real, but was losing my grip. It was life as only a rock star would know it, but it was twisted, and I was living it in public. I was a young man leaning into the wind of his aspirations with a kind of desperation that twisted the world into the view I had of it.

I knew once I got out on the road the reign of tyranny—my bad habits—would kick into overdrive. At the start of the tour I began to snort coke, and then everything was ratcheted up a notch or two or three. Booze, coke, broads, and Mary Jane ruled. Beginning at the Spectrum in Philadelphia in April of 1987 and ending five months later in Sydney, the party rolled on and on in an overabundance of sound, fury, and wild energy.

In addition to Steve Stevens, my band for the tour included Kenny Aaronson on bass, Thommy Price on drums, and Susie Davis on keyboards. We had experimented with a lot of technology in the recording process, and the band was feeling the constraints of trying to reproduce everything live, as we had some keyboard-driven songs that had to be locked in with the synth. Everyone tried to make it work, but unfortunately the high-tech demands grated on the band. It was the early days of combining live and prerecorded shit. The techniques we used had to be babied into place, and it took forever to set up and make sure that everything was working properly. I was asking a great deal of everyone, and to their credit, both band and crew rose to the occasion.

The Whiplash Smile tour wasn't as much fun or as carefree as the Rebel Yell tour, for many reasons. The dynamics of the relationships had changed. Everyone was a lot higher, and we were all partying our asses off. As the leader, I should have played to people's strengths, not simply made them adhere to my ideas for the sake of it. A true leader should set people free, not make them feel trapped. But I was too high on drugs to realize that, let alone make it happen.

Despite the emerging tensions, the gigs somehow came off well to the outside world. But that old joie de vivre was harder to conjure up. Concert arenas all looked alike, and it was hard to reach the fans like we could in clubs or theaters, even though I encouraged the audience to pull up to the barrier at the front of the stage. We missed playing in smaller venues where the audiences were allowed more freedom, more connection. In these larger venues, the music had less dynamics, and sometimes it all became a blur in the big, cavernous spaces.

Still, one thing about Idol audiences—they go nuts no matter where they are. There were tons of girls with their cutest '80s gear, highest fuck-me pumps, going crazy with their teased hair and short skirts. Some wild punks were still there, too. You couldn't help but reach into that audience and take what you wanted. I was turning into a rock 'n' roll monster, but I liked it, and basked in the greatest drug of all—adulation.

It was about midway through the tour and Mike Bone, the new head of Chrysalis Records, was looking for a way to make an immediate mark. He proposed doing a live version of "Mony Mony" to go with a collection of our remixes since 1980 compiled into one album that we would call *Vital Idol*. It was the closest thing to a dub album I could make, and up until that point, no one had done anything quite like it. Keith Forsey came to one of the shows and we recorded a live version of "Mony Mony." We released it as a single because Mike felt our studio version didn't receive the exposure it deserved when it came out in 1981.

The new live take was more guitar-oriented, and when the single was released it went to number one (knocking off another Tommy James song, teen mall queen Tiffany's cover of "I Think We're Alone Now"). *Vital Idol* also did well, breaking into the Top 20 on the *Billboard* chart. The luck of the Irish was still with me. Or was it?

"IT'S MY BAND!" SCREAMED STEVE STEVENS in my face one night. The little Jewish kid from Far Rockaway is as strong as an ox, by the way. I'd discovered this when I tumbled with him during a momentary argument and he pinned me to the floor. Now, as the tensions of the tour finally boiled over, he was confronting me and being very belligerent. I shot back at him, "Your band? It's *my* band!" Somehow, my drug- and paranoia-fueled ego got the best of me and we were having a full-on shouting match in front of the rest of the band, the traveling party, and the backstage workers.

Nothing more was said, but after the tour, Steve went off to pursue a solo career for Warner Bros. If Bill Aucoin had been around, I think he would have found a way to hold it together. As the tour progressed, I succeeded in driving Steve to the end of his tether, forgetting all he'd done for me. Sorry, Steve, you didn't need your mate disappearing in front of you, but that's exactly what happened.

PART III
LOS ANGELES

CHAPTER THIRTY-TWO

WE NEED A MIRACLE JOY, WE NEED A ROCK AND ROLL BOY

Astral Drive, Hollywood Hills, Los Angeles

BY THE END OF 1987, PERRI and I had fully reconciled and had a new goal in place. We set out for California, moving into a house on Astral Drive, a side street in the Hollywood Hills, where Van Morrison supposedly lived in the late '60s and got the inspiration for his classic album *Astral Weeks*. It was a time of change for me on multiple fronts. I had a new home in a new city and, once again, a new manager to help guide my career. Freddy DeMann had done a fine job under the trying circumstances created by Aucoin's disappearance, but our partnership just never felt right. With the *Whiplash Smile* project having run its course, I finally had a chance to think about my management situation and decided to hire Tony Dimitriades.

Our new home on Astral Drive was right down the block from Tony D.'s house. I'd met Tony during Christmas 1986 while on a brief vacation in Hawaii. Perri and I were staying in a hotel in Maui, but everywhere we went, eager fans and curious holidaymakers recognized us. We wanted to go somewhere that was quieter, and John Diaz suggested we call his friend Tony, who was in Kauai. We ended up sharing a house on the beach with Tony. I got to know and like him.

Tony is an Englishman of Greek Cypriot descent. He had been a lawyer in the UK in the late '60s and began managing artists in the early '70s before moving to Los Angeles in 1976. Turned out it was a lot more exciting than practicing entertainment law and British constitutional law, although he did have some wild stories about litigating as the British Commonwealth began breaking apart.

When I got to know Tony, he was managing Tom Petty and the Heartbreakers ("You Got Lucky" was one of the few songs I actually liked on early-'80s U.S. radio) as well as Yes and Stevie Nicks. I liked Tony the moment I met him and thought he was what I needed: a fellow Brit to guide me.

Relocating to L.A. was a deliberate move: Perri and I wanted to get away from the craziness of New York and give our relationship an honest chance. Steve Stevens had also moved west and had begun working on a solo album with a two-record deal at Warner Bros. Now "the man behind Billy Idol," as the press dubbed Steve, was no longer there for me, which was frightening. At the same time, I was really trying to pull myself together and get back to square one, both personally and professionally. I knew it would take a while to rewire my brain.

Trying to cool out and settle down, Perri and I decided to have a baby together. About a month after we moved to L.A., Perri announced she was pregnant, which was very exciting. We began to make preparations for our new life, which represented a welcome change in my state of mind. The impending arrival of our child gave us a fresh focus as a couple. I began to work out to try to build my depleted body back up, hoping my brain would follow suit.

Perri was in seventh heaven during her pregnancy; we soon found out she would be having a boy. One morning, she woke up, turned to me, and said, "I just saw his face." I believed it, too, as mother and child are so connected to one another. She would practice her yoga and take walks regularly. Perri decided she wanted a home birth, believing a drug-free delivery would be better for the baby. We went to Lamaze classes, where we learned breathing and birthing practices, and I was taught how to coach Perri through the delivery. Perri is pretty tough, and after a couple more classes at home, she seemed mentally prepared for the experience.

With "Mony Mony" at number one on the Billboard singles chart, I decided to celebrate. I bought myself a Harley-Davidson Wide Glide motorcycle, which I still own to this day. I also purchased some gym equipment and a treadmill, so I could work out at home and build up the physical strength to ride her. I'd always loved motorcycles, and would talk all the time to Derwood about his BSA Gold Star in our Generation X days. But the Harley is a big American bike equally suited to the freeways as well as to the local streets, and that meant, at some point, I would take her on a road trip.

It was good for me to learn on something lighter and smaller—you don't want to ruin a big bike by dropping her because of your inexperience. For a couple of months I learned to ride on a Kawasaki 454, which Keith Forsey gave me after he bought a Harley Softail. The Kawasaki was a very light bike, so if you dropped it, it wouldn't sustain real damage. Even if it did, it was my learner cycle. As I was riding it one day, some biker pulled up next to me on a Harley and sneered, "Why don't you get a real bike?" Moving to the Harley was the next step after doing a hill start and riding a few times on the freeway on the Kawasaki.

I taught myself how to ride the Harley in my neighborhood. Plenty of people I knew were riding in L.A., such as the Sex Pistols' Steve Jones and the Stray Cats' Brian Setzer. At first, the bike was a way to get a buzz without needing chemicals. I was getting stronger working out, but I still felt a bit too small to ride her, which is why I tried to bulk up. In my enthusiasm I may have overdone the workout regimen, but you have to be able to pick up this 750-pound bike. If you can't pick her up, you can't ride her—Harley rules prevail in the motorbikin' world!

Scooting around Hollywood on a bike gave me a real sense of freedom compared to being cooped up in a tiny New York apartment or living in a bubble behind the wheel of a car in Los Angeles. It was a blast to be out there in public on a motorcycle in the pre-helmet-law days. While I could still be seen and recognized by others using the road and the sidewalk, being on the bike made me feel one step ahead of the ever-attentive fans and paparazzi. I didn't need security around me to guard against the crazed multitudes who knew me from MTV. I felt empowered and free, and what could be better than that?

You have to be fairly together to ride a bike, especially at first.

All the preparations—prepping her for a ride, being safe, maintaining her—gave me something that was fun to do, but I also had to be responsible. I'd grown up on push bikes in England, so here I was at thirty-three once more with two spoke wheels beneath me just like a kid, except this Harley boasted monster horsepower and could go hundreds of miles at top speed. It was and still is one of my prized possessions. Today, my black and chrome beautiful Glide has a name— Boneshaker, as she is not rubber-mounted. "Get your motor running, head out on the highway . . ." Yes, it was Easy Rider time for the punk rocker to get out of his head on adrenaline!

At the time, all the lads, including Keith Forsey and John Diaz, were riding, so we formed our own biking enclave called the Rude Dudes, after a name I was dubbed by the UK magazine *Smash Hits*. I designed a ring that was a fist, with R-U-D-E on the knuckles and D-U-D-E on the fingers, that I presented to anyone who became a regular member of our group. I met a chap named Harry Johnson, whom I proclaimed the Rude Dude leader, as he was our most experienced rider and knew the L.A. area like the back of his hand. Harry would later become my full-time assistant.

It was fun riding with a small coterie of friends. It was safer, too. Knowing everyone's style of riding allowed us to practically predict what each of us would do while riding on the open highway. With my crew united, we explored the highways and byways of the Golden State. One of the first places we visited was Vasquez Rocks, the formation that *Star Trek*'s Captain Kirk stands on after he's beamed down to a planet surface on the TV show. I felt relaxed and liberated as we rode along the Angeles Crest, the Pacific Coast Highway, or up to central California to a bike festival in Visalia, in the San Joaquin Valley, where one day we ended up jamming on a festival stage.

Having the freedom to go anywhere I pleased was so different from those stoned years locked away in the Barrow Street apartment, smoking that "glass dick." I still feel best in my biking gear, as you eschew fashion for what will be most comfortable while riding a chopper. Why else would you wear leather clothes in L.A. if you weren't on a bike? On a motorcycle, leather and denim are a necessity—your armor. It was great attending rock shows on my bike as I could scoot in and out without having to wait in long lines of traffic. I hate stretch limos and I can't stand being driven. Now I was at the wheel, in control, and that felt good to me. Free at last!

It was wonderful living with Perri, spending time together on Astral Drive, living a normal and nurturing life. But even as Perri was pregnant with my child, my ability to curb my womanizing tendencies was being put to the test—and I failed miserably, with consequences beyond my imagination. Naomi was part Asian and part American Indian, and had a personality that made her seem to be at least a quarter male. A friend of mine went out with her in New York when I was living there. She was on heroin then, but had cleaned up upon moving to L.A. and was riding a Harley Sportster with a girlfriend who rode Harleys, too. She was riding with several groups of people, a lot of them using the motorbike as a way to get a buzz now that they had given up substances. She, too, was finding riding the bike to be a therapeutic experience.

Naomi and her friend gradually started to ride with us Rude Dudes, as we were always going somewhere scenic or fun. Over the course of a few months, Naomi and I started to get closer, and ended up having a full-on affair.

How could I on the one hand be reveling in the fact that my first child was coming but at the same time be full-blown involved with someone other than Perri? The addict in me had never really stopped being in control. Out of sheer self-preservation I had attempted to clean up, but the drug addict who is somewhere deep in my center was still in need of heroin. I didn't want to take heroin, as I was determined to put that behind me, so I started substituting other activities that were ultimately much worse for me and those around me. The multiple effects could make me unpredictable and incapable of separating William Broad from Billy Idol. Too often, the core Idol tenet drove me: Do what you want. The problem is, I didn't stop to think what that truly was. I acted on impulse, for the ephemeral high.

Back on Astral Drive, Perri was doing wonderfully, pregnancy giving her a natural high that I could only marvel at. From the very moment we found out we were having a boy, we began thinking about his name. Somehow, I always had the idea I would call my son William, to keep the family name going. Now was my chance. But Willem Dafoe had just done *The Last Temptation of Christ*, and was therefore my generation's Jesus. And a wild one at that! After I saw the film, the name "Willem"—the Dutch spelling of William—stayed in my mind. As we pondered his middle name, we considered that we liked the film *Amadeus*, in which Mozart's wife, Constanze, was always calling him "Wolfie." And I had also always admired General James Wolfe, who was famous in England for taking Quebec from the French, though dying in the effort. In his writings, he had predicted the American empire, saying that whoever controlled America could control the world. So, with such fanciful ideas as these, my son was named Willem Wolfe Broad. I always thought when he grew up he could use Willem Wolfe as a stage name, and that is in fact what he does today when he DJs.

Perri was happy as a clam while pregnant, and it was fantastic to see as she bloomed to the final stages of her pregnancy. On June 14, 1988, we were eating lunch at The Source, a legendary vegan restaurant on Sunset that is now a Mexican place, when her water broke. So we came back to Astral Drive to start to prepare for the birth. From Lamaze classes, we knew all about the "hee, hee, hoo" breathing exercises in preparation. We had two midwives in attendance during the day and night of Perri's twelve-hour home-birth labor. Perri opted for a drug-free delivery, and Willem had a completely natural birth. At one point halfway through her labor, when she was standing in our bathroom and we were alone, I could see how much distress she was in, and, feeling powerless to help her, I started to cry for her. It was incredible seeing what women can go through to give birth. Any thoughts of women being in any way the weaker sex, or not tough, go right out the window once you witness what they endure during labor.

After several more hours Willem arrived, weighing 8 pounds, 6 ounces. He seemed to come through it all right, and the next minute, after the midwives had cleaned him off, Perri was holding him in her arms. Soon it was my turn and I took a picture of his head in my hands, his body along my inside forearm.

CHAPTER THIRTY-THREE

LA VIE ENCHANTÉ

Hollywood Hills, Los Angeles

As I CELEBRATED THE BIRTH OF my son, I began to refocus on writing songs and preparing to record my fourth album. It was daunting in many ways, particularly because this would be the first Billy Idol album without Steve Stevens on board. I was nervous without my partner, but Keith was still at the helm and I was determined to move forward, this time with Mark Younger-Smith on lead guitar. Once we returned to the studio, it wasn't long before I was back to acting as if the attempts to clean up and create a more conventional family life never happened. Old habits die hard.

A few months after Will was born, I caused the incident that would finally and irretrievably end my relationship with Perri. When Will was napping, we would place a baby monitor near him so that we could step away and have some time to ourselves but still hear him when he awakened. On this particular day we were out by the pool around lunchtime, sunning ourselves. Taking a quick break to get some drinks and towels, I went into our bedroom, where Will was also sleeping, and phoned Naomi to check in on her and to fix up our next date. Upon gathering the towels and drinks, I walked out towards the pool. As I got nearer to Perri, she started to get up, an expression of distress on her face. "Who's your baby?" she asked me. "Who do you love?" To my great surprise and dismay, she was repeating parts of the conversation I had just had with Naomi. When she saw the look on my face, she angrily brandished the baby monitor. Horrified, I realized I'd forgotten about the monitor in sleeping Willem's crib, which transmitted my entire conversation back to the receiver next to Perri. She gathered her things and left the house, taking Will with her. She went to England to be with her family and although she returned a few months later, it was never the same between us. I had crossed a line and was unable to return. In August 1989, with the words "I've had enough of this," she left for good.

I don't blame her at all. I found a house not too far away from me for Perri and Will to move into. We were determined to do our best for Will, and though it would be some time before I fully settled down to parent earnestly, a regular routine eventually emerged, with Will spending every other week with me.

Self-sabotage is one of the things I'm truly gifted at. I'd worked so hard to build a life with Perri, and now with Will, and I threw it all away. The rock star's ingrained mind-set—*do what you want when you want to*—often thrust me into a miasma of sex and drugs, short-circuiting my most important relationships.

The English poet Alexander Pope said, "An excuse is worse than a lie, for an excuse is a lie, guarded." No excuses here. Once Perri was gone, I became umoored. I'd made my bed: now it was time to fully lie in it.

DURING THE MAKING OF *CHARMED LIFE*, Tony Dimitriades asked us if we'd like to perform at the second annual Bridge School Benefit, a charity concert that Neil Young leads in support of a special school near San Francisco. Neil and his wife, Pegi, helped found the school, which offers education and opportunity for children with severe speech and physical impairments. Tony asked me if we'd like to appear at the benefit, as Neil had asked him.

We were deep inside "Boots and Scarves" territory, which bore no relation to the real world outside our sex-club studio. Our performance was to be acoustic, about half an hour long. With the instrumentation of Forsey on snare drum and me and Mark Younger-Smith on guitars, we planned out the set in some rehearsals in the studio at off moments. The day before the concert we flew up to a hotel near Neil's home, just south of San Francisco, a million sheets to the wind. The following day at the performance we were incredibly hungover, so much so that we could hardly play in the sound check. David Crosby was there watching, and remarked as much to me.

Still, we pulled ourselves together for the early evening half-hour set, which was better than the sound check, as we'd had one or two drinks prior so we could overcome our hangovers enough to physically play. We somehow performed the songs, and congratulated ourselves by dropping ecstasy and drinking to get our highs back. Then, while out of it, we met an assemblage of living legends whose records I'd listened to or I had seen in concert. Stephen Stills, David Crosby, Graham Nash, Bob Dylan, and Tom Petty were all there.

Tom Petty went onstage and something (probably the ecstasy) took hold of me halfway through his set. I crashed the stage while Tom was between songs, walked up to the microphone, and said, "You wouldn't believe, we are managed by the same person!"

It was meant as a joke, but in those surrounds, with differently abled kids at the back of the stage and Tom's fans out front, no one needed me bringing our studio party up north from L.A. and onto his stage. But that's what happened. Thinking about the incident today—which I try not to do—I am horrified and embarrassed. Sorry, Tom.

On a positive note, I'm thankful to have been invited back to the Bridge School Benefit and have played it four times altogether now; each subsequent time it's gone very well. I play to the kids at the back of the stage and generally have a blast. Neil is a great person, and it's an honor to know him and to be involved in such a worthy cause.

But that evening, I left the stage not quite realizing my faux pas and ended the night being shot up with speed by some bird. When I saw Tony D. the next morning he was shocked at my appearance, as I was sheet-white. I felt awful, as I don't like speed much, let alone the explosive effects of shooting it up.

I was taking it all too far. Once again I was a junkie in search of a high on whatever drug was available. That's dangerous territory. I was a loose cannon and no one, certainly not me, knew what I might or might not do next.

Tony D. couldn't really have known just how fucked up we'd become at that stage of the record, as he wasn't attending the sessions every day. Junkies are quite good at disguising when they have to, but one step too far, one Bridge School incident too many, and all would be exposed.

CHAPTER THIRTY-FOUR

CITY OF NIGHT

Sunset Strip, Los Angeles

Halfway through recording *Charmed Life*, I was approached by Oliver Stone to be in his upcoming biographical film about the Doors and their iconic singer, Jim Morrison, who was to be played by Val Kilmer. I went for a reading of a few lines of the movie, watched by Oliver, who decided to cast me in the part of Tom Baker. A close friend of Jim Morrison's, Tom was an actor among the superstars of Andy Warhol's glory days at his studio, the Factory, when they met.

I went to a dinner to meet Oliver and some other actors at Le Dome on Sunset. I expect in some form or another he was putting people together and watching them interact to see if he could use them in his movie. Somehow I managed to pull one of the girls away from one of the actors at the table. The girl said he was her boyfriend, but we made it in the toilet, which was quite obvious to all at the table when we returned.

Oliver Stone is an incredibly gifted man who envisions exactly what he's trying to achieve. It must be a wild process directing a movie and trying to combine all the elements needed to complete one's vision. I considered the opportunity to play a role in one of his films a true gift. Between *Salvador*, *Platoon*, *Scarface*, *Talk Radio*, and *Wall Street*, Oliver was the king of memorable dialogue at that moment—he had the most colorful dialogue of any director in the '80s. Everybody in my band had memorized nearly every line from *Scarface*—for which he wrote the script—from watching it so much on our tour bus.

Oliver had a true love of the Doors, and of Jim Morrison in particular, as I think that music meant so much to the world in the haze that was Vietnam. "Lost in a Roman wilderness of pain and all the children are insane, waiting for the summer rain, yeah!"

The music meant a lot to us, but those who served in 'Nam lived and died it. On reading the script, it was great to see someone so gifted handle the Doors' story, which is intellectual but still somehow primitive. It was a difficult story to convey on-screen without becoming too pretentious and boring, but I thought Oliver's script met the challenge well.

While Oliver stressed that I should act as natural as possible in the film, I started to attend some acting lessons to rehearse my scenes and generally prepare. Much of the class focused on sense and memory work, which involves bringing some of your own experiences to fuel the emotional background of the character. It was really interesting to see the amount of work actors go through to achieve the level of performance necessary to convince an audience that they are truly that character.

I went down to the Ambassador Hotel in L.A., a location Oliver was considering for replicating a New York hotel for a single scene. It was there I met Val Kilmer. Val was great and I watched him over the course of those weeks as he came to grips with convincingly playing Jim Morrison.

Val and I went out one night to meet a friend of Jim's who'd been part of Jim's intimate circle and knew my character, Tom, as well. We ate out at the beach and later we went to a small bar down in Topanga Canyon where he and Jim had hung out. After being there a while, I drifted across the bar and chatted up a girl. When I returned to the guys, Jim's old pal told me that he'd been unsure about me at first, but now he could clearly see me in the part of Tom. This was an incredibly gratifying endorsement.

Meeting the Doors was great as well, although only John Densmore and Robbie Krieger were present, as Ray Manzarek had had a disagreement with Oliver and was not involved with the film. I also hung and spoke a lot with Danny Sugerman, who had managed the Doors at a very young age. He was a terrific guy and I liked his book *Wonderland Avenue*, about the house on the street of the same name where Jim and Iggy Pop had lived at one time or another. I also enjoyed his biography of Jim Morrison, *No One Here Gets Out Alive*.

Meanwhile, we were still putting the finishing touches to the *Charmed Life* album, mainly in perfecting "Cradle of Love," which we made and remade four times before Keith gave it his seal of approval. So I was moving between these two roles: that of real rock star and that of playing a friend of a rock star.

I FELL HARD FOR LINDA. HER glistening body slowly writhes to the sonic boom of the bass. In the flashes of overhead light, her skin glows in a soft, tanned sheen. Her wild smile holds something of the exotic as the corners of her mouth curl up and she flits a glance at me as she moves, dancing in place. She revolves in time, undulating with her message to me. Through her almond-shaped eyes, she sends an unmistakable psychic thought: *Be with me*. I can't resist. The attraction is mutual; the moment is framed, emblazoned forever in my memory. The smoke in the room veils her for a moment, but, like the sun, she shines forth. The blast of her light goes straight to the heart of me.

That blissful moment would yield one of the great joys of my life: my daughter, Bonnie Blue, born a year after Willem. Before she was due, Linda Mathis chose to go home to Oklahoma to have Bonnie, and I wasn't always understanding. The substances I took in abundance often made understanding impossible. But Linda is a lovely, forgiving person, and Bonnie is a glorious female version of me—headstrong from Day One, that little love. A risk-taker with no fear at the playground, which is where I first met her, in an L.A. park—face to tiny princess face. We played together on the swings and monkey bars. I was terrified she'd get hurt, but I helped her along as she climbed the top bars. I held on to her the whole time, to make sure she wouldn't fall, and I told her, "You are such a clever girl." Because not only do I see myself in her, I see my dad. Very clever indeed.

Now I revel in the delight I get from both my children. It was having them that enabled me to finally rehabilitate myself and stop being quite so cavalier with my life. My fear of leaving Willem and Bonnie without a father as a result of my drug addictions has been *the* positive force of change in my being. As they grew older, I knew the last thing they truly wanted was a drugged/alcoholic/sex-addict father. I have done my best to be there for them. I haven't always succeeded, I'm afraid, but that is the lot of a parent: you find yourself constantly second-guessing, so you must rely on your best intentions and instincts and hope it all comes out to the good.

But during the recording of *Charmed Life*, while they were infants being looked after by their mothers, I wasn't there for my son and daughter. I was a slave to my addictions and lifestyle. The wagon was rolling, the wheels were turning, and I was caught underneath. And I was about to record one of my biggest chart hits.

CHAPTER THIRTY-FIVE

TROUBLE WITH THE SWEET STUFF

Sunset Strip, Los Angeles

CAROLE CHILDS WORKED AT GEFFEN RECORDS and was Tony Dimitriades's friend. She had a song she wanted me to record for the Andrew Dice Clay movie *The Adventures of Ford Fairlane*. The song was called "Cradle of Love," and she was anxious to get our take on it. I messed with the lyrics a bit, but David Werner had written most of them already. The song just needed a little finesse and interpretive work on my part. We wanted to inject some character into the music. The song was about some of the great cradle robbers in rock 'n' roll, and included a shout-out to Jerry Lee Lewis—"It burned like a ball of fire / When the rebel took a little child bride." The plan was for the song to appear on both the movie sound track and on *Charmed Life*. "Cradle of Love" turned out to be the album's lead single and a huge success.

Another tune on the album, "Trouble with the Sweet Stuff," started out as a medium-paced Idol rocker—much like "White Wedding"— but turned into an epic, six-minute torch song. "Pumping on Steel" came out more true to my initial intention, which was to write a fuck song about screwing on my motorcycle. "Prodigal Blues" has a beautiful elegiac quality. Maybe I knew I was saying goodbye for a bit, because it's an encapsulation of my story, my journey up until then.

During this time, producer/director/writer Michael Mann asked me to record a version of the Doors song "L.A. Woman" for his TV movie *L.A. Takedown*. I admired Michael's work, and readily agreed to record the song that would be featured on the film sound track and would also be the second single on *Charmed Life*. When Steve Stevens and I first started jamming together in '80 we sometimes jammed on "L.A. Woman," as it was a song that interspersed vocals and lead guitar lines, and we had no others like that at the time. In those early days, when we got near the end of an Idol set, we sometimes threw it in for fun, and to blow off some steam. Since I was working on the Doors film at the same time as recording *Charmed Life*, including our version of "L.A. Woman" on the album seemed very appropriate. We did a very up-tempo, cocaine-driven version that sped along a little differently than the original Doors version, which was a slightly slower barroom honky-tonk piano boogie. Our version remains a staple of Idol set lists to this day and is always a blast to perform.

The making of *Charmed Life* continued through a variety of recording studios, including Conway, deep in Hollywood, where we recorded a '50s "death" song, "Endless Sleep," also suggested by Carole and Tony D. I liked the idea of trying to sing one of those death-wish songs that poured its Cadillac blues all over the studio speakers. The song was originally recorded by 1950s rockabilly singer and songwriter Jody Reynolds, who had a Top Five hit with it in 1958, and was later covered by Hank Williams Jr. Those speakers vibrated and whirred as the recording and mixing inexorably ground their way to the conclusion.

Mark Younger-Smith made some excellent contributions to the album. It was Keith Forsey who introduced me to Mark, a six-foot-tall, Harley-riding Texan. He plays a mean Texas-blues-rock-style guitar, which was interestingly different from Steve Stevens's "shock and awe" electronics. But at the same time, Mark could execute the Stevens-era guitar sounds in his own way when he had to, while bringing a slightly different blues vibe to our entire sound. He is a great guy who was all about enjoying life to the fullest. When it came time to do press for the album, I asked him how he would answer the inevitable question, *How on earth are you going to fit into Steve Stevens's shoes?* His inimitable reply was, in a laconic Texan drawl, "I don't wear them—there high heels." Which I thought was fucking perfect, a great way to diffuse the questions.

During the recording sessions I watched *The Loveless*, a 1982 film. Codirected and cowritten by *Zero Dark Thirty*'s Kathryn Bigelow, it was her feature film debut. The film also introduced Willem Dafoe, starring in his first credited screen role as a member of an American biker gang who finds trouble in a small southern town during a cross-country escapade. The title, *The Loveless*, seemed especially fitting to me in describing my own increasing feeling of disconnectedness.

> I KNOW SHE'S WAITING FOR ME / OUTSIDE OF SOCIETY.
> —"THE LOVELESS"

When you're making an album, the pressure to come up with ideas is huge; it's the new ideas and the associated pressure that ultimately push the record forward. Sometimes, Keith Forsey would be there all night into the next day. When we arrived, the music on the playback would be so loud and distorted, it was hard to discern what song it was. Keith could hear through it all, fine-tuning with that sorcerer's magic of his, squeezing the beat into that special place dubbed the "Forsey World." Keith worked hard to put the drums into a certain groove that, musically speaking, if you were a woman, would tickle your musical G-spot. For a dancer, that means the beat is nonstop, working its way to your insides, creating a flow of endorphins that spur greater intensity. In that way, they accompany the rhythm, so instead of a drumbeat going "boop bat," it seems to say "oooh" and "ahhh," as you surrender to a quality that is more than just "in time." It's masturbating with the tempo, working in and out of it, making a simple drumbeat say more by filling out the meaning to the words, driving them home in a way that is instinctual. Keith always said there should be an animatronic "pussy" between the studio speakers that would react to the beat we were creating. As it became more intense, the pussy would cream its juices and tell us we were getting it right.

We worked together to get the vocals to a point we were all proud of. Keith would often look at me as I strode to the vocal booth, intent on delivering my main vocal track. "Bill, when you're in there, don't forget to have a good time," he would say, and it broke whatever tension I had, so I could approach the vocal with a joie de vivre. As the track started to take shape, after some careful consideration, he would jump up, spin around in a crouch, and clap his hands when he thought we were getting somewhere. He would then position himself in between the smaller speakers in the studio and put his head between them, listening intently, eyes closed, to figure out what needed to be fine-tuned. He would examine the blur and roar of disparate guitars and drums and spot an instrumental color that would help bring the mélange of noise together, solidifying it and claiming the space it occupied, so that it became virtually undeniable. Sometimes, he would do this with a faux Italian cry of "I must produce!" as if he was a grandstanding, big-name foreign producer. Keith always came ready to work. He is a true professional with a heart big enough to always see the potential, however minuscule, in me.

CHAPTER THIRTY-SIX

DRUNKEN, STUPID, & NAKED

Three weeks in Bangkok, Thailand

I REGRET VERY MUCH HOW THINGS ended with Perri. She deserved better from me, especially at such an important time. With Perri gone, I was left completely to my own deviant devices, and felt guilty that I had fucked up in such a massive way—making a mess of my relationship with the mother of my child. Once again, I was very depressed, and though I tried to carry on regardless, my condition did not go unnoticed by those around me. Rude Dude leader Harry Johnson urged me to take a break from recording, so, at his suggestion, I chose this moment to fulfill a wild fantasy. We struck out via jetliner for Bangkok, throwing caution to the wind, along with any fear of the Golden Triangle. What made us decide that this was the time and place to seek out our destiny? Was it the stories of young damsels to be found there? Or the overabundance of crazy things one could get up to? Whatever the reasons, it was with no trepidation whatsoever that we braved the high humidity, which I personally dislike, and danced into the mystical realm of long-lost tales.

Harry is a small chap of stocky build, a little older than me, who was even then losing his hair at the front slightly. He had once been a hairdresser, although his reason for being one was not completely mercenary. It was purely his love of the fairer sex that led him, scissors in hand, to beauty school. He knew most of the other men in that line of work would be gay and that he would have a clear field among the women who were also learning the art of hair cutting, coloring, and styling. He had, Warren-Beatty-in-*Shampoo* style, once owned his own salon, where he regularly had sex with his clientele while hearing all their personal stories and gaining an insight into the workings of the female brain unlike anyone else I have ever known.

We flew out of LAX, telling each other we were only going to drink and not do any drugs while we were there. The plan was to just spend as much time in the brothels as possible, with as many girls as possible, and that is exactly how it was for the first few days. We settled in at the Oriental Hotel, in the presidential suite on the top floor, with a panoramic view of the city. We were perched high above the dirty Chao Phraya River that lazily wound its way past the hotel and through the busy, overcrowded capital, disappearing into the distance. The brothels around town were many, and typically each had about fifty girls behind a huge glass window, all scantily clad in blue see-through sarongs, wearing numbers to allow you to easily identify which girl (or girls) you wanted. After a while, all the women started blurring together, and so I would say to Harry, "Just pick me a few you'd think I'd like, mate," and we'd go back to the hotel.

Harry took Polaroid photos of our female companions and had over a thousand shots by the time our trip was over. Things were in full swing after a week, when we both decided drinking and jet lag were taking their toll. So we thought, quite innocently, *What if we scored a little blow just to even out the booze?* We asked a taxi driver if he could get some and a twinkle appeared in his eye as he exclaimed, "yes!" in Thai, and drove off to get it for us.

After about an hour he returned. We climbed in the back of his tiny cab, where he slipped us a long, thin vial, about eight inches in length, filled with white powder. The size of the vial looked suspicious, so Harry took the vial and, with his little finger, tasted the powder. I could see by the look on his face that something wasn't exactly right. *This isn't blow*, he mouthed to me. My eyebrows raised and my eyes widened as I incredulously asked him—without actually saying a word—*What could it be, then??* Though I had a fucking pretty good idea. . . .

On getting up to the hotel room we examined the powder and yes, sure enough, it was the strongest China White heroin I'd ever touched. You only needed to smoke a pinprick of it to get high. And when I say high, I mean zombie high.

Shit, my best dream was coming true—or more likely, my worst nightmare. I hadn't had any smack since halfway through *Whiplash Smile* in '86, and here was the best stuff in the world. A junkie just can't say no to that! I definitely couldn't.

One big problem was that we didn't have any tinfoil. After a few hours spent searching through Bangkok markets, we eventually realized they didn't seem to use tinfoil at all in Thailand, so we headed back to the hotel and used the chocolate-bar wrappers from the minibar. Junkies are nothing if not resourceful!

The hotel staff were embarrassed by the seemingly continuous parade of hookers through the lobby and corridors at all times of the day and night, but we didn't care. It was an over-the-top kind of fun. I still have a little bit of video we took: there we are, pale ghosts flitting through the suite, zombielike and somnambulistic. We had slack facial expressions, our muscles sliding beneath our skin, hollow and nightmarish, avoiding the light and unwelcome scrutiny, dressed in sheets, shunning the ordinary.

The hotel asked us to move so that the president of Cambodia might have the entire top floor. We refused, thus continuing to wear out our welcome at the Oriental. The king's bodyguards stood glaring at the other end of the hallway night and day, but we were so high we didn't give a shit about that, or anything, really.

Eventually, about two weeks into the trip, the dope started to run out and we started to think about our next moves. We decided once the vial ran out, that had to be it, or we would just keep going. But we were so hooked at this point, we knew the heebie-jeebies would be hell if we stopped cold. We went to a pharmacy and bought every knockout pill they stocked. You can get everything over the counter there, so I'm sure we got some codeine and the like, but nothing made much of a dent in the descending agony of coming off that stuff.

We decided to get out of Bangkok. Our time was up in the hotel anyway, but not before Mel Gibson and family, horrified, saw me passed out in the elevator with the door opening and closing on me. Harry, who was trying to help me to my feet at the time, later told me that Mel offered a polite, "Excuse me," and led his family to the next elevator.

Next we moved to the Royal Cliff Hotel in Pattaya, a seaside resort to the south. Harry had met a Vietnamese bird and she came with us, too. The only English she knew was "boom boom," and "out go the light." I suspect Harry had taught her. With the heroin gone, we used the pills. So now, instead of lying low and staying quiet, we were loudly roaming around, getting drunk and tranquilized at the same time. We hired Jet Skis, and while playing chicken with Harry, I didn't steer out of his way in time and my Jet Ski got dinged and started to sink. For good measure I took off my swimsuit and was nude as it sank. I gave the family $25,000, which hopefully set them right. The Jet Ski was their livelihood. Looking back, I feel just awful about it, but I was really too sick and stoned to fully appreciate the situation at the time.

We repaired to our hotel and downed more pills. Before long, I passed out in my bed. When I came to, it was nighttime and Harry had gone out, leaving me with two hookers. I became enraged, and with all the power I could muster through the workouts I'd been doing for a year and a half, I picked up the five-foot log that was serving as a table and threw it through the glass sliding doors that filled an entire wall of the room. When the hotel owner saw it in the morning, it took $20,000 to calm him down and stop him from calling the police. We decided it was best to get out of Dodge, or in this case, Pattaya, and head back north to Bangkok.

This is where things get hazy. I have only flashes of the rest of the visit in my memory. Phone calls were coming in for me thick and fast, insisting I return home, but I knew I had to get through a week or more of coming off smack before even thinking about the fourteen-hour plane ride back. In '86, I had smoked crack to avoid the hell I was now facing, and coming off heroin is increasingly worse each time. All I remember now is people pleading with me to take my friend and leave. I'm sure my mate was dead worried. I was such a loose cannon smashing things up in a tranquilized hell that I'm sure Harry thought we would be arrested at any moment. I was crazy, then sane, and then crazy again. One minute you could reason with me and then I would be gone again—the Billy Idol version of "acting out," I suppose. All told, I smashed up three hotels and dished out many thousands of dollars to placate hotel management.

In the end, the Thai military were called to help escort us to the plane. I think they got a nurse to come and give me a shot, and they strapped me to a hospital gurney and wheeled me away out of the hotel to the airport with four soldiers armed with rifles marching beside me. I remember seeing them in one blurry moment of consciousness before I blacked out again to wake up puking at the airport. Wonderful!

It was during this mad vacation that Harry coined my crazy side's identity by calling me Bilvis. Zool had been usurped by Bilvis. We returned to Los Angeles to finish making my fourth solo album.

CHAPTER THIRTY-SEVEN

I BEAR A CHARMED LIFE, WHICH MUST NOT YIELD

San Fernando Valley, Southern California

THE TITLE *CHARMED LIFE* TOOK ON ironic significance in the light of future events, but the making of the album was a never-ending party. Every few days, it seemed like I was recovering from yet another sex, booze, and drug binge where it took seventy-two hours just to feel normal again. I realized that in many ways I had reverted to the behavior and feelings that permeated my life during the recording of *Whiplash Smile*, but I simply could not, or would not, stop myself.

Whatever studio we were in became our lair. Twenty-plus years on and I hear they still talk about our exploits at the Record Plant—we orgied like Roman times. Of course, the ecstasy played a big part. The control room in the studio took on the look of a spacecraft with its panels of LEDs as we literally took off into the stratosphere. I remember standing naked in the studio, looking at the blinking lights of the control room and thinking our spaceship was about to blast off. Sometimes, when we were out of our minds, Hollywood's lights became an extension of the studio as we proceeded to explore the sexual boundaries of this strange galaxy accompanied by the roar of motorcycles that we rode night and day, sober or fucked up, as we delved into the seedy side of Tinseltown. We entered the black hole ahead willingly, skated near death, and reveled in the experience.

Life happens in front of you, and you have to react to the stimulus. The stress and pressure built up because I cared. I cared about the music. First and foremost, I wanted to satisfy my own creative drive, but I also cared whether the critics and the fans would like the album. I did not feel that I had given my best on *Whiplash Smile* and I knew that I had to step up my game. But I didn't have my trusted partner Steve Stevens to lean on and I battled fears of mediocrity and failure by dancing with Mr. Death. At least that's what I told myself. I was about to reach the pinnacle of success, but also plummet at the same time through overindulgence and leading a deranged life. I had been living as if there were no tomorrow, and had nearly made that a reality.

THE FEBRUARY 6, 1990, MOTORCYCLE ACCIDENT left me severely injured and helpless in the confines of Cedars-Sinai Medical Center, just a few months before I would have a number 2 single with "Cradle of Love" and a hit video directed by David Fincher. We had a world tour booked to start in the summer and an album to promote, but here I was in February, not knowing when I would be able to leave the hospital, or even if I would have a leg beneath my right knee when I did.

In fact, the press in Britain initially reported after the accident that I'd been killed. My sister heard this on a London radio station, and even though the story was later corrected, I feel awful that she had to hear about my accident in this way. Of course, it wasn't the first time I'd been reported deceased: an article in the *New York Daily News* in the mid-'80s also prematurely reported my demise. As Mark Twain once put it, "Reports of my death have been greatly exaggerated."

Luckily, in my previous visits to Cedars, I had struck up a relationship with a Dr. Michael Smolens. The other nurses were aware of this and immediately sent for him. At the time of the accident, he had just left his night shift in the emergency room, and he graciously returned to the hospital to help organize and oversee my treatment. When the police were considering charges, he also reasoned with the cop on duty that I would likely lose my leg, and wasn't that punishment enough?

Dr. Smolens organized a specialist team of doctors to work on the various aspects of my injury, meaning I had a single group working on me from the start. Friends and fans from around the world sent flowers, cards, and their best wishes. Ron Wood sent me a case of Guinness.

I very nearly lost my leg, but the stellar team of doctors managed to see me through, intact. I would need a series of operations to correct the butterfly break in my right leg, along with some plastic surgery. The doctors would have to move a muscle from my calf to do the job of the one that had been blown apart by the impact of the car that broadsided me. Essentially, I was slammed on the right side, and as the car impacted my leg, the pieces of bone exploded through the skin where my shin had been, creating a hole the size of a baseball. My leg broke in three places in the center of the lower leg bone. As my orthopedic surgeon, Dr. Jack Moshein, put it, "If you're going to break a leg, this was the best location to break it." If it was nearer to the ankle, he said, "we wouldn't be able to reconstruct all those little bones."

Dr. Moshein was a nice, ruddy-faced man who always gave me hope that I could return to normal. Dr. Robin Yuan was the plastic surgeon who told me that moving the muscle to cover the hole would be "very complicated, but not impossible." If grafting skin on top of the transplanted muscle didn't work the first time, it might not be feasible to try a second time, but we forged on anyway. "Ten years ago, we would have just cut off your leg," he said. Shit, this was serious, but through the dreamy glow of the morphine, I remained confident they would fix me up.

The morphine drip and the toot of the pain medication became an every-twelve-minute occurrence. I was in heaven. I had never taken morphine before, and it was incredible. I could see the hole in my leg, the size of a baseball, a bloody gap, and not give a shit about it, as I was floating in Never-Never land.

Getting hit by a car was a drastic way to get wildly out of my mind, but in the cushion of morphine, the womb felt more hospitable than ever. Outside my body, I was in a world of hurt; inside, an unborn baby safe inside my bubble. And don't fucking burst it, either! I floated weightless, spinning in space, one with the universe. I was trancing with myself.

I HAD MY OWN ROOM ON the eighth floor of Cedars-Sinai. Next door to me were Sammy Davis Jr. and the jazz singer Sarah Vaughan, who were both dying of cancer. Sometimes, Sarah's beautiful daughter, Paris, would visit, and after she saw her mother, she would drop in on me, which was incredibly kind of her. It helped me pass the time. A doctor told me Sammy had asked him how much one of the pain medication delivery boxes cost, and when the doctor wondered why, the Candy Man answered, "I want to strap one to the dashboard of my car!" It got me thinking.

OLIVER STONE CAME TO VISIT ME one day, accompanied by *The Doors* producer A. Kitman Ho, and I was very glad to get their best wishes. As I was expecting their arrival, for a laugh I pulled myself out of bed, dressed, and posed in a chair on the other side of the hospital room, holding an open bottle of red wine, like I was still having a grand time—which, on all that morphine, I was. He asked me if I ever thought I'd walk properly again. I told him yes, as I was determined that somehow or other I was going to make a full recovery.

I also spoke to Val Kilmer about my recovery; I asked him to do what he could to help me keep the part. He was really understanding and caring, but what could he say? It soon became apparent that I would not be physically able to take on the role I'd been cast in, as my accident and injuries meant I would be recovering throughout the entire shoot. Keeping the part was impossible.

I acquired some music equipment for the room, along with a TV and videos. I also asked to have posters put up on the wall, to liven the place up. I had a coterie of people working for me who brought me whatever I needed. My trainer visited and we worked out the top half of my body. My son, Willem, would lie with me on the hospital bed watching cartoons in the afternoons. But I still had the constant visits from my doctors and the sight of my disfigured leg and a very open wound to remind me of my plight. I broke my forearm, clavicle, and a couple of ribs too, so I quickly underwent surgeries to start the mending process. After each operation I was back in my room, high as a kite.

I would often listen to albums while stoned. Free's *Fire and Water* was a big one, especially "Heavy Load." "Oh, I'm carrying a heavy load / Can't go no further down this long road." Their music was at its height on that album, extending those blues jams into classic songs, especially the slow-rising funk bass surrounded by ringing guitars on "Mr. Big": "Mr. Big / You better watch out . . . Oh for you now / I will dig / A great big hole in the ground."

I found myself alternatively laughing and very sad, leaning toward despondent, as I felt around inside my emotions, pondering my condition, not quite knowing what I'd done to myself as I lay motionless, confined to my living coffin. Friends brought me David Bowie's *Hunky Dory*. I love "Quicksand" and "The Bewlay Brothers." I certainly was sinking into quicksand myself, seeing everything and everyone through morphine eyes.

In my altered state, Elvis performed solo concerts for me as I watched his whole career stretch out in front of my hospital bed, each fold of the linen bouncing back a rock 'n' roll tale of success, excess, and distress. "Just take a walk down lonely street / To Heartbreak Hotel." Brother Elvis sang the blues, and the emotional content he could bring to a song elevated the nursery rhyme southern slang into an art form. He may not have written a song himself, but does that really matter? Only music snobs worry about shit like that. Just look at his effect on the Beatles, and that's all the argument needed. His early Sun Records stuff was my favorite, but he had a musical journey to take, and I was riding along, strapped to IV lines and surrounded by blinking monitors.

The nineteen-year-old young man who blew out of the South like a tornado, creating rock 'n' roll along the way as one of the four pioneers along with Little Richard, Chuck Berry, and Fats Domino, seemed like a staggeringly tragic dream. Yet Elvis had this golden voice, and all who heard it fell under his sway. For a time in the '50s he was untouchable. The number one records fell like rain and it took the Beatles to unseat him. The world knelt at his feet and he spent the rest of his life deeply wondering what benevolent force had bestowed it. His celebrity was unfathomable, a mystery to him. When fans would shout, "Elvis, you're the king," he would smile and answer, "There's only one king and that's Jesus." Missing the point of their adulation, he spoke his mind, even while in Colonel Tom's fetters.

From my hospital bed, I also watched the Marlon Brando movie *The Wild One*. I recently saw a documentary about Brando that showed how he, after a certain point in his career, avoided emotional, gut-wrenching performances like *A Streetcar Named Desire* and *On the Waterfront* in favor of lighter fare like *Sayonara* or *The Teahouse of the August Moon*. He found it difficult to keep reaching down so deep, as it stirred up disruption in his soul. His last real attempt at artistic control was *One-Eyed Jacks*, a western he was directing before he was pulled off by the studio, who grumbled as he held up production by spending a fortune on retakes due to his perfectionism. Even after that, Brando had a number of groundbreaking turns, among them *The Godfather*, *Last Tango in Paris*, and *Apocalypse Now*.

Sometimes it takes a crazy do-or-die attitude to get to the heart of a piece. It would be simpler if it was easy, but it's not. Even the greats struggle with this. "That's All Right" was a song Elvis, guitarist Scotty Moore, and bassist Bill Black were just foolin' around with in the tiny Memphis Sun Studios in 1954, and after hours of trying every other style, it was only then that Sam Phillips heard the magic.

Tortured by my own actions and the pain they caused me, I knew only that I could and would make the long haul to recovery. At least I had rock 'n' roll music to get me there—in fact, I had a whole album in the can to release and a projected summer tour to get better for! Could I do it? Would I be healed in time? Would I even be able to walk across a stage, let alone "wiggle about a bit and fuck off," as the director David Mallet once described my live act? Somehow I would make it, wouldn't I? The pulsing IV seemed to gurgle an indistinct reply—*Charmed Life*, indeed.

Today I don't like to think about the motorcycle crash. While I was in the hospital I couldn't wait to be twenty-plus years away from it, and that is exactly where I am as I write these words. I only think about it today in terms of its having made me a better rider. I've been down and I don't want to go down like that again, all big-time pain and hospital madness. I was a victim of my own hubris. I had been willing something to happen because it was all getting to be too much for me. Life became complicated and I had a date with disaster, a need to test the boundaries, whatever the cost, whatever the price, forever rushing toward death. The Grim Reaper rides today on a Harley made of human bones and skulls, looking for victims. He tried to take me, poured all of his will into making me embrace an early death. I smiled, as if I sought a pass into both dimensions.

While lying there in the street, I had an "other realm" experience I can't quite explain, though it happened to me once before in a spiritualist ceremony I attended when I was sixteen. Then I was sitting in a circle of people who channeled voices of others, speaking through them. My friend's girlfriend was particularly gifted as a medium, with many spirits coming through her, fielding questions posed by the circle. We meditated, each sitting in a chair, head bowed in a silent, respectful prayer. The séance lasted twenty minutes before the spirits could be contacted. This period of quiet concentration was needed to calm the room and allow the spirits access to their chosen vessels. Nothing took place my first two times, but on the third, I rose above myself into the red dimension of love and warmth, the spirits surrounding me. I stayed there for an instant, or a lifetime, and came down to find the circle awakening to begin their conversations with the other side.

I went through seven operations in a month before I was back limping around. Though not for everyone, for me it's an insane rush, riding the edge between life and death. I experienced morphine for the first time, the king of downers, the Big M. It was murder to detox, especially in a hospital bed with a broken leg. The nurse had to change my bedclothes once an hour for several weeks, as I was sweating profusely during sleep. But I got off the stuff. That is quite the accomplishment, according to my doctor. "Mister Broad . . . How can I say this to you? You are 'drinking' the pain medication in. Is there anything you want to tell me?" I confessed to being a massive junkie but promised to get off the gear when the time came. And I kept my promise.

CHAPTER THIRTY-EIGHT

HOLLYWOOD PROMISES

Tinseltown, Los Angeles

ONCE HOME FROM THE HOSPITAL, MY mum came to help nurse me to health. Mum was a nurse by trade, so in addition to having her moral support, it was great to have her professional aid. As I sat in my chair in the front room, she would skillfully clean my leg wound using a long cotton swab coated with hospital-strength Betadine antiseptic. One day, Mum remembers little Will got into the cotton buds and started to touch my leg with one, and when Mum asked him what he was doing, he said, "Cleaning Daddy's boo boo!"

It was great to have her there, as she could care for my injuries properly, which meant I could dispense with the expensive professional help. But more than that, it was a special bonding time for us, as we were alone together for long periods, the most in fact since I was a very young child, when my mother first got her driver's license in America and the two of us took long road trips together. She is an excellent nurse and has a very loving but deliberate way about her that is both full of concern as well as she won't allow you to dwell on the negative.

At night, we would often read from the bible together—I still had a long road to recovery ahead of me, and I wanted everything possible on my side. Besides, how could I say no to my mum? It's not like I could get up and walk away.

Once Mum returned home, reporters questioned her about my rehabilitation, and she mentioned innocently that we had been reading the bible together nearly every night, saying that the accident had "certainly changed my life." The UK press ran with the story, saying I was "born again." *Devilish Billy Idol becomes an angel!*

And so when it came time to do press for *Charmed Life*, in a satellite interview with journalists from UK and Europe all gathered in one room, I knew the first question asked me would be, "Billy, so is it true, born again??"

I came prepared, thrilled to hear the question first out of the gate. I responded, "I think everybody heard it wrong. When people were saying I was born again, it was actually that I've got back into *porn* again . . . I think there's just a little bit of a mistake there, when my mother was telling everybody. Because I mean, my church is still the dirty bookstore." Yes, it was worth a good laugh, but the real purpose of the statement was fulfilled; it put a swift end to those questions before they'd begun.

FILMING OF *THE DOORS* BEGAN THE same month I was released from Cedars-Sinai, with a newly implanted steel rod in my leg, a long road of rehab still ahead of me. I was feeling very down, when Oliver kindly reached out to offer me a less rigorous role, and I gratefully accepted. Oliver was extremely generous in offering me the part, as neither he nor I knew whether I would be able to walk by the time my scenes were to be filmed. I was given the smaller part of Cat, a film director and hanger-on to Jim's entourage, and I would be playing across from Dennis Burkley, a character actor appearing as Dog, whose large size meant he usually played bikers.

Once I was feeling well enough, I first went down to the production offices and met up with some of the other actors, but I found it difficult being in a wheelchair. Eventually I was able to go to the set on crutches with a cast on my leg, and tried to execute my role as Cat. It wasn't easy.

I was extremely impressed with Val's commitment to his role. He did everything he could to stay in character, such that he had given instructions that no one speak to him when he arrived on the set, among a number of other stipulations. Some thought this was excessive, but I thought there was a complete validity.

One location was in a house off Laurel Canyon where they shot the now-infamous "the duck is dead" scene, in which Val's Jim Morrison struggles with a knife-wielding Meg Ryan's Pamela Courson. The scene ends with Val's Jim stomping on the duck he'd burned to a crisp, exclaiming, "And I'm still killing your fucking duck!"

The house was down about 150 steep steps that I had to negotiate from the trailers. I spent the majority of the time that afternoon getting up and down those fucking steps. I got just one line in that day: "Fuck you, Ray." I said it with venom, pissed at my own stupidity that had led to losing my original part. The late Dennis Burkley steals the scene when he picks up the flattened duck carcass from the floor and says to no one in particular, "Fuck it, man, let's eat this thing."

It was really interesting to see all the props in the house. They were all of the period, down to the Marlboro cigarette packets lying on the table, featuring the vintage design. Occasionally Oliver would ask me if I thought the film's concert scenes were true to the era, as he had spent a lot of that time as a grunt in the U.S. Army in Vietnam and had not witnessed the Doors' gigs firsthand. As far as I could see they were accurate, although sometimes the Doors' concerts in the film would show the audience in a modern standing-on-their-feet way of watching a band perform, whereas I remember everyone sat on the floor at concerts in the '60s. But in my opinion, the audience being involved and on their feet made the gigs in the film seem rebellious or wild in a way that was important. It showed Jim's ability to stir an audience to action.

I wore a wig of long brown hair for my part as Cat, and it was amusing to me, as it reminded me of what I looked like in my teen years. I felt daft to be on crutches doing every scene, but I think Oliver liked having me there for a rock 'n' roll ambiance, and for the steady flow of chicks.

The Doors movie was not the only major film part I lost due to my accident. I was still a long way from fully recovering when I got a call to audition for James Cameron for the part of the Terminator 1000 in the sequel to the first *Terminator* movie. Of course, I was excited beyond belief, as I was told one of the scenes would have me throwing Arnold Schwarzenegger through a wall! I had dinner with James Cameron, and the following day I went to his offices in the valley, where he explained to me what he was thinking. His description of the movie and what my part would entail was pretty wild.

His offices were next to Stan Winston's special effects studio, and James gave me a guided tour. After meeting Stan and upon going round the different studio offices, I began noticing various drawings on the walls, where I was already depicted as the new Terminator! James personally shot a little screen test were he got me to say a few lines and then shoot a gun a few times. I believe it was the scene where the T-1000 is in his L.A. policeman guise, asking young John Connor's foster parents some questions before returning to kill them both in the classic "Your foster parents are dead" scene. James seemed quite happy, but I couldn't help wondering if he really would want someone as recognizable as myself for the role. I was all over MTV, entertainment television, magazines, newspapers, and the radio. But in the end, it was the state of my recovery from the accident that decided my fate in the film.

Terminator 2 had scenes where the T-1000 had to run very fast, chasing Arnold, and my limp was still quite noticeable. Running in the film would be a difficulty, to say the least. Cameron pondered whether he could produce it all as a CGI effect, or with a double, but even walking really fast made my limp more pronounced. In the end, I knew he would need to move on to someone else. He eventually gave the role to Robert Patrick, a still relative-unknown at the time who had a brilliant cold veneer, devoid of feeling, which he was able to bring to the part. In retrospect, that probably would have been a little out of my acting range. I did receive a very nice letter from James Cameron, who told me he thought I could act and was very complimentary. It was great to have met him, and even to have been considered was fantastic. And it would later come in handy that I had met Stan Winston and his crew, as on my video for *Cyberpunk*'s "Shock to the System" I was able to enlist their help for the special effects.

Other film-related opportunities seemed to elude me during this period. For years Keith Forsey had worked with Kathy Nelson, an executive who enlisted musical artists to come up with songs for movie sound tracks. She asked us if we could create a song for a racing sequence in the Tom Cruise film *Days of Thunder*, directed by Tony Scott. The producers Don Simpson and Jerry Bruckheimer already had "Gimme Some Lovin' " in the scene as a placeholder. But it was quite difficult to come up with something that beat "Gimme Some Lovin'," so they eventually just used that.

Some months later, record producer Trevor Horn was working on the sound track to the same movie and was looking for someone to write lyrics and sing them over Hans Zimmer's *Days of Thunder* theme music. I didn't know Trevor at the time, but he contacted me and I agreed to give it a go. He came to my house and we put together a rough demo, with me singing over the theme. He was very enthusiastic and thought I would be perfect for the movie, so we proceeded to record it right then and there. It was fun working with Trevor. He is a rhythm player, a bass player originally, and a Brit with some of the same sensibilities as Keith. Like Keith, he has also produced and played on a vast number of records. Trevor, Don, Jerry, and Tom Cruise all liked what we'd recorded. But then it turned out that the movie was scheduled for release during the same time period as *Charmed Life*.

Initially, the plan was for "Days of Thunder" to appear on both albums, but in the end the timing didn't work, as we already had "Cradle of Love" in *The Adventures of Ford Fairlane*, which meant there was no way to avoid both singles coming out at the same time, and my record company was not going to agree to that. Ultimately, David Coverdale sang "Days of Thunder" for the sound track, but the experience of working with Trevor was a good one and opened a doorway for the future.

CHAPTER THIRTY-NINE

HAVE A FUCK ON ME

The Americas and Europe

I NEEDED A VIDEO FOR "CRADLE of Love," which was to be the first single from the new album. I was out of the hospital, but I was unable to walk without the help of crutches. How the hell could I perform in a video? David Fincher had contacted Tony D. to let him know he would love to make a video with me. Tony explained to David that he would have to figure out a way to make it without having me dance around on crutches. The next day David called Tony and said he had a concept that would overcome my handicap. Boy, was I curious to find out what it was! David arrived at my house with Tony and his producer. It took him less than two minutes to describe his concept and I knew right away the guy was a fucking genius. He explained that I was to be inside a framed picture on a wall that comes to life. The frame prevented you from seeing me beneath my waist. In the video, an alluring Lolita-type young girl enters a geek's apartment and attempts to seduce him while I watch and perform inside the art frame, visible only from the waist up. *Rock the cradle of love!* The video would go on to become a huge hit on MTV, helping the song reach number 2 on the singles chart. At the 1990 MTV Video Music Awards, the video was nominated for Best Male Video and Best Special Effects and won the award for Best Video from a Film. And it was the easiest video I ever made, thank you, David. Of course, the whole world today knows what a great director and producer David Fincher turned out to be. We would work together on another video, for the album's second single, "L.A. Woman," shot in downtown Los Angeles. In the video I was chasing—with the aid of a cane—an elusive image of a girl, who amazingly enough steals my keys and ends up in my bed. A true music video fantasy that was in actuality very close to my real life. MTV refused to play this video until a scene showing a Marilyn Monroe look-alike crucified on a telegraph pole was edited out.

As summer approached, I knew that it would soon be time to commit to the Charmed Life tour that Tony D. had lined up. I was nervous but felt I would be ready to go, so I gave the green light. I had worked very hard to ready myself and had done everything my doctors had told me to do. The album was a huge success and I was keen to go on the road. I was healing well from the motorcycle accident, although I hit a serious bump in the road to recovery. Initially, the doctors put a cast on my leg for a month or so to see if it would heal without inserting a steel rod down through the center of the leg. Well, the top part of the break fused together and began to heal nicely, but despite the cast, the lower half of the leg and my foot were still free to move about. It looked like I was Mr. Fantastic from the *Fantastic Four*. As a result, in April, the doctors decided to insert the metal rod in my leg. They also put chips of bone taken from my hip around the rod, to help the lower half of my leg receive blood via the bone. This would make it possible to heal. Amazingly, it worked. By the early summer the doctors began to offer me encouragement that it would be possible for me to tour.

With the doctors' endorsement, the Charmed Life tour was booked and scheduled to begin in late August. But there were additional medical procedures to deal with first. The doctors took the metal rod out (my seventh operation!), a procedure that took a little while to heal from. Then, two weeks before the tour, my bone specialist decided the final measure would be to remove the remaining lower two screws that had been holding the rod in place. He told me it was a simple operation that could be done in his office. It turned out not to be so simple. He numbed the leg with a local anesthetic and made an incision near my ankle to take the two screws out, but unfortunately for me he had trouble locating them and was cutting around my ankle searching for them, arguing with the nurse along the way about which screw was which and where it should be located. By the time they figured it all out, quite a lot of damage was done to the ankle, and it would still be healing when the tour started. Oh well, another stumbling block. A few Percocet pain pills, some bandages, and *voilà*! Idol was ready to tour.

I started the tour using a cane to help me move about. I had a few different canes, including an Irish walking cane—a shillelagh—and a Chrome Hearts stick with a silver skull on top. I was a bit of a gimp moving about, but I know the audience enjoyed our big stage production featuring a woman's hosed thighs being parted to create the space for the band and me. Above the stage we had a fist with RUDE DUDE tattooed on it, which rotated at the start of the show and extended its middle finger to flip the whole audience off. The crowd would inevitably laugh, clap, and go wild when this happened. The drum riser had skulls, and other Halloweenesque stage accoutrements dotted the stage. The entire stage set was documented in the "Prodigal Blues" video that was partly shot in front of a live audience in Florida.

The tour began in Greater Sudbury, Ontario, Canada, on August 22. I had made a good recovery in the six months since the February crash. We played throughout the U.S. and Canada until the end of November, with Faith No More as our opening act. They were having lots of success, and it was exciting to give a really strong bill to the audience. We enjoyed having them on the tour and became quite friendly with them. As the North American tour drew to a close, my personal assistant and sometime bodyguard, Art Natoli, started to think of practical jokes he could play on them during the final U.S. show, which conveniently fell on Halloween, in Seattle. At the time, Faith No More had a video out for their song "Epic" that ended with a fish gasping for breath. Taking a prompt from the video, we placed a vat full of sardines above the stage in the rafters, out of sight of Faith No More and the colorfully dressed audience. After the band played the last note of their set and began taking their bows, the vat opened up, dropping the sardines on them. The weight of the fish pushed singer Mike Patton to the floor of the stage. He good-naturedly started to put fish down the front of his pants and the guys threw them about at each other. They probably thought that was all, but when they returned to their dressing room, they found it occupied by a lamb and two goats eating hay and what was left of their deli tray.

They quickly found a way to repay me. During my show four naked men wearing only brown paper bags came out and danced round me, much to the surprise of the Seattle audience. Faith No More were really great guys to take it all so well. Thanks, lads!

After the U.S. portion of the tour we headed to Europe and began there with a show in Helsinki, Finland. In Dublin, my mum came to the show with about fifty of my Irish relations. For the special occasion I wore my ERIN GO BRAGH emerald-green shirt with a gold inlaid Gaelic cross on the back.

In Switzerland, a transvestite came to the backstage entrance and asked for "Billy." Everyone was shocked, thinking I had gone out on the town the night before and somehow snagged myself a little something. But it turned out the transvestite was looking for a different Billy on my touring party.

In Germany, a fight started after we left a club in Munich. Art, Keith Forsey, and my bodyguard, who had a black belt in karate, ended up in the fight with some locals over a cab we were all hailing at the same time. I hailed another taxi and got the hell out of there. Maybe I was learning a little, as later, when the police came to our hotel to arrest whoever was involved in the fight, I did not have to spend the night in a German police cell.

The tour had gone extremely well. The band played great and the audience reaction was overwhelming in every country that we visited. Most importantly, I had behaved myself—relatively speaking. Compared to the drugs that had been consumed on previous Billy Idol tours, this one had been tame. But we were especially looking forward to returning to the UK. After a gig at the National Exhibition Centre in Birmingham, we excitedly drove down to London for two shows at Wembley Arena.

Getting off the bus at the hotel in the theater district of London, we headed straight to the bar. There we were joined by the heavy metal band Anthrax, who sat against one of the walls watching everything we were doing. Over on the other side of the hotel bar was an old couple seated with two young men on either side of them, each looking resplendent in evening dress, obviously after a night at the theater. In the center of the bar we were drinking and having fun, happily celebrating the end of the tour, with only the two London shows to go. After a while, one of the young men came over to me and asked politely if I would meet the old couple and the other young man. I nearly declined but thought they looked harmless enough and that it would be nothing to say hello to his party. I went over and shook the other young man's hand and greeted the older couple. As I turned to leave, without warning, the young man who had approached me unceremoniously full-on kissed me, tongue and all. I returned to our group in a state of shock and tried to tell Art what had just happened. But with the hubbub of the bar he didn't hear me quite properly so I grabbed him and shouted in his face, "That guy just full-on French kissed me!" Pointing in the young man's general direction, Art went right over to the wrong guy and started to try to tip him up or pull his pants off or something. I was saying, "No, that's the wrong guy!"—pointing to the other young man. Art decided to leave it at that and we carried on drinking. But sometime later the young man who kissed me came across the bar and tried to talk to me. By now I was somewhat inebriated, and though I was making it perfectly clear I did not want to talk to him, he continued to try to engage me in conversation. This irritated me to the point where Bilvis reared his ugly head, and I took my glass in my hand and smashed it on the bar in disgust. Luckily for him (and me), he wasn't cut, but the furor of people trying to separate us before things escalated any further became quite heated.

On the walls of the hotel bar were autographed photos of famous actors and performers. We were particularly offended by an autographed photo of fifteen-minute pop sensation Milli Vanilli. Just one month earlier, they'd been stripped of their Best New Artist Grammy after admitting they hadn't sung a single note on their debut album. And so, Art took the opportunity to rip their signed photo from the wall, throw it to the floor, and jump up and down on it. That did it. We were thrown out of the hotel, the first time on this tour—but we upgraded to a better hotel as a result.

The next night was the first of two nights at Wembley Arena. We had Gene Loves Jezebel supporting us on this leg of the tour. I was in my dressing room putting on my gear and preparing for the show and I could hear their bass player flubbing his notes, but the rest of the band sounded good. *Hmmm, strange*, I thought. Thinking nothing of it I went back to getting ready, but then the guitar player started dropping a load of notes. *What the fuck?* I thought. Then I started to hear the drummer flubbing his fills, and then the bass player again. "What the hell's going on out there?" I said to somebody within earshot who could see the stage. Art was standing at the front row of the audience, right in front of each band member in turn, looking up, as if something might fall on the band. It was our end-of-tour practical joke! Word of our final-night prank on Faith No More had obviously spread, and each member of Gene Loves Jezebel was trying to play his instrument while craning his neck to see into the dark of the rafters of the arena in case something was about to drop on his head.

The Wembley gigs were excellent nights all around. They concluded with a large number of balloons falling from the ceiling onto the audience with condoms attached to them and the following words written on each one: HAVE A FUCK ON ME.

And with that, the Charmed Life European tour came to an end.

After Europe we had a short break, and in January '91 we embarked on a short South American tour where we were guest stars supporting the great Joe Cocker in gigantic outdoor stadiums. We played three shows in Argentina and found the girls there to be very beautiful, tall, leggy, and blond. They were also very willing, so the gigs were great. We played Punta del Este in Uruguay and finished the short tour leg by playing the first night of the Rock in Rio festival in Brazil, which also was held in a gigantic stadium attended by 250,000 people. In Rio, we supported INXS the first night, and when Robert Plant had to cancel his support slot before Guns N' Roses the next day, we were asked by GNR and the promoter to take his place. This translated into playing in front of half a million people in two days!

We hung out with GNR after the show and partied hard. All I remember now is Slash making what seemed like a million sweet vodka
drinks, which we all dutifully drank. Cocaine was in abundance and
as we weren't leaving the next day, the partying went on until almost
daybreak, when we decided to repair to the hotel before the sun came
up. I'd been asleep for just over an hour when loud, crazed screaming
awoke me. It was a shrieking chorus of young girls greeting New Kids
on the Block, who were also playing the festival and had just arrived
at the hotel. We'd known they were coming. Art had prepared for the
moment, buying a NEW KIDS SUCK T-shirt in Virginia Beach, and he
took this opportunity to show it off. He was out in his underpants with
the T-shirt hanging over the railing in full view of the arriving band
and screaming fans. *Rolling Stone* was covering the festival, and a photo
of Art made it into the next edition of the magazine, standing there in
his skivvies on the hotel balcony, showing off the shirt. Donnie Wahl-
berg saw Art getting photographed and later went to Art's room with
a few of his bodyguards. He threatened Art through his door and Art
said he'd open the door and fight him if he sent all of his bodyguards
away. Donnie left.

Our tour in South America coincided with the first Gulf War's
Operation Desert Storm, and during the day we watched the attacks
taking place in Iraq. It was an incredible thing to witness the impact of
modern weapons, so clearly shown on TV.

In between shows, when we had a few days off, we went to a little
peninsula resort northwest of Rio called Búzios, a rather appropriate
name as about all we did there was drink, party, and go into the little
town to pick up girls. One day Mark Younger-Smith felt the effects of
partying too hard and called for a doctor and nurse. He wouldn't say
he'd overdone it, just that he didn't feel well and thought he needed a
doctor. Later, as we were making our way to a little boat that would
ferry us back to Rio, we ran into the doctor who was just coming from
seeing Mark. When we asked the doctor his diagnosis, he said simply,
"Intoxication."

"We could have told you that!" we all replied.

CHAPTER FORTY

THE MADAM AND THE PREACHER

MY CAROUSING AROUND TOWN RESULTED IN my entanglement in an episode notorious in American tabloid culture. In late 1990, Art Natoli had gotten to know a woman in her twenties named Heidi Fleiss. One night, Art took me to meet her and a few of her girlfriends at Trader Vic's. Over the course of the next few months, Heidi invited Art and me to some parties she'd planned in West Hollywood. A plethora of beautifully coiffured and fashionably dressed girls in their late teens or early twenties could always be found at these parties, as well as some well-known actors. It didn't take long to realize that these girls' "charms" were for sale. Art and Heidi had become close friends, and I would often snag a girl or two or three. They were very lovely, and nothing was asked of me in return. As a bachelor in my early thirties, why would I say no?

We remained friends with Heidi, and as the months passed and her business grew, she told us that she wanted to expand. She started to talk about wanting to buy a more private place, so as to avoid disturbing the neighbors. She spoke to Art and me about how she was going to buy Michael Douglas's old house in the Hills. We both warned her that a young woman buying a place like that, at over $2 million, might draw some attention from the authorities—tax or law enforcement—

but she seemed quite unaffected by our concerns and bought it anyway. Her business continued to expand, and it was almost as if what she was doing was an open secret in Hollywood. She even gave an interview for a piece in the *L.A. Times* discussing her business, although it didn't mention her by name. She was described in the article as the "Hollywood Madam."

During the U.S. tour to promote *Charmed Life*, Art met a girl in Florida called Miami. Though she was only eighteen, he brought her back to L.A. to live with him on Camino Palmero in Hollywood. They seemed very happy, but after a few months they had a fight and Miami ran off to Heidi's. The girls there were among the few friends she had made in L.A.

Art really liked Miami and was distressed when she left him. When he found out she was staying at Heidi's, he freaked at the thought of Miami possibly working for Heidi. He told me he felt betrayed by Heidi and that he wanted Miami to return to Florida.

He called Heidi's house often, trying to speak to Miami, but she wouldn't come to the phone, and he felt that Heidi was taking pleasure in his frustration. He told me that Heidi was winding him up that Miami was going to become one of her girls. Art became incensed, and it seems that the phone calls between him and Heidi were becoming particularly unpleasant. Each complained to me about the other. Heidi seemed to delight in the idea that she could keep hold of Miami and show her a good time, but at the same time, she claimed Art was threatening her. Art, in turn, griped that Heidi was taunting him and had driven past his apartment with Miami in her souped-up red sports car, honking the horn so that he would see that his ex was with her and not him. Threats went back and forth between Art and Heidi. I did my best to stay out of it.

Heidi even had prominent people in the film industry phone me to tell me to fire Art. I wondered whether the calls were motivated by concerns about the info in her famous black book, rather than concerns for me. But I said to those who called me, "Why doesn't Heidi just let the girl go? She's got plenty of eighteen-year-olds up there—why does she need to keep this one around?" Heidi herself even called me a couple of times, telling me to fire Art. I responded by appealing to both her logic and her ego, telling her she was bigger than this feud. But Heidi wouldn't listen to me: it seemed that she and Art were well past listening to logic from anyone.

I was a little dumbfounded, but feuds often make no sense, and when emotions are stirred up, things can get crazy. The situation was getting nasty, and I was trying my best to not get caught up in it. Other former girls of Heidi's sided with Art, and the two cliques feuded for over a year with no resolution until finally, Art told me Heidi had been caught using some stolen credit cards somewhere in Beverly Hills. When she was questioned by authorities about the stolen cards, she said she had gotten them from Art Natoli.

When the police confronted Art, he became angry that Heidi would try to set him up, and he saw it as his opportunity for payback. He told the detectives, "Do you know who you have here? I don't think you realize who this woman is!"

He referenced the newspaper interview she had given anonymously, and though they were aware of it, they hadn't known exactly who the Hollywood Madam was—until now. Art told the cops the story of his girl Miami and how Heidi was involved. He told them how all he wanted was for the girl to go home to her mum, and that he hadn't given Heidi the stolen credit cards. He told them her accusations were all part of this feud. The police went into action and busted Heidi.

The next time I heard of her was on the news, in the headlines and on TV. She was in court and going down. I felt sorry for all parties involved, as I liked Heidi, Miami, and Art, but I felt fortunate to be removed from it all, as the entire situation had devolved into a reality TV nightmare for all involved.

BACK WHEN PERRI AND I FIRST moved to L.A., we went to the Comedy Store and were lucky enough to see Sam Kinison perform. Sam was a former Pentecostal tent preacher who had turned his oratorical gifts away from the church and toward comedy. I first saw him in 1984 on HBO's *Young Comedians Special*, hosted by Rodney Dangerfield, which was Sam's big break, alongside fellow comedians Andrew Dice Clay, Louis C.K., and Dave Chappelle. We ended up hanging out with Sam and his comedian mates after the show that night at the Comedy Store. The evening spawned a friendship between Sam and me.

We hung out fairly frequently, and eventually Sam asked me to appear with other rockers in his video for his comedic cover of "Wild Thing" that also featured a big-breasted Jessica Hahn rolling around in a mud-wrestling ring (minus the mud). We went to Bowie's Glass Spider tour together one night and ended up backstage to see David. When he saw us, he good-naturedly said, "Oh no, not you two, together," with a big grin on his face. Madonna was also in the room to see David, and a photographer captured all of us lined up backstage, laughing and having great fun.

Around this time Sam was consuming a lot of blow and was beginning to act more like a rock star than like a comedian. He truly loved rock 'n' roll and played a mean guitar—the insane rush that comes from putting oneself well out on a limb to play a live rock set in front of a crowd must be similar to what one feels when delivering a comedy act. Sam occasionally came shopping with me looking for rock 'n' roll duds, but finding cool pants to go around his fifty-eight-inch waist was difficult. He favored long coats to minimize his substantial bulk.

Soon, his cocaine consumption began to bring out his paranoid side. He had a lovely young girlfriend who had a sister and they would dress up as Vegas showgirls and generally serve as eye candy for Sam's act. He became unpredictable and without warning would suddenly pick a fight with someone in the room, claiming they were out to steal his girl.

Sam began featuring music in his comedy act, and I occasionally went to Vegas when he was appearing there, to get up and do a song or two with him. On one occasion I went with Mark Younger-Smith to do two shows in a single day with Sam at the Sands Hotel. It was on this trip that my friendship with Sam Kinison came to a crashing end. Sam called me up onstage at the end of his afternoon act. Mark and I did "Mony Mony" and then we supported Sam while he did "Wild Thing."

Sam was a high-decibel comic, and his guitar playing echoed this, as he came out playing three times louder than anyone. While he was soloing wildly on his axe, I was over to one side of the stage, and I got in between the two sisters dressed as Vegas showgirls. I was doing nothing particularly suggestive, but Sam, paranoid and jealous, concluded I was up to something. I could see at the end of the song that he was looking particularly bothered. He couldn't get to me, so he punched Mark, who was playing near him.

Well, that's really out of order, I thought. We had come there to support Sam, not to end up in a fight. We tried to get out of Vegas that night in an effort to defuse the situation as much as possible, and actually went to the airport but couldn't get a flight. Returning to the Sands, I saw that Frank Sinatra was also performing there that night. We ditched Sam's second show and decided to see the septuagenarian Sinatra instead. Hotel management comped us great seats. They were aware of the fracas with Sam and understood why we wouldn't want to return for an encore.

Frank was marvelous! He arrived on the stage fresh from a penthouse suite that delivered him via elevator, straight onto the stage. His son Frank Jr. was directing the orchestra for him, and Frank Sr. would occasionally consult with his son about which number they were doing next. His son would now and then lean down from his perch, where he was conducting the orchestra, and whisper in Frank's ear. At one point Frank audibly said, "I'm not doing that!" His son gave a funny look and offered another suggestion, to which Frank nodded. The show featured numbers spanning his entire career, including "Soliloquy" from the musical *Carousel*, an eight-minute song about an expectant father awaiting his firstborn and wondering what the future will be for the child. During this song, Frank touched his forehead several times, feigning concern that he was sweating, and making sure the audience took notice. He began to remove the orange handkerchief from the breast pocket of his own midnight-blue jacket but, thinking better of it, quickly reached out and used his son's matching handkerchief to mop his own brow. He made some comments about how he couldn't regularly smoke or drink, but had a cigarette and a hit of Jack during the show. It was special, my first and only time seeing Ol' Blue Eyes live.

I was sorry that my relationship with Sam ended the way it did, but if he hadn't gotten so paranoid and jealous that evening in Vegas, I never would have seen the Chairman of the Board. In his mid-seventies, he still sounded good and seemed to be enjoying himself. It was truly inspiring and made me think that if you work hard and have the desire, there is no reason you can't sing professionally well past retirement age.

I was terribly saddened when I learned of Sam's tragic death in a car accident in April 1992. He was sober and drug-free, driving from L.A. to Laughlin, Nevada, where he was going to perform before a sold-out audience. Sam's brother and manager, Bill, followed Sam's Trans Am in a van, along with two assistants and Sam's dog. A couple of teenagers in a 1974 Chevy pickup truck were approaching from the opposite direction on U.S. Highway 95 near the California-Nevada border, drinking and driving fast on a Friday night. That's when the pickup crossed the center line, colliding head-on with Sam's Trans Am. With only minor cuts on his lips and forehead, Sam stumbled from his mangled vehicle and lay down, after being begged to do so. He said, "I don't want to die, I don't want to die." And then he paused, as if listening to someone only he could hear. "But why?" he asked. "Okay," he finally whispered. "Okay . . . okay."

CHAPTER FORTY-ONE

MIND FIRE

Golgotha Studios, Hollywood Hills, Los Angeles

DRAWN BY THE RETREATING RUSSIAN ARMY, Napoléon pushed on harder into the unwelcoming Russian hinterland, ignoring the star that had guided him. He hurriedly readied his Grande Armée, which was beginning to feel the strain of the three-month march, along with the lack of food and rest. "They must turn and face me at the walls of Moscow," he said. "Then I'll have the decisive battle I seek." And so the march continued and Napoléon doggedly followed in the forlorn belief in his destiny, which had been so right up until then. *One more big battle and I'll have them beaten*, he thought to himself, as the blistering heat of summer burnt his nostrils and the hot wind blew eternally over the vast Russian tundra. Caulaincourt, his Master of the Horse, shook his head in vain as they moved deeper into the stark unknown. Napoléon lay sprawled out while he studied his inaccurate maps, languishing behind the lines while letting Murat and Davout fight the Russian rearguard, who had outfoxed the French and kept the mighty Grande Armée at bay like a snapping dog chained at its heels, just out of reach. "One big battle," he muttered underneath his breath to no one.

Despite various frustrations and distractions, I was basking in the sunshine of a dramatic recovery from my accident and a successful tour (that I hobbled through on a cane). I felt the satisfaction of accomplishment and rocking while doing so. I didn't let my injury get me too down. I just went hell-for-leather to get better to be able to perform the album that I had completed prior to the crash. Maybe that was what spurred my recovery; I had something to get better for . . . the thing I loved. At that point, I was happy just to take care of Willem, then a toddler, and see Bonnie whenever I could.

As Errol Flynn put it in *Captain Blood*, "Faith, it's an uncertain world entirely." I was at the top of my game and at the top of the charts all over the world. My production and management teams were coming up with the goods.

Still, some deep-seated fear was taking hold of me that I couldn't explain. My drug and alcohol consumption left me feeling lifeless. I wasn't bouncing back from my binges like I had come to expect. What was wrong with me?

Had the making of *Charmed Life* and the motorcycle accident taken more out of me than I could have imagined? Had I toured too soon after the accident? A life-threatening accident, seven operations, and straight into a five-month world tour without even thinking about taking a break, and I had still found time to party during and after the tour. What was I thinking? Like Napoléon, I ignored my symptoms, as I hoped to open a new vista for myself. I had aspirations of taking advantage of the momentum of a successful album and tour to come up with something new and unanticipated, but I was feeling hamstrung by fame and expectations. I found that I often couldn't think clearly regarding musical decisions, where before, my instincts had rarely failed me. I was listening to a lot of dance music from England, stuff like early Prodigy and Future Sounds of London. The rave scene was in full swing, almost making rock 'n' roll seem quaint and old-fashioned. I had become interested in the techniques these bands employed: home recordings, samples, collages, musique concrète. John Joseph Wardle's post-PiL Jah Wobble records, The Orb's dubbed-out house, and On-U Sound Records' reggae-influenced productions. I liked this new world but, looking back, I may have gravitated toward it at that moment because I didn't have enough energy to commit to any more rock 'n' roll records. Plus that world had been taken over by grunge, which to me was nearer to heavy metal and hard rock than it was to punk. While this description didn't necessarily apply to Nirvana, I felt it was the case with Pearl Jam and Soundgarden.

I started to become interested in the prediction of the cyber-revolution and the possibilities intrigued me. At the same time, I wanted to make an album that was completely dance-oriented just as *Charmed Life* was rock-oriented. I wanted to explore musically and take some risks, whether it was the right move for a long-term career or not. I should have allowed myself to take stock and perhaps take the break I never had after the accident, but I didn't.

I had survived fifteen years of serious drug use, and enough drugs for another fifteen years in just three weeks in Thailand. And then there was the breakup with Perri. All this had taken a bigger toll than I had been prepared to acknowledge. I had no energy. I was shattered and I couldn't sleep. I was paying the piper.

I was flailing about like a beached whale gasping for air, out of my element, far from my beloved rock 'n' roll. Like John Lennon sang in "Yer Blues," "Feel so suicidal / Even hate my rock 'n' roll."

Trying to be a trooper, I plowed on regardless. The scholar and poet Rossiter W. Raymond once wrote, "Death is only a horizon; and a horizon is nothing save the limit of our sight." I felt I had arrived at one musical horizon and wanted to pass through to see what was on the other side.

I decided to try a different producer for what would become the *Cyberpunk* album and found Robin Hancock, who recorded using an early Pro Tools rig, with its array of samples and effects. Bringing in my new guitarist Mark Younger-Smith, we started to write and record new songs, such as "One Touch of Venus," "Tomorrow People," "Shock to the System," and "Power Junkie," which featured a sample of Muhammad Ali yelling, "I'm a bad man! I shook up the world!" after upsetting the allegedly unbeatable Sonny Liston.

I got the idea for the album from an interview with Legs McNeil, who interviewed me in the hospital and, seeing my leg hooked up to this electronic muscle stimulator, dubbed me "Cyberpunk." In the mid-'80s, I'd read William Gibson's classic books, including *Neuro-*

mancer; now I immersed myself in the genre of cyberpunk fiction and began reading books such as Neal Stephenson's *Snow Crash* and Gareth Branwyn's influential 1992 manifesto, "Is There a Cyberpunk Movement?" I began seeing cyberpunk as a new way to reexplore my punk roots.

I had no desire to emulate the recording process and the partying of *Charmed Life* so I decided to record the album in my house. It was my attempt to do an indie record, but the world had already decided I was a mainstream artist and expected a straight-ahead rock record as the follow-up to *Charmed Life*. I realized that the emergence of affordable technology would have a major impact on bringing about a new era for DIY punk music. "It's 1993," I told the *New York Times*. "I better wake up and be part of it. I'm sitting there, a 1977 punk watching Courtney Love talk about punk, watching Nirvana talk about punk, and this is my reply."

Cyberpunk was originally supposed to be the sound track for a film. I was introduced to the film director Brett Leonard by Tony D. He had made the original cybermovie, *The Lawnmower Man*, and let us sample any effects we wanted from the film for the record. He talked of a sequel called *Mind Fire*, for which we started to write songs. The thinking was that the album would be the film's sound track, not just a regular release. So I wrote with that in mind. This process sent me deeper into the cyberworld. The script for *Mind Fire* was really imaginative, a futuristic love story. At one point, the two lovers are locked up together, so Robin and I wrote a song called "Prisoners of Love," which we didn't use in the end. We were well into the album when Brett informed me that the film studio didn't want to give him the money to make the new film bigger and better than the first one, so the entire project stalled. The studio cut the film's budget in half and made what turned out to be a flop with another director, which we declined to be a part of. That left *Cyberpunk* on its own, as a Billy Idol album.

Released on June 29, 1993, it was my least successful album to date and was mocked and labeled a failure in both content and concept at the time by critics. Musically, the album was ambitious in style, but the direction was scattered. My creative instincts and possibly even my taste seemed to abandon me this time around. Even so, I am still proud of the album. The ideas and themes I was exploring and the methods I insisted on using to record, promote, and share the album with my fans have proven to be far ahead of their time, as they would come to dominate the record industry in the years ahead.

Cyberpunk was recorded entirely on software such as Pro Tools and featured songs that dealt with the oncoming onslaught of technology on our daily lives. I was the first artist to include his or her e-mail address on an album jacket, and I used early online communities like The WELL and Usenet to connect with my fans and solicit ideas from them. The first single, "Shock to the System," was released on a floppy disc, a medium that is a precursor to the MP3 that is now the norm. We were the first to release a digital press kit for an album on a diskette, which featured clips from the album, artwork, lyrics, and commentary: all elements that are staples of modern music websites that are naturally taken for granted now but that seemed strange to many at the time.

I'm not sure if it was an inability on my part to explain the album's themes fully, or an overarching hesitance amongst the public to accept the themes as realistic, or both. Or it may have just been that people didn't like the inconsistent music. But the result was that the press and probably many of my fans found my attempts to do something new like *Cyberpunk*, and promote the impending prevalence of technology in music and daily life, as comical and reason to subject me to ridicule. Even the small yet burgeoning 1993 online community, which I went to lengths to embrace and present in a new and relevant light, accused me of attempting to co-opt their world and use it for my own selfish gain.

The immediate reaction to the album humbled me, and I declined to speak much further on it at the time, but now I hope that those who initially criticized what I was doing with *Cyberpunk* can at least appreciate how much I was going out on a limb to do something different and push the envelope, challenging myself and my audience, even if it led to failure. As I said in an interview around the time of the album's release, I feel that I was honoring my DIY punk roots by moving

ahead and making an album entirely on computers at a time when—
especially for a prominent artist—to do so was exceedingly rare. I feel
that having the courage and commitment to use the computer exten-
sively as creative tool, despite being a novice in the computer world,
was a move in the tradition of the punks who had the courage and the
commitment to write songs and play music on instruments, when they
more often than not lacked musical skills.

Being an artist is about putting aside your fears and going for it.
This was my code in 1976, and in 1993, and it still is today.

CHAPTER FORTY-TWO

BITTER PILL

Southern California

AFTER *CYBERPUNK*, I WOULDN'T MAKE ANOTHER album for twelve years.

Toward the end of 1994, I was asked to write a title song for the Keanu Reeves and Dennis Hopper movie *Speed*, so I used the opportunity to call Steve Stevens to see if he wanted to work with me on it. I was delighted when he agreed. Steve is a massive part of the Billy Idol sound and, quite simply, he's a virtuoso with staggeringly proficient technical skill. I really liked Mark Younger-Smith's Texas-blues-rock style, but in the end, no one can hold a candle to the incomparable Steve Stevens.

We began to work in Steve's apartment off Sunset Plaza and finished writing "Speed" in just a few hours. It ended up being the title song to a very successful movie. Steve and I decided to keep going, mulling over recording ideas, going through tons of work tapes, and actually wrote quite a lot of material in addition to "Speed." One day I would love to look back on those ideas and listen to what we were doing. "Speed" was a fun song to write, and I hoped we would reunite with Keith Forsey to produce it. Unfortunately, the chap selecting the artists for the movie wanted to produce it, and I didn't think the end result was as good as our usual singles. I think that was reflected in its chart position, although it seemed to do really well in Europe's former Eastern Bloc countries, as they had all just opened up to MTV.

Steve and I wrote a lot of good music around this time, but somehow we never moved beyond the demo stage with those songs. As a result, for a while we were in a kind of self-induced limbo. I am inclined to look back at this period of my career with disappointment. Why, you may ask? Well, I wanted to move forward into something different creatively and not be stuck repeating myself over and over, and Steve felt the same way. It was easy to write "Speed" because "a sound from the past" is what the music supervisor and the producers wanted, so we gave them what they asked for. But if Steve and I were going to make another album together, then we had to break some new ground. I had reached the twenty-year mark in my music life and career, and it's true that many artists hit a fallow period at different times in their careers. This has to be overcome by sheer persistence. "Genius is one percent inspiration and ninety-nine percent perspiration," Thomas Edison said. But that did not mean that we should compromise.

Steve and I kept at it, writing songs together until the late '90s, but none of the creative roads we tried to go down seemed to click. Looking back, I think a combination of factors led to this period of discombobulation. I found myself, for the first time in my career, unsure about which creative direction to turn in next. I had lost the musical thread of what we had been doing prior to *Cyberpunk* and was struggling to come up with my next move. Nonetheless, I continued to try.

As I was wondering what to do next, I received a script to read that would lead to one of my most enjoyable experiences working on a movie to date. Even at a young age, Willem was a fan of Adam Sandler movies, and we used to watch them together. I enjoyed them, too, and liked Adam's work on *Saturday Night Live*. I received a script called *The Wedding Singer*, a spoof '80s movie that would star Adam and Drew Barrymore. Drew used to come to my New York club gigs when she was ten years old. On reading the script, I found it used "White Wedding" as a central motif and that it was quite amusing. I enjoyed the idea of playing myself, but also sending myself up. As time goes on, one can't help but see the cliché side of what happened musically and culturally in the '80s.

I turned up on the day of shooting to find Adam had a guitar, drums, and bass set up in his trailer so we could jam between takes, which was a fun idea. Many comedians from this period loved rock 'n' roll and wanted to be musicians. Like Sam Kinison, Adam could play guitar.

My part called for just a one-day shoot, but those first scenes went well, and soon Frank Coraci, the director, and Adam decided to ask me to come back for another day. I was tasked with continuing to help Robbie, Adam's character, finally get with the love of his life, Julia, played by Drew. So my character was given additional lines on the airplane near the end of the movie where I pretend to be the captain of the plane speaking to the passengers over the PA system explaining how "We let our first class passengers do pretty much whatever they want," bringing Julia and Robbie together. I was, in effect, playing a rock 'n' roll cupid! Frank told me he would have liked me to play the best man when they marry at the end, but that scene had already been shot.

I always thought, somewhere in my imagination, that I could be good in a movie, and in some ways here was evidence of that, although I was playing myself—not much of a stretch. I really enjoyed the camaraderie and the comedy of the film and the shoot.

WHILE MY EXPERIENCE WORKING ON THE *Wedding Singer* was a great diversion, musically, I felt unmoored. Compounding the problem during this time, my label, Chrysalis Records—which had been a strong supporter of my work from the days of Generation X—was beginning to fall apart. They had fought fiercely to remain independent for many years but succumbed in 1991 when half the company was sold to EMI. In 1992, EMI acquired the other half and systematically proceeded to tear the company apart until it no longer existed. EMI became my label through no choice of yours truly. But then I heard that Gary Gersh, the president of Capitol Records, a part of the EMI family of labels, wanted me to be on his label. That suited me fine, as Gary was a friend of my manager Tony D. He had also been the executive who had first signed Nirvana when he was at Geffen Records. The added bonus was that the Capitol offices were in Los Angeles. Gary hooked me up with producer Glen Ballard, who was hot off his multiplatinum Alanis Morissette album. Steve Stevens joined in and we got halfway through making a record. We even played a proposed single, "Bitter Pill," which had a distinct rockabilly feel, at the European Midem convention. But just as we were finishing, Gersh was fired from Capitol. The new regime dropped me from the label without even listening to the album we were working on with Glen. That was the end of that. After negotiations with EMI, I did manage to hold on to the rights to the recordings, so it still could be completed one day; in fact, a new version of "Bitter Pill" will appear on my latest album, *Kings & Queens of the Underground*.

IN LATE 1998, I BECAME VERY interested in the idea of a new digital music model, somehow utilizing the people power of the Internet. During the making of the Capitol album that was never to be, we recorded a song called "Sleeping with an Angel," a ballad I wrote with Billy Steinberg. On being unceremoniously dropped by the label, I took the song and gave it to a free Internet service called MP3.com, founded by a guy named Michael Robertson, who clearly had the major labels in his crosshairs. I thought this syrupy tune might end up being a bit revolutionary in its release, helping promote, as it did, the breakdown of the record company monolith. John Diaz, who later worked at MP3.com, knew the people over there, so it was easy to make happen.

As a result, I was one of the first wave of prominent artists to make their music available for free on the Internet. Later, I gave MP3.com another song, called "Find a Way." It was fun to see the music come out instantly, and to add weight to the growing insurrection.

Shawn Fanning had yet to launch Napster, while Facebook was still several years down the road, waiting to be born in Mark Zuckerberg's Harvard dorm room, but my punk roots were showing, and I was beginning to daydream of a way to mainline the music directly to the listener. Twenty-plus years prior, mainlining the music meant performing inches in front of fifteen people on a tiny stage I helped build, exchanging sweat and saliva. Disenchanted with record label conglomerates, I began to ponder a digital parallel.

I appeared on *NBC Nightly News*, interviewed by Tom Brokaw as the first major artist to go digital. "Sleeping with an Angel" was downloaded more than 100,000 times in the age of the dial-up Internet connection, when a single song often took fifteen to twenty minutes to access. Releasing the song and in effect pirating my own music was a Christmas gift to my fans and a middle finger to Capitol. While my manager, Tony D., quickly came around to the idea, he was aghast when he first learned about it, which was why we buried it during his year-end holiday!

CHAPTER FORTY-THREE

MY ROAD IS LONG, IT LINGERS ON

Redwood Valley—and beyond

FOR SIX YEARS, I DIDN'T SET foot on a single stage. Performing in front of a live crowd had been central to who I thought I was for most of my adult life. The backlash following *Cyberpunk* made me think it was best to take a break from the road, and even once I was able to put that album in my rearview mirror, I had no desire to tour again unless I had something new and relevant to say. But an experience born out of my insatiable love for riding motorcycles helped get me back onstage, launching the next chapter of my touring career.

In January 1999, my friend John Diaz introduced me to Stephen McGrath, aka Evil McG. Steve had his own recording studio, and I was looking for someone to help me bring mine up to snuff. I immediately liked his friendly, outgoing personality, and as we talked, we found we have many things in common. In addition to being a musician, like me he's a voracious reader and loves to ride Harleys. We decided to take a ride together to the Redwood Run biker rally in Northern California. Since my early childhood I have been fascinated by the images of the redwood forest that I saw in books, never expecting that one day I would see those trees in real life. On our way, we stopped in Ukiah, California, and spent the night at the house of a friend of McG's.

The next day we rode farther north on 101 and into Redwood Valley, en route to the rally site. McG and I had a fantastic trip to the redwoods and California hill country, south of Eureka. We posed for a photo right in the middle of one of those majestic trees, together on our bikes. You can actually drive through one of the trees, and I had once seen a truck with a trailer going through it in a children's picture book. Visiting this natural temple was a wild feeling; it was easy to imagine a bit of what the settlers must have felt when they came across the many natural wonders of America.

Once at the rally, we pitched a small tent next to our bikes in the campground. A stage had been set up where various local and blues bands were going to play. Later that evening, Los Lobos took the stage. I ended up onstage with them performing "Train Kept a-Rollin'." As the music picked up pace and I got into it, I found myself having a semi-out-of-body experience, feeling as if I'd been transported into another realm of feeling and consciousness. Quite honestly, I felt like a spinning top. It was a powerful sensation and I thought, *If this is what being back onstage feels like, I need more, more, more!* It was too good a feeling to miss. McG and I took many road trips together that summer and became close friends.

Back in L.A., I began to make plans to return to the road and live performing, and in December 1999, I reunited playing live shows with Steve Stevens, with McG as our bass player. We have been touring the world fairly consistently ever since.

In addition to Steve Stevens and McG, my touring band in the early 2000s also included keyboardist Derek Sherinian and drummer Brian Tichy. Brian is also a songwriter, and the two of us collaborated on many songs, some of which appear on my 2005 album *Devil's Playground*.

Brian had worked frequently with Ozzy Osbourne and was partial to hard rock, heavy metal, and classic rock. So apart from making music in the Idol vein, we also experimented with some styles that didn't make it onto *Devil's Playground*. Two of these songs, "Hollywood Promises" and "Whiskey and Pills," were recorded with Trevor Horn for my *Kings & Queens of the Underground* album.

I was also writing with Steve Stevens around this time, so with the songs I wrote with Brian, plus my own solo contributions, three song-writing teams combined to produce *Devil's Playground*.

Most of the songs I wrote with Brian had been written around his guitar riffs, including "World Comin' Down," "Super Overdrive," "Body Snatchers," "Cherie," and "Evil Eye." Sometimes when you sit with demos you become very attached to them, and you come to believe all ideas on the demos must make it to the finished record. I was cer-tainly guilty of this when it came time to record *Devil's Playground*, and so this meant that Steve Stevens sometimes needed to emulate Brian's guitar licks and reiterate them exactly as on the demo. This didn't give Steve much opportunity to come up with his own take, and I know that was frustrating for him. He did what I asked, without complaint, but the situation would eventually lead to friction between Steve and Brian, particularly when we went on the road.

We recorded *Devil's Playground* at the Jungle Room in L.A., with Keith Forsey once again at the helm. The Jungle Room is run by Brian Reeves, who engineered the first Billy Idol album, so it was the old team back together for this one. Brian is an excellent engineer and fun and easy to work with. It was especially helpful that Keith Forsey was involved, because at that moment we needed someone who could bring the album to fruition by helping the varied sources of material jell properly.

Many of the lyrics on this album deal with a sense of impending doom, or a determination to keep going in the face of adversity, but fortunately, it's not all gloom. The record also includes "Cherie," an ode to Perri. She gave me love, and that love produced our son, and she put up with a lot from me in the years we were together. She stood by me during the heady days of the '80s and was by my side as our roman-tic journey took us around the world. Venice in the spring; Paris in the fall; all the hot, sweaty, and humid New York City summers we lived through; and London's winter chill. The song "Cherie" is my way of saying *Thank you . . . for everything*.

Looking back, I was still feeling somewhat insecure about putting out another album, and I relied too much on the opinions of others when some hard choices needed to be made. I sometimes felt that I had to allow Brian to dictate the arrangement since he'd cowritten and produced the demo, but I also felt it was unfair to Steve to have to play Brian's guitar arrangements. Either way, I couldn't win. I should have known better, since I had learned many years ago that compromise for the sake of compromise has negative repercussions when recording an album.

Sanctuary Records released *Devil's Playground* on March 22, 2005. Unfortunately, the label was struggling financially at the time, and disintegrated not long after the album was released.

We plowed on regardless and toured with Brian as our drummer in 2005 and 2006, but the relationship between Brian and Steve continued to deteriorate until I knew I had to do something about it. After we worked with producer Josh Abraham on two new songs, "New Future Weapon" and "John Wayne," for the greatest-hits package *The Very Best of Billy Idol: Idolize Yourself*, I made the decision to let Brian go. For his part, Brian was probably ready to move on, too, so everything was amicable. After this shift, the vibes in the band improved dramatically.

Soon after Tichy departed, Steve came to me with the idea that the live show would benefit from having a second guitarist. In fact, this is what you normally hear on our records: two interweaving guitar tracks. So at Steve's suggestion, we brought in a second guitarist, Billy Morrison, who had previously played with the Cult. He has proved a perfect fit for many reasons, including his talent as a songwriter. In fact, six of the tracks on *Kings & Queens of the Underground* emerged from the Idol/Stevens/Morrison trifecta.

Billy is from New Eltham in South East London, not far from Bromley, where I lived with my parents when the punk explosion began. He is ten years younger than me but got into punk at a very young age. By hanging with Guy Jardine, another Bromley punk who I've known for years who was older than Billy, he managed to bunk into gigs for free, so he saw a number of the early punk bands, including Generation X. He was a big fan of *Valley of the Dolls* when it was released in 1979, so when he joined the band, we started to play some selections from that album live. Not only is Billy Morrison a good mate and a link to my days of punk in the UK, but he's also become an integral part of the new Idol sound. And as if that is not enough, he has also been our battlefield reporter, taking fans for a ride around the world with his colorful Idol Live tour diary entries on BillyIdol.net, our official website.

Over the past few years the band has jelled into what is without question the finest band I have ever had. We have toured the U.S. and Europe several times over and have had the pleasure of visiting several countries that at one time were either behind the Iron Curtain or part of former Yugoslavia, including Russia, Serbia, Bulgaria, Croatia, Slovenia, Hungary, and Macedonia. Who would have thought it? A punk from Bromley bringing joy to ten thousand screaming fans in Moscow. Too wild for the chemistry teacher from South East London who called me "Idle" to comprehend, I'm sure. And does my older music still hold up? Blimey, I think it does!

To think it was just two years ago in a tent in Munich that I saw one of the greatest moments of total audience participation ever, where the whole, and I mean the whole, audience had their fists in the air during the encore song "White Wedding"! The band was so overwhelmed they stopped playing, and no matter what I did the crowd wouldn't stop cheering or shouting out in exultation. These are human moments of communication where for a short time we feel connected by the music, by the energy, and the sheer will to rock out. It is in these moments that I find validation of my life's work.

These moments also encouraged me to contemplate another album. Steve and I continued to write together and we also brought in Billy Morrison to contribute to our writing sessions. I also wrote some songs with a wonderful young artist named George Lewis Jr., aka Twin Shadow. I couldn't wait to get back in the studio again. When it came time to think about a producer for my new album, Tony D. reminded me of the time I had worked with Trevor Horn on the *Days of Thunder* sound track and how much I had enjoyed that experience. We contacted Trevor and sent him some demos of the new songs. He quickly responded that he thought they had a lot of potential, so I went to London to see him in May 2013. One of the first things he said to me was, "Why do you want me to produce your record? I do prog rock!" I said, "Bollocks, you've done everything—you can do it all!" And that he has, from Rod Stewart to Art of Noise, from Frankie Goes to Hollywood to Seal. Then, of course, there was Yes's "Owner of a Lonely Heart," which turned prog rock on its head with regular back-to-back airplay with "Flesh for Fantasy" back in 1983. After that, we were on!

Trevor's studio in London, Sarm, was due to close for a remodel, but he agreed to keep it open so he could make one last album there. The studio is in a former church in Basing Street, just around the corner from Portobello Road where, in that white-hot summer of 1976, from a top-floor window, I witnessed young disenfranchised Jamaicans demonstrating before being subdued by battalions of blue-clad bobbies. Like their punk brothers, they also left their indelible mark in the history books on behalf of England's youth.

Sarm Studios' storied history goes back even further, to the days when it was the studio and headquarters for Chris Blackwell's Island Records. Legends such as Bob Marley, Traffic, Free, and Cat Stevens were signed to Island Records and recorded there, as did many non-Island artists, including Led Zeppelin and the Rolling Stones. If those walls could talk.

Trevor worked from our demos but instead of relying on sampled or drum machine automation, he got Ash Soan to play live drums while he played bass. I put some guide vocals on Trevor's tracks while I was visiting my parents and left him to it. He sent me the tracks he had worked on, and I was so impressed that I returned to London a few weeks later with Steve. We recorded five more tracks that we felt would work best if recorded live. These include "Love and Glory," "Kings & Queens of the Underground," "Hollywood Promises," "Ghosts in My Guitar," and "Postcards from the Past." I redid some vocals and Steve put down his guitar tracks on the keyboard songs that Trevor had recorded while we were in L.A. Later Billy Morrison joined us. We worked on some string arrangements that Trevor was keen to put on "Kings & Queens," "Eyes Wide Shut," "One Breath Away," "Nothing to Fear," and "Love and Glory" and when they were finished they sounded like the new anthems we hoped they'd become.

Before we left, we discussed some overdubs that Trevor then added.

These were basic sweetening overdubs using smatterings of keyboards played by Trevor's Buggles partner, Geoff Downes, and also strings and backing vocals.

Working with Trevor was exhilarating. In some ways it wasn't so different from working with Keith Forsey, as both are English and started out as primarily rhythm players, Keith on the drums and Trevor on the bass. But there the similarity ends. Trevor has his own style completely and it was this that he brought to the album.

Trevor sent me the mixes after I returned to L.A. I was very happy with what we'd produced, but I felt that I needed one or two more songs to complete the album. In 2013, I met Greg Kurstin, a prolific songwriter-producer, and we discussed writing together, but the timing did not work for either of us. While listening to Trevor's mixes, it occurred to me that a song we'd put aside—"Save Me Now," written with George Lewis—might be great with some revisions. I contacted Greg to see if he wanted to help me finish writing it. In the song, I'm calling out to a loved one to rescue me and restore in me faith in humanity that has been cruelly shattered. No one wants to do it alone, ladies!

Greg's finishing touches made us both very excited about the song, so I asked him if he might also produce it. "Save Me Now" came together so well, we both felt we were onto something, and we decided to write another song with the help of Dan Nigro. With Greg once again producing, "Can't Break Me Down" carries on the message of defiance to those who seek to beat us down in this world. With the two new songs wrapped, the album was complete.

In the entire album, I tried to stick to themes that affect us all in our daily lives, universal themes of love and loss. As the world continues to find new ways to tear itself apart, humans still love, hate, feel rejected, and yearn to be close to someone.

Give the future enough time and it will speak for itself. Now, with this new album and excellent iteration of my band, including Steve Stevens, Stephen McGrath, Billy Morrison, drummer Erik Eldenius, and keyboardist Paul Trudeau, the forest no longer seems impenetrable.

MY GREATEST INSPIRATION ON THIS ALBUM has been my family and the opportunities I've had to reflect on my life. It's been great fun to watch Bonnie and Willem grow up, first as small children, then through their teen years, and now as adults. One thing's for certain: the DNA doesn't fall far from this tree! Whether I see them individually or together, relaxing at my house or sitting with them over dinner, it's always a great time, as they are both terrifically bright, loving, and funny. They crack me up with their rapid-fire banter, fueled by youth and wonderment. Seeing them makes it easy to remember when I saw the world with the same curiosity all those years ago, wanting to drink up every last drop.

Ever since Bonnie was young she's been a prankster, and she gets me every time. When she was in her late teens, I became anxious she might get a tattoo, as they were popping up on her friends' arms, legs, and torsos. A friend of hers had just had two pistols tattooed on her stomach—Dad was worried! I know ink is truly forever, and that many times young people get a tattoo they later regret, so it was the one thing I told her I really didn't want her doing. A few days later she came to me and showed off a tattoo on her arm, a massive anchor with the word *Mother* emblazoned upon it. I started to get worked up and I was about to go berserk, but she was proudly admiring this tattoo. Then, looking up at me so seriously, waiting for my reaction, she flashed that 100-watt smile. "It's fake, Dad!" Bloody hell, she got me good and proper! I just had to laugh, as that's exactly the sort of prank I might have played on my parents.

Though she no doubt has her playful side, Bonnie's always been particularly serious about her education. Not long after starting at a new high school, Bonnie became noticeably unhappy about the quality of teaching she was receiving. One afternoon, I went to see her as school let out, and instead of that blinding smile, I was greeted with a face full of thunder, bottom lip pushed out, pissed-off and sulky with her situation—exactly how I used to look when I was teed off with my own circumstances! I wanted to laugh at recognizing myself in her, but I buried my laughter. I knew if I were in her shoes, I wouldn't want to see my silly parent taking my predicament lightly.

"This school just isn't the level of education I'm looking for," she said, spitting the words through gritted teeth.

"All right love, I've made a mistake, we'll sort it out immediately,"

I said, backpedaling. I know full well that parents don't always get everything right, and the best thing to do was simply fix it. Seeing her reaction to this situation made me realize just how alike we really are.

And yet, she's her own woman, following her own star, set on a top-level education with a vision for her future. She once asked me what I thought she should do for a living, and I said, "Only you can truly know what that is. I can *guess* at what it is, or try to steer you in the right direction, but, in truth, only you know your dreams." Well, she's working hard at college right now to pursue those dreams; this Broad knows what she wants and goes the hell after it.

Willem is also incredibly motivated, particularly when it comes to music. He has his own band, FIM, they gig regularly and have put out a couple of self-produced albums. He also makes his own EDM and chill music as Willem Wolfe, and sometimes collaborates with other like-minded musicians via the Internet. We always chat about music, recently venturing into our first collaboration together, a song called "Airport Blues," for which he wrote most of the music and lyrics. We've occasionally talked about a follow up to *Cyberpunk*—undoubtedly my most controversial album. "What do you think, Pops?" he'll say. (He always calls me *Pops* instead of *Dad*. I've said that it makes me sound like I'm his grandfather, but that's his way, so *Pops* I am!) I can't wait to see what we dream up together in the future.

It's a breath of fresh air for me to be with my children and share in their world, no matter whether they are going through good or bad times—as we all do. When I'm feeling a little lost, a little hazy, or a bit out of place, they anchor me. They are my clear reality when all else is fuddle.

I visit England each summer, primarily to see my family, my mum and dad, and my sister's family. In recent years, I've spent the better part of those sunny English summer visits with my dad on the golf course. Funny, he taught me how to play when I was eleven, but I was always complete crap at it. But strolling through the putting green gave my dad and me so many pleasurable, cherished moments of bonding. I never thought I'd treasure those endless golf lessons as a child as much as I do today.

EPILOGUE

The road of excess leads to the palace of wisdom.
—WILLIAM BLAKE

WHEN I FIRST ARRIVED IN AMERICA with my parents in '58, because I felt the change so deeply, I developed a limp in my right leg, as if it was slightly shorter than the other. The doctors could find nothing wrong; they told me it was psychosomatic, all in my head. But considering my motorcycle accident some thirty-odd years later, which in fact did shorten my right leg and return my limp, I believe it was a foreshadowing, a harbinger of what was to be.

As I got older, I began to feel a disenfranchisement from life, an eerie emptiness that grew inside me for a long time. I had the curse of feeling too much, dreaming too big, suffering slights too deeply. Moving around all the time had made me feel that my attachments in this life would be short and end quickly. I lived inside my brain, a soulful person squashed by belittlement, failure at school, failure in the eyes of my parents. I had demonstrated only mediocrity, and I felt the need to abandon their way of life with its fears and boldly go where no Broad had quite gone before.

A sixth sense drove me to follow my dreams, for anything else would lead to feelings of sickness or frustrated anger when I found obstacles in my path. From an early age, that fury was fueled by a fear of desolation. To be well meant I had to realize my chosen destiny. I was forced to leap and fly or accept the nightmare of knowing I would be ill from not doing so.

I AM HOPELESSLY DIVIDED BETWEEN THE dark and the good, the rebel and the saint, the sexual maniac and the monk, the poet and the priest, the demagogue and the populist. I feel the pull of emotions when these characters appear in my actions. I can find justification for any of it, but inside, where it really matters, the fullness and the void struggle to assert dominance over each other. I feel pulled by tides of passion, anger, lust, corruption, madness, sin. . . . The corporeal body struggles until its death, the wind was sown, and the whirlwind followed.

With my dad an atheist and my mom a Catholic, I grew up with conflicting ideas that are wholly incompatible. One is a mystical philosophy, the other a cold, hard truth that there's nothing spiritual anywhere. The two opposing creeds have battled inside me. One means life goes on after death and everything we do here counts; the other, that all is vanity and we are doomed to an eternal sleep from which none awake. The tide pulls me and its undertow submerges me. I drown and grasp for the foam; I'm turned topsy-turvy in the flood until the tide recedes. My bruised and battered psyche lives on. Sound becomes hollow as I crane my neck to see the next consequence my actions will bring.

But this ideological schism has enabled a birth of musical notes that fly on the wind, blaring in my mind. It has created me in its fashion, and my music is its manifestation. The peaks are so high, and the valleys so low, that it became easy to question my own sanity. Freedom is not free. Achieving that state of grace can numb the mind and destroy it. What was it James Russell Lowell said about Jean-Jacques Rousseau? "Talent is that which is in a man's power; genius is that in whose power a man is." I may be talented—genius, of course, continues to elude me, but the very thought of exuding even a flash drives me on.

When I say *genius*, I'm talking about the small spark or flame of invention that burns in all of us, waiting to be fanned by our thoughts. Together we innovate, freeing our minds and propelling ourselves forward on our separate paths. Each of us has an ember we can blow on with our breath of mind and see the sparks glow red. I'm no genius and never will be, but with your help, I can run the galaxy of thought and plunder the hidden secrets of the universe. And that's what you have done for me by helping me touch my artistic side, creating a tongue of fire above your head. I speak in tongues. I lengthen my horizon. I see new worlds.

THIS DREAM OF LIFE BEGAN WITH my first friends, my mum and my dad. As I work to get down the final pages of this book, my family is going through a crisis. My dad's health started to deteriorate in the spring of '13. He began losing weight and knew inside that something was very wrong, as he had no appetite whatsoever. Nothing tasted good, and he began to talk gravely during a summer holiday to Portugal, where I joined my parents with Willem and Bonnie Blue, my sister, my niece Naomi, and my nephews Matthew and Mark.

Dad started to say to Mum within my earshot that this was probably the last holiday we would all take together. A lump was growing on his shoulder and we were all concerned, but I was in denial, as my dad has always been so healthy, playing golf in his late eighties through two hip operations and a near-fatal MRSA infection. But he knew what all the signs meant. Upon our return from the holiday, a battery of tests confirmed that it was cancer. Over the course of the following year it gradually spread from his bones, to his lungs, to everywhere, really.

My first friend was dying while I made the *Kings & Queens of the Underground* album. We recorded in England so I could be near to my parents and spend as much time with them as I could. Now, Mum tells me that Dad puts on the recordings I gave them of the finished record, that he listens to it in the morning sometimes, and that he likes "Save Me Now" a lot. I knew also that he'd been listening to some Generation X songs, as he shared his thoughts with me on "Wild Youth."

In May 2014, Dad began to suffer real difficulty breathing as the cancer reached his lungs, and I returned home to help my mum before hospice care began. He was to be cared for at home, as Mum was a

nurse and still is the greatest at what was once her profession. My niece
Caroline is a doctor, and her fiancé, Ahmad, is a leading oncologist, so
Dad had the best medical care within arm's reach. But I came home to
help Mum during the vital days before the extra help and a stairlift arrived. My arrival gave my sister a much-needed break, as, with Mum,
she was bearing the brunt of it all.

I would help Dad upstairs: as he had great difficulty climbing the
stairs, he would become exhausted by the effort. Doing simple things
for himself became terribly difficult, like putting on his pajamas after
taking off his clothes at bedtime, or brushing his teeth. One evening,
I was alone with him, helping him get settled for the night, and when
he was finally lying in bed and comfortable he became quite emotional
and said to me, "Billy, did I upset you that I didn't understand about
you choosing music as your career?" We had had our ups and downs
over the years, as all sons and fathers do, but it was all in the past now.
I replied, "Dad, I was crazy to think I could do it," and the look of relief and love that passed between us crystalized a truth: however upsetting his present state, this feeling between us at that moment was our
true relationship, and had always been.

There were other moments when we saw the shining look of love
in his eyes as we did our best to make him comfortable under very
trying circumstances. This time spent with my dad was so precious—
horrible and beautiful all at once—that in private I cried with both joy
and sadness. My sister had told me this might happen when she asked
me to come to the UK to help Dad, but the experience was more affecting than anything I could have imagined. My father is a great man, and
I am privileged to be his son.

Now I wonder about the red dimension of love I entered while
gone from this world, in the moments after my motorcycle accident,
and I contemplate whether it is there that we will truly meet again.
Maybe that loving presence is so close at hand that we just don't realize
it unless terrible pain or exhilarating joy propel us into it—shock us
into contact with the other side, as it were, while our emotional core
lies bare and vulnerable. *Would that be something an atheist would wish
for?* I would never say anything to my dad in his present state of health

to make him wrestle with any such earthly questions, as he gets so easily anxious or upset, precious oxygen being denied him. Besides, the answer will be apparent to us all in due time.

As I see his life ebb away I find a disquieting horror there. I feel a tightening of the throat, a sense of panic, and I long to see him once again, whole, the young man in the Fleet Air Arm uniform, pictured in his fighter plane in the waning days of World War II, paisley scarf around his neck catching the wind. Or the man I knew as a boy, diving for clams off Long Island, hunting and fishing, living his life to the limit as he saw it. The man who told me at sixteen that if I really wanted musical instruments I should get them myself. I'm proud to say the do-it-yourself attitude I maintained through all my endeavors was instilled by my father's words. The same man who came to the U.S. during my darkest days of isolated addiction, stepping off the plane carrying a big walking stick he did not need, resolved to save me from myself. A man who always took the moral high ground in any argument or business deal—it's hard to defeat what is right, and if it does suffer a blow, it holds fast and comes back stronger. He taught me this. He was tough on me at times, and yes, I've bridled against his hopes for me, but the young buck is bound to. But I know it's because he loved me, and in the end, a considerable part of the person I am can be attributed to him. Oh, if only I could impart a small piece of my energy to help bolster his. I can only be there for him and understand how the moral high ground he stood upon in his life was his power. He wielded that power so deftly and with such sublime intelligence that I once wondered if his dreams had truly been fulfilled. The look of love in his eyes says yes.

Still, right now, as he knows what each day means, I take comfort in my contact with the other side and hold on to this as my answer to why we must experience this love and glory that walks hand in hand with our existence, yet is invisible and omnipresent, but nonetheless real and welcoming, and is but one breath away.

TODAY, WHEN I'M NOT TOURING OR working on a new project, I enjoy being "busy doin' nothin'," to quote the title of a Brian Wilson song I didn't understand at first but do now. I like to roar along on my Harley, blasts of wind burning my eyes, the lead rider guiding the way to no direction known, my soul feeding, my mind expanding, my senses exploding with delight. The guy in front signals, *Look out for this dirt patch*, a burst of fuel and time as heaven unfolds. The road is blue, the sky yellow, the sun burning. I can't remember the sea being quite so lovely as we ride by, drinking in the vistas.

That's what biking does. It opens you up to see the wild in raw nature that is just an acceleration away. A massive orgasm of gas and flame ignites and powers my dragon, and, like St. George (Harrison), we face our demons down. When I was battling my own many-headed hydra, I prayed to George Harrison that, whatever he thought of me down here, he'd look out for us from up there. An afternoon long on human movement does the heart good.

I watch a pair of hawks descend to the canyon floor. They survey the valley below and then rise up on a flow of air unseen by the human eye, created by uneven heating of the earth. The thermals push and lift them higher until, standing on the rock, they see far into the distance. We climb through a winding elevation of road unknown to cars, pull over to stretch our legs, and stand like lords of all we survey.

Green and cream, she cools by the road waiting, her chrome gleaming. She wants you to know she's traveled more than thirteen thousand miles through all manner of terrain and weather. We turn to scan the windswept promontory, a vista of emerald, for it's a day after rainfall, and the flowing surface looks like water-carved rock. I stand with a 360-degree view of the Pacific Coast Highway, the mountains stretching away from the sea, high above, in a place I would never be if I didn't ride a bike. Life is sweet.

ACKNOWLEDGMENTS

FIRST AND FOREMOST, I'D LIKE TO thank my parents, Joan and Bill Broad. My father passed away on August 7th, 2014, 9:45 p.m. BST, 1:45 p.m. L.A. time.

When my dad entered hospice, though my first instinct was to rush back to his side and support my mum, Dad wanted me to continue working even when he was in the final stages of cancer. He believed once you had made a commitment, you had to see it through: the courage of his convictions never stood down. Mum would ring and tell me he was listening to early mixes of songs from *Kings & Queens of the Underground,* which I'd sent along once they were in good enough shape to share. She said they comforted him.

One day my mum put on the mixes, and it was to the sounds of "Ghosts in My Guitar" that he relaxed and fell asleep. My incredible father, my friend: I will forever remember you as one of those ghosts in my guitar.

For decades of unwavering service and friendship, Tony Dimitriades and Brigid Waters. For cheering me on through thick and thin with this book, Laurence Freedman.

For past services, Bill Aucoin (RIP). Pure matesmanship and incredible musical partners, Keith Forsey and Steve Stevens. To my loves, Perri Lister, Bonnie Blue, Willem Wolfe. For my little sister, Jane Cheese, and family. For my confederates, Brian Tichy, Trevor Horn, Greg Kurstin, Billy Morrison. Fellow "chalatwin" and Prime Mover in Generation X, Tony James; also Derwood and Mark Laff. Matesman and bass man no. 97 "Yammamatao" says Hi to "Sagamahachi" no. 98 Stephen McGrath. Rude Dude and mate John Diaz (fuck off). Mates and musicians, Terry Chimes and Steve Jones. For press and love, Sharon Chevin. Styling and love, Gwen Mullen, Mitzi Spallas, and Lindsay Morris.

Invaluable in editing and discussion phases of this book, David Falk. To Jessica Roth, Brian Belfiglio, Susan Moldow, Meredith Vilarello, Lauren Friedlander, Laura Flavin, Elaine Wilson, Cherlynne Li, Polly Watson, Sarah Wright, and everyone on my Touchstone/Simon & Schuster Team BFI for their support and creativity. For her foresight and early belief, Stacy Creamer. For valuable contribution in the early days of this book, Roy Trakin, John Albert, and Steve Dennis. To my literary agent, Laura Bonner, and William Morris Endeavor. To web sage Jim Bullotta, a true cyberpunk.

For their unstinting service, press agents Ellen Golden, Howard Bloom, Mitch Schneider, and Marcee Rondan. For booking and promotion, John Marx, Barry Dickins, and Prue Almond. My lawyer, David Altschul. Road kings and mates, love and respect to Rex King, Karel Hamm, Mark "Rangi" Williamson, and Matt "Toast" Young. For art and friendship, Amanda and Shepard Fairey. To all my road crew mates through the years, there are too many of you to mention. To Evan Bright and Tiffany Goble at East End Management.

And to you out there, you and your priceless help, for good or evil as we work through this nutty gift we've been given, I thank you for making my life so fucking great, even when it's not easy. That's life—sometimes it's bittersweet, like "Sweet Sixteen," sometimes dark and moody, like "Eyes Without a Face," or shouting and triumphant like "Rebel Yell." It's true, I've been down a sick and twisted path strewn with darkness but also glowing with life and love, striving to do what I could with the tools I've been given. My life, this life, is so fucking great. You and I together have made it so.

This book was written through my perspective and I quite understand that others may remember things differently, but I hope they look beyond that and see it as a postcard from the past. If it can provide a reader who wonders about those days a glimpse from one who participated, then I hope you will see the greater good. This book is intended as a testament to a life lived on its own terms.

INDEX